How to be Real

A Survival Guide in Challenging Times

By Stephen Frosh

UNCORRECTED PAGE PROOFS

Please do not reprint without publisher's prior approval

VERSO

Contact: Anthony Korum
anthony@versobooks.com

ISBN 9781804299197 • $26.95

256 pages • Hardback

On sale September 30th, 2025

How to Be Real

A Survival Guide in
Challenging Times

Stephen Frosh

London • New York

First published by Verso 2025
© Stephen Frosh 2025

The manufacturer's authorized representative in the EU for product safety (GPSR) is LOGOS EUROPE, 9 rue Nicolas Poussin, 17000, La Rochelle, France
contact@logoseurope.eu

All rights reserved

The moral rights of the author have been asserted

1 3 5 7 9 10 8 6 4 2

Verso
UK: 6 Meard Street, London W1F 0EG
US: 207 East 32nd Street, New York, NY 10016
versobooks.com

Verso is the imprint of New Left Books

ISBN-13: 978-1-80429-919-7
ISBN-13: 978-1-80429-921-0 (UK EBK)
ISBN-13: 978-1-80429-922-7 (US EBK)

British Library Cataloguing in Publication Data
A catalogue record for this book is available from the British Library

Library of Congress Cataloging-in-Publication Data
A catalog record for this book is available from the Library of Congress

Typeset in Sabon by MJ & N Gavan, Truro, Cornwall
Printed by Integrated Books International, United States of America

To Judith

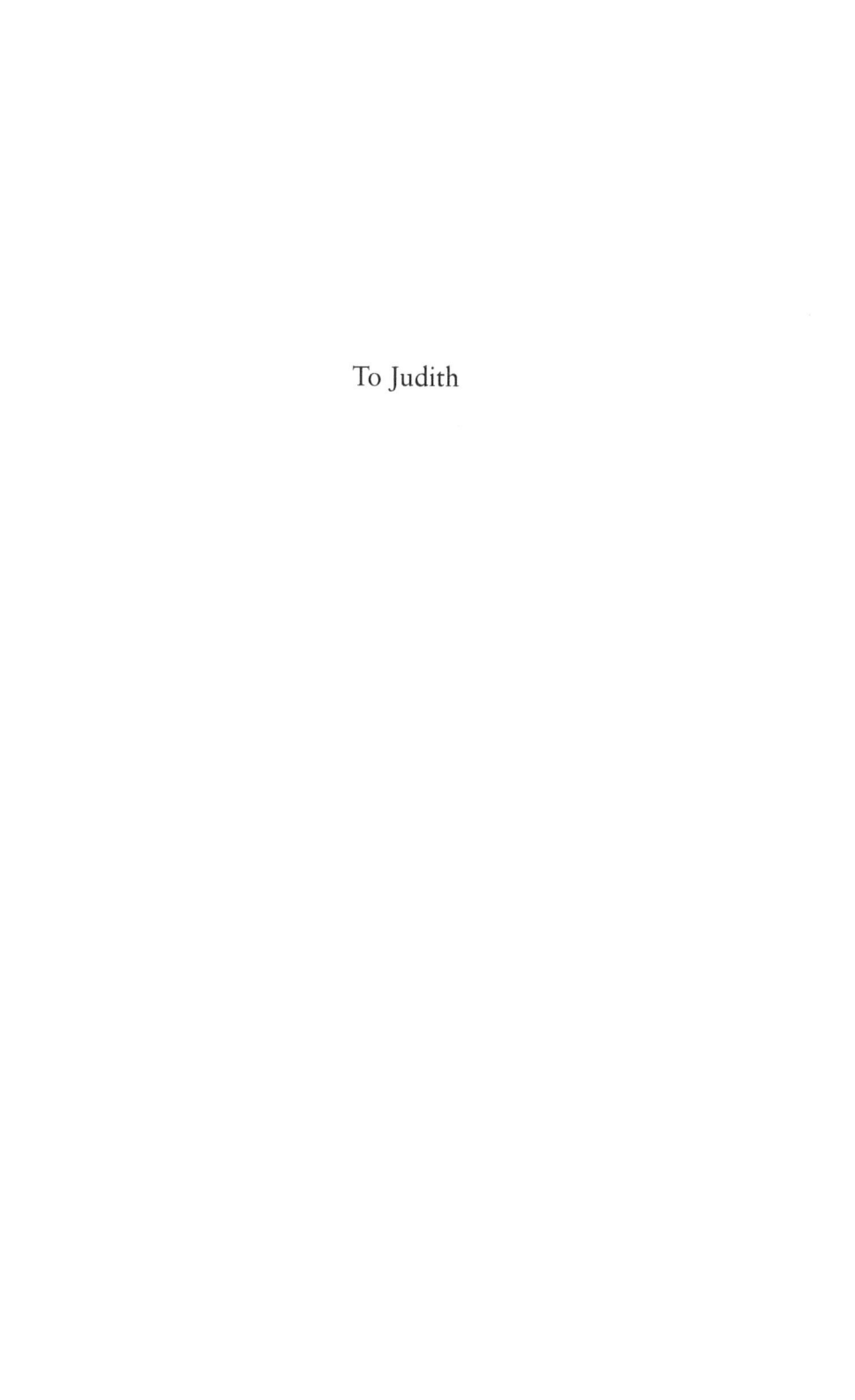

Contents

Preface   vii

1. Being Real   1
2. Recovering Childhood   35
3. Hate   63
4. Defending Ourselves against Reality   91
5. Ghosts and Ancestors   119
6. Psychopolitical Reality   147
7. Endurance   181
8. The Sense of Ending   207

Notes   227

Preface

One day in October 2024, after I had drafted this book, I decided that it needed a Preface to start it off and to guide readers as to what to expect. It was quite late and I was tired, so I did what is becoming increasingly common: I asked ChatGPT for help. 'Write a Preface for a book called *How to Be Real* in the style of Stephen Frosh,' was my request. This is what it produced, instantly:

> In a world obsessed with appearances, performance, and the relentless pressure to craft a perfect image, the concept of being 'real' becomes elusive, almost slippery. The very question of what it means to be authentic often feels submerged beneath layers of social expectations, digital representations, and self-imposed demands. The notion of 'realness' confronts us daily, yet its substance remains tantalizingly out of reach, as if the more we strive for it, the more it dissolves.
>
> This book, *How to Be Real*, is an exploration of the complexities of authenticity in contemporary life. It does not aim to offer quick fixes or definitive answers. Rather, it seeks to unravel the tensions that accompany our attempts to live honestly and meaningfully in a fragmented, hyper-mediated world. At its heart, the book poses a series of provocations: What does it mean to be real when our identities are increasingly shaped by forces beyond our control? How can we reconcile the desire for connection with the alienation so many of us feel in a world that seems, paradoxically, more connected than ever?
>
> The question of the real, however, is not just an intellectual one. It is also profoundly emotional. Being real involves confronting uncomfortable truths about ourselves and the worlds

PREFACE

we inhabit, exposing the fault lines that often lie hidden beneath the surface. It demands vulnerability, an openness to uncertainty, and a willingness to inhabit the cracks where our defences falter. The real is not a fixed state to be achieved but a process – one that unfolds in the messy entanglements of relationships, identities, and social structures.

This book draws on a range of perspectives, from psychoanalysis to sociology, to examine how the pursuit of authenticity is fraught with contradictions. In our efforts to be real, we are often drawn into performances of authenticity that are just as contrived as the masks we seek to remove. Yet, these performances, however flawed, tell us something important about the human condition: that being real is not simply about stripping away artifice but about acknowledging the complexities and ambivalences that define us.

As you read this book, I invite you to approach it not as a manual with concrete solutions but as a conversation – a dialogue about what it means to be real in a world where the boundaries between the self and society are increasingly blurred. Together, we will reflect on the possibilities and limits of authenticity, knowing that the search for the real may never lead to final answers but can still offer us profound insights into who we are and who we might become.

After reading this, I wondered why I bothered to write the book at all. The irony of AI describing what it means for humans to be real will not be lost on anyone. But my response was more personal: has ChatGPT somehow tapped into my general style and been able to replicate it so accurately because my writing is cliché-ridden and obvious? Does this collection of cobbled-together truisms really represent the limits of my thought? It's not that it is wrong – if things were that simple, I would not be so disturbed. It is rather that this simulacrum of my thinking is pretty good, and it makes many of the points that I would like to make. Nevertheless, as the book was not yet available to be read when I asked ChatGPT my question, how could it know so much about how it would come out? If I were to include this AI-generated Preface as my own, would anyone notice? It is certainly not written by me, but is it nevertheless 'authentic', to use the language it deploys, or 'real'?

This is one of the ways in which the question of being real arises. If human thought-processes can be modelled and imitated so precisely, what is it that constitutes the specific nature of humans? If such a specific nature exists, it clearly must amount to more than the ability to string some points together in a way that is vaguely meaningful (I corrected this sentence on the advice of the grammar checker in Word, though it is still my sentence). In itself, responding appropriately to stimuli – which in the case of ChatGPT is a question or request – is not enough; something else must be going on to mark the difference between the seemingly 'authentic' and the real.

I have long been haunted by the epigraph to E. M. Forster's novel *Howards End*, 'Only connect.'[1] This has always seemed to me to be a very challenging injunction. It refers to the connectedness of events and to how relationships intertwine, so that what happens in one can set off effects in others. But it also conjures up an ambition to *feel* connected, to have a capacity for emotional alertness and thoughtfulness that immerses us in the events of our lives, most of all in our encounters with other people, granting them significance and meaning. That is not something that I have found easy, despite being a psychologist and making my living out of offering therapy or, in later years, teaching and writing about psychoanalysis. Being real and connected, finding myself wholly in tune with my situation, facing up to conflict and loss, admitting love: these are difficult accomplishments. It is much easier, I find, to take refuge from, or defend against, the too-close, the demandingly intimate, the startling moments when something looms up in front of us to challenge us to make an honest response. Ducking and diving to make our way through or around these without being dragged fully into them, without having our self-image challenged or our emotions stretched too far, is an attractive prospect if our ambition is to keep on an even keel. Yet if we occupy ourselves too fully with these avoidances, the chances are that we will narrow our experiences and our capacity for responsiveness to such an extent that everything will seem artificial. We will lose track of what it might mean to really 'connect', to become fully immersed in life, to be real. At least, that is my experience.

It will be immediately obvious that the sense in which I am using the term 'real' is quite psychological, although I would prefer to call it 'psychosocial' to indicate that it deals not just with the actions and feelings of individuals, but also with the way society is structured – how it promotes certain ways of being and social arrangements, and values some lives more than it does others. 'Real' here is quite specific, if not exact and precise: it means having an engagement with experience that does not back away from trouble but knows when to confront it and when to let it be. As ChatGPT says, 'Being real involves confronting uncomfortable truths about ourselves and the worlds we inhabit, exposing the fault lines that often lie hidden beneath the surface. It demands vulnerability, an openness to uncertainty, and a willingness to inhabit the cracks where our defences falter.' I cannot improve on this, and hope that it is something that has been extracted from my writing rather than generated from elsewhere. Being real is a process of becoming, in which we learn to face reality as it impinges on us, acknowledging its contradictions and our own. It also involves something that ChatGPT seems not to have noticed: that being real is an *ethical* project, in which the question of truthfulness comes to the fore. Deceiving ourselves is a way of hiding from reality, as are the deliberate lies and subtle or commonplace deceptions of the social world. They can make our lives easier to manage, but they also do great damage, distorting our appreciation of how things are as well as actively oppressing large groups of people, sometimes in violent ways. To this, the ethical response is to insist on truthfulness, even if we know we will never achieve any 'absolute' truth; and truthfulness involves a commitment to not turning aside when what we encounter is something uncomfortable, distressing or personally and socially challenging. Some things are very painful to come up against, but this does not justify pretending they are not there.

How to Be Real is an attempt to articulate this kind of being real and to explore where the pursuit of it leads us. It proceeds through an examination of what it might mean to be real in a deeply complicated and conflictual society, looking at childhood and the development of the self, at why and how we put up defences against reality, and at what hate means. The book describes how we might turn the ghosts that trouble us into ancestors that enrich our lives. It asks us to seek solidarity with others and, finally, to find community in death. Throughout the book, I draw heavily but hopefully accessibly on psychoanalysis as the discipline that offers a vocabulary for, and set of insights about, emotional and intellectual intensity, while also providing an account of how social practices and structures make life more, or often less, real. The 'message' of the book is one that I state early in the first chapter: that being real involves facing our experience of the world without flinching too much, allowing ourselves to think about it honestly and to feel moved and affected by it. This is not just an individual project; our society too must face up to its inconsistencies, its modes of oppression and its lies, if it is to facilitate growth in its members. In this book, I try to identify some of the obstacles to this kind of truthful pursuit of reality and to suggest how we might overcome them.

I would like to thank Leo Hollis and John Merrick at Verso for their encouragement and excellent editorial help. And for the avoidance of doubt, no other part of this book is AI-generated.

1

Being Real

It might seem obvious that we all have a sense of our own reality and that 'deep inside' we know who we are. Yet this is not necessarily the case. For one thing, it is not completely clear what is meant by the idea of 'being real'. It can refer to facing up to what others regard as reality, so 'get real' can be an accusation that we are living in a fantasy world, usually a naïve or unduly optimistic one. It can refer to a more personal sense of authenticity, in which being a 'real person' means having a sense of connection with something genuine in ourselves, something that strikes us as truthful and honest.

It can also be a matter of ethical standing, especially in the context of relationships with other people. Being real means being honest and open (think of the difference between a real smile and a false one); being the kind of person who makes others feel that they are in the presence of someone who is centred and reliable and attending to them properly. It almost certainly means not hiding from experience by pretending to ourselves and to others that the world is simpler than it is. Indeed, this book is premised on the idea that gaining a sense of reality requires us to appreciate the complexity of modern life, to think more clearly and bravely about it, and to allow ourselves to develop a depth of feeling that may sometimes be uncomfortable or even distressing to live with. Much of this depends on the quality of relationships we form with each other, in particular our receptiveness to other people's suffering. It requires a form of endurance that means we can remain connected to those who make a 'call' on us, even when this call stirs up difficult feelings. It involves being able to stay with trouble without denying it, offering different forms of human solidarity. This all sounds like a requirement to develop a set of personality traits that enable us to face up to the world, and in some ways this is true. Yet we also need to recognise that the capacity to 'be real' is not just an individual achievement. The social contexts in which we live affect it greatly. In societies which are based on denial and falsehood, it is ever harder to gain a resilient sense of reality. Consequently, the question of 'how to be real' has political as well as psychological and ethical implications.

There are many aspects of the contemporary world that make it hard to develop and sustain a sense of ourselves as real. The complexity of events, the rapidity with which they happen and the way in which we might be powerfully affected by things outside our control and which seem to have little to do with us, all contribute to the difficulty of locating ourselves firmly in time and space. Making sense of the 24/7 news regime – especially when there is little agreement about the nature and meaning of events that might feel both distant and of immediate importance to us – is one of the challenges here. Too much happens, too fast, for many of us to grasp; and its mediation by outlets with competing interests means that interpretation of these events is increasingly hard. Who are we to believe? Anchoring ourselves in a reliable, comprehensible world is more and more difficult as it spins (in all senses) more rapidly. How can we navigate our path through this?

While world events are confusing, their impact on us is ever more immediate. As we discovered during the Covid pandemic, a virus that may have escaped from a laboratory or market in one country can cause lockdowns and deaths throughout the world; similarly a war that is confined to a small geographical area can so spiral that its social and economic effects are felt everywhere. In an age of environmental catastrophe, a drought in one region of the world can provoke migration by desperate people, resulting in political crises in distant places.

We are bombarded with messages about these events, with no reliable way to judge their accuracy, yet we somehow need to find a way through them. We are helped and hindered in this by the cultural resources at our disposal, both traditional (newspapers, mainstream radio and television broadcasts, films and other artistic materials – all of which might show biases of different kinds) and new (the explosive growth of internet and social media). While these resources offer some guidance as to how to make sense of the world, we are very likely to suffer from information overload, with information itself becoming a source of stress. We might notice this especially at those times when we cannot tear ourselves away from news about particularly troubling occurrences. This can be very draining, sometimes drifting into what has been called 'vicarious trauma', a state in which observers of terrible events come to experience them almost as if they are themselves participants, showing patterns of distress and disturbance that are characteristic of those who have been directly involved. In this sense, space (and on occasions time) collapses – the whole world is present in our life, weighing on us, and when we cannot fend it off we might feel overwhelmed by it.

A further force adding to existential confusion is the remarkable acceleration of technological change. How many of us understand how anything works? In the virtual world, reality is ever more difficult to tell from fiction. The very term 'virtual reality' expresses this well: it refers to something that seems like reality; it is almost ('virtually') real but is in fact a kind of parallel universe in which we can find all sorts of excitements and rewards but might also be tripped up by miscalculations and deceit. How can we tell the difference between a person and a bot – and does that distinction really matter anymore? If, for example, a chatbot makes you feel less lonely, or a therapy bot helps you overcome your anxieties, does it matter if they are not 'real' in the sense of being attributable to a person? And what about when it is made *deliberately* unclear whether or not the responses we receive online are coming from a robot? Do the developments in AI that are undeniably progressive in some ways (medical advances, access to information, connections with friends and family in far-flung places, reliability and cheapness of communications) also disrupt our sense of ongoingness in who we are and who we are connected with? Does it *actually* matter, if it does not *seem* to matter, where someone is when they text or talk to you on the phone?

It is already difficult to tell the difference between artificial intelligence and human activity. Three-quarters of a century ago, Alan Turing proposed that a machine can be thought of as 'intelligent' if, without seeing it but only observing what it does (its 'outputs'), you cannot tell that it is a machine.[1] The thought experiment he developed, which became known as the Turing Test, was quite crude. Put simply, it works as follows: if a machine can be programmed to respond to an input (for example, a question) in the same way that a human being would do, and the responses from the human and from the machine cannot be told apart, then just as we would say that the human is 'thinking' or showing 'intelligence', so we must say the same of the machine. It seems likely that the threshold for this was passed some time ago – certainly since the advent of Machine Learning, but also in more everyday online encounters. The situation is complicated, however. One of my students researched the moment in discussions (on what was then called Twitter) when a human realises they have been conversing with a bot.[2] Apparently the discovery is often marked by the statement, typed in amusement or anger, 'You are a bot!' – and this happens hundreds of times a day. Intriguingly, it backs both sides of the argument about whether humans and machines are equivalent. On the one hand, the human is 'duped' for a while; on the other, they eventually realise that they are engaging with a machine – which means that the machine has failed the Turing Test. The level of betrayal they may then feel perhaps reflects the extent to which they were fooled. On the other hand, again, it is remarkable how attached people can get to AI bots, even when they know they're not human. Reports of people feeling comforted by Siri or Alexa or their equivalents are legion. This relational oddity has been around for a long time. There is a – possibly apocryphal – story about Joseph Weizenbaum, who created the natural language program ELIZA in the mid-1960s.[3] The aim of ELIZA was to simulate conversation, but its most famous version was a therapy programme which worked mainly by repeating back to the human interlocutor the last part of whatever they had just said, accompanied by some open, encouraging questions. People interacting with the computer understood the situation perfectly well, yet this did not stop them becoming attached to ELIZA and treating it as if it too were human. The story is that Weizenbaum's secretary, who was trying out the programme, asked him to leave the room when she was speaking to ELIZA so she could have privacy in what she was experiencing as an intimate relationship.[4] The effectiveness of therapy bots ('You can talk to me at any time') does not depend on creating the simulation of a human-to-human relationship: most of the companies promoting these make it clear that the bots are not human, sometimes, as with the commercial programme Woebot, including it upfront in the name. This, however, does not stop users from relating to them *as if* they were human – and sometimes preferable to genuine therapists. The issue is not, therefore, one of deception; it seems rather to be that people like to suspend their knowledge that they are dealing with a bot and instead treat it as if it were a person. Or, perhaps, the human status or otherwise of the people we talk to does not matter as much as we usually believe.

AI, Machine Learning, bots on social media, psychotherapy bots, satnavs – they can all appear human even if we know they are not. Even the confirmation required on many websites, 'I am not a robot', is set and analysed by a robot. And – as the film *Blade Runner* dramatised – the difficulty of telling a person from a machine might not be restricted to our judgements about others. We cannot even be fully sure of ourselves. Are we human? Or are we just set up to believe we are human, when in fact we are machines? How would we know? What does it mean to be human anyway? Is the only criterion that we are made of biological 'stuff', muscles and bones and internal organs, or is something else necessary? Given how many people are full of artificial elements (manufactured knees and hips, stents, plastic lenses in the eye), is there a point at which we are mainly non-human? Or at least, not completely 'real'? As we will see, it is not uncommon to mistrust our bodies or believe that they do not represent our true identities, that there is a mismatch between our biological state and how we imagine and feel ourselves to be. Bodily reality is not the same as feeling real, even though it is clearly connected to it.

Another famous thought experiment throws a slightly different light on the issue of what it might mean to be human as opposed to a machine; or rather, since it is possible to think of the human brain as a machine, suggests what might be the difference between this and a computational machine (that is, AI). In 1980, the philosopher John Searle published a paper arguing that there is a fundamental difference between AI, which relies on the manipulation of symbols, and human intelligence, which is about understanding. The famous experiment is what he called the 'Chinese Room'.[5] When first published, it was a provocative enough experiment to generate twenty-eight different responses from a whole string of Searle's opponents, and this debate has scarcely ceased in the near half century since. The essence of the Chinese Room thought experiment is as follows. Suppose a non-Chinese-speaker is locked in a room with a large number of uninterpretable symbols on cards, plus a rule book in the person's language. More symbols are fed in from outside the room, and the rule book tells the person what symbols to push out in response. The rule book might say: 'When a symbol looking like this comes in, push out a symbol looking like that.' Suppose also that the people pushing the symbols in from outside are Chinese speakers, asking questions in Chinese, and that the rule book is so complete and the person inside the room so adept at following it, that the answers are indistinguishable from those of a native Chinese speaker. From the point of view of the Chinese speakers outside the room, it looks like the person inside is speaking Chinese. But, as Searle points out, for the person inside the room, Chinese remains as mysterious as ever and, importantly, there is no way that person could ever learn a word of Chinese through this procedure.

We can get a fuller notion of this if we now assume that the person inside the room is an English speaker and the people outside are putting questions to that person in English. The questions and answers might be identical to the Chinese example, but the process is radically different. This time, the person in the room understands what the questions mean and responds accordingly. Searle's point is that even if a machine passes the Turing Test and can therefore be taken to be showing 'intelligence', the kind of intelligence being shown is different from that of the human. In the first case, that of the machine, it is simply manipulating symbols; in the second case, that of the human, it is understanding what is going on.

As I have mentioned, Searle's claims and his example have been the subject of much controversy.[6] He nevertheless identifies an important principle: humans, if they are machines, are meaning-making machines, and this in turn refers to a realm of subjective being in which we make connections between words and things, ideas and feelings, perceptions and their inner significance. This may also be true, or become true in the future, of machines; but we cannot really know this, as we must assume their 'inner life' will be different in important ways from our own. For the present, we should focus on what the discussion makes clear: that we possess consciousness and intentionality, and that these are central features of the way in which we relate to ourselves and to others, and to the physical and social environment. Our lives are governed by how we make sense of the complex array of forces that operate on us, and on which we try to have an effect.

Being real has a lot to do with the context in which we find ourselves and with a sense of *belonging* – geographically, communally and relationally. While being grounded in a particular place remains important to most people, much of the sense of belonging that we have, rooting us in our own reality, comes from our relationships with other people. There is no evidence that these relationships have become any less central, despite the prevalent moral panic about the impact of social media and smartphone culture on relationship quality. With regard to young people who are internet and smartphone 'natives', it is often feared that their numerous 'contacts' are substituting for the real relationships that previous generations of young people forged with one another. Yet there is little evidence that this is the case, and it seems more likely that these contacts sometimes turn into more intimate friendships, at other times are used to bolster relationships by maintaining links across time and space, and at worst are simply *different* from close friendships – more centred on fun and social excitement. They may also expand the range of people's connections across boundaries of ethnicity, class and nation, even though the contrary phenomenon in which social media become an 'echo chamber' for prejudicial views is very apparent, and favours the dissemination of conspiracy theories and manufactured hatred.[7] Nevertheless, the need for more intimate relationships remains strong and these relationships provide the ballast for a sense of self that might offer psychological stability. It is this kind of stability that potentially enables people to approach the confusion of the world with a capacity to discriminate. If we have a sense of who we are, it will help us to locate ourselves in relation to the multiple messages that surround us, facilitating selection between those that matter more and those that matter less, between those which are clearly false and those in which is lodged some truth. Given the power of the 'post-truth' dialects that govern much political discourse, this is – or would be – a valuable achievement.

There is an important set of difficulties here. Even though the sense of personal reality rooted in strong relationships with others is a crucial attribute for survival and growth, it is under great strain precisely because these relationships are so difficult to find and maintain. This may always have been the case, but the contemporary forms of alienation from others are of a special kind. The chance of making connections that feel real is reduced by a social environment in which such connections are actively undermined by the kinds of process I have described – chaotic, overly rapid, highly mediated, of uncertain veracity, sometimes mendacious, often shrill, and at times traumatic. This last point is especially significant in what has come to be called 'trauma culture', in which personal and social suffering demands to be heard. This suffering is important and often systemic. It can be inflicted on individuals and groups in the present, and it can also be produced by historical circumstances that continue to affect people, as a kind of haunting of the present by the past, with the legacies of slavery, of colonialism and of the Holocaust being prime examples. As an ironic and poignant contrast with the rapid flashing across different surfaces and tendency to move too fast that characterise the 'postmodern' difficulty of forming relationships, these intense, trauma-centred experiences maintain themselves over time and keep repeating. They are hard to respond to because they are so emotionally draining, both for sufferers and for those drawn into their orbit. They call for resources that we might not have, sometimes precisely because of the shallowness and uprootedness created by the conditions of superficiality generated in modern society. They require of listeners or witnesses to pain an ability to hold onto their own sense of reality while allowing others to testify to the damage done to them. This is what is meant by 'staying with trouble'.

Finding ways to respond to others' traumatic experiences is important for therapeutic and ethical reasons yet can be very difficult, and the temptations to withdraw from such encounters are many. They may take the form of a defensive turning-away that reflects an inability to deal fully with another's suffering because it is too personally painful; or, in a contrary, equally defensive move, an over-identification with that suffering that makes it our own rather than promoting recognition of the specific experience undergone by the sufferer. These kinds of withdrawal exemplify how hard it is, in the face of the demands of other people, to respond in ways that acknowledge the force of those demands and, where appropriate, our implication in them, our responsibility, direct or indirect, for aspects of their suffering. These defensive responses can also be shared by whole societies, as we see sometimes in the 'denialism' produced by war, the disputes over memorialisation between countries each claiming the status of 'victim', or the selective turning-away from the impact of racialised inequalities by those who are implicated in sustaining them. I will discuss all this in more detail in later chapters.

I imagine most people have a sense of themselves as real, but not everyone does, and it is probably true that most of us do not *always* feel real or feel real only in part. For some people, the experience of unreality is of being taken over by an outside force. This might get labelled as 'schizophrenia', but it basically boils down to the feeling that someone or something else is in control of us, that our thoughts and feelings are not our own, that they are being manipulated by others.

A hundred years ago, the troubled early psychoanalyst Victor Tausk described the fantasy of an 'influencing machine' controlling a patient remotely.[8] Tausk writes that the construction of this imaginary machine, as complained of by certain schizophrenic patients, 'cannot be explained, but its function consists in the transmission or "draining off" of thoughts and feelings by one or several persecutors'.[9] The influencing machine is envisioned as a technological device of no knowable construction, mystifying but intensely powerful, able to enter into people's minds and manipulate their thoughts. It is best understood as a representation in machine terms of the age-old experience of being operated on from outside by a force greater than oneself. We can see it as an early recognition of the deeply unsettling power of information machines to persuade and influence us, in ways that are hard to track and make us feel uncertain about whether we are thinking our own thoughts, or thoughts implanted from outside. This experience also fuelled strong anxieties and fantasies about 'brainwashing' in the Cold War period that persist today, as recent conspiracy theories testify.[10] Nowadays, with the extraordinary penetration of social media and general online scrutiny into everyday life, the paranoid fantasy of thought-insertion is a common one and might be well-founded, if the claims made about the prevalence of surveillance and the potency of propaganda (not to say advertising) are true. The reach of contemporary media is such that thinking for ourselves – and in this sense feeling real – is ever harder to sustain.

Being influenced is not, of course, the same as being unreal. In a way, the fact that we might fear being influenced assumes that each of us is able to recognise the possible impact of the influencing machine. We might be taken in by propaganda, for example, but we might also have an uneasy sense that this is happening to us, which implies some capacity to distinguish between what is real in our experience and what is not. Nevertheless, the idea of the influencing machine vividly describes the feeling that a force is eating away at us, reducing the space in which we can be ourselves. Finding ways to navigate a world in which influences of this kind proliferate (and it is perhaps relevant that social media figures with big online followings are called 'influencers') and in which their truthfulness is frequently open to dispute, is a challenging task. With information, opinions, claims and lies swamping the multiverse that media have become, and with so much that happens being highly complex, technical and hard to understand, how do we locate ourselves as thinking beings with a sense of our own reality and that of the surrounding environment? Attributing everything to an external influence – a malign influencing machine – simplifies things greatly, as is visible in the appeal of conspiracy theories and of racist and antisemitic beliefs. It offers a firm, if poisonous, structure through which everything that happens can be interpreted – above all, everything that goes wrong.

Although nowadays the belief that we are being used in this way sounds like conspiracy theory, historically it often had religious sources. Prophets worked with the conviction that they were a channel for something greater and more important than themselves, calling on them to speak or act as messengers from God. In cultures in which such experiences are valued, they might actually make people feel *more* real than usual, perhaps in touch with the divine. The ordinary, superficial self is transformed into something profound, and we come to feel that we are living more fully. The intensity of prophetic states exemplifies this, as do more mundane but still mystical 'out of body' experiences. Losing the ordinary confines of the self by channelling something greater can be exhilarating and can give a person a sense of meaningful depth that they may feel they usually lack. Perhaps mystics really do know something about how to deepen the connection we have with ourselves as well as with the world.

The potential gains of relaxing our usual self-boundaries can also be seen in the excitement that we might get from being part of the crowd at a rave, for instance, or a sports event or a political rally. Losing ourselves in this can paradoxically be a way of finding ourselves, becoming freer of the inhibitions we place on ourselves by 'overthinking' or self-inspection and critical self-judgement. Under those circumstances, the impact of forces that do not seem to be truly 'ours' can feel liberating rather than persecutory. The ability of a crowd to lift people off their feet – metaphorically but sometimes literally – can make us feel empowered, living more brightly and intensely and with a greater capacity to participate in life. Less positively, this is also a source of the power of demagogues and charismatic speakers who can generate a sense of belonging to something exciting, in which petty concerns are left behind and we are united with others in some great project. Huge rallies energise these demagogues and reflect back on their followers, who in turn feel linked to the leader and to one another, freed of their usual inhibitions – for better or worse. Suddenly, everything seems to make sense. Unfortunately, this is often in the form of a manufactured hatred directed towards those who do not belong to their privileged group, and the loss of inhibition can have disastrous consequences. The fascist rallies of the 1930s were prime examples which have lately been reworked to disturbing effect, especially by right-wing agitators.

Possession states of various kinds might at times be liberating, freeing us from our usual constraints, but losing control of our mind and body in this way can also be frightening. We may experience a panicky sensation of the self being overwhelmed not in order to become part of something more meaningful, but as the result of a kind of invasion by a malign force. Those who try to resist the crowd can feel this acutely: such resistance is very difficult, given how strongly group dynamics function to pull people in. Holding to our values and sense of reality in the face of a mass of people who seem to think and feel differently is a very hard task. Under those circumstances, the sense of our reality falls away and a different kind of artificiality comes into play, directly confronting us with the question of what it means to be an autonomous human. 'Groupthink' is relevant here, understood as the tendency of members of groups to become more alike in their thinking and less able to diverge in their views, sometimes leading to misreadings of reality and to bad mistakes, notably in organisational and political contexts.[11] More profoundly, we might find ourselves unable to think at all, because our thoughts have come to be owned by others.

There are various ways in which the struggle to make sense of the world we live in can be thought about. One useful approach is to consider the kinds of vocabulary that our society makes available to us, as a way of understanding and relating to the states of mind characteristic of different phases of social life. Three main psychoanalytic concepts have been used over the past fifty years to conceptualise these cultural orientations or 'discourses', understood as ways of describing and to some degree diagnosing the contemporary situation.

The first of these is 'narcissism', which refers to a way of being that is characterised by a kind of 'thinness' of the self. This reflects a state of mind in which there is very limited capacity to care for others or for intimacy, and in which our dependence on other people can be felt as a great threat. The narcissist may be bullying and Machiavellian, with little compunction about using others to achieve advancement and showing a willingness to deceive and betray, apparently because the only thing that matters is the self. Yet most narcissists need the admiration of others to validate that self; without this adoration, constantly renewed, they are deflated and empty. Aficionados of the film *American Psycho* will recognise this in its famous business-card scene, which can be taken as a paradigmatic vision of narcissistic rage.[12] A group of more or less identical business executives compare their new cards. Patrick, the lead character, becomes increasingly upset as the others' cards (all of them white and embossed, and indistinguishable from each other) seem smarter than his own. By the end of the two-minute sequence, he is engulfed in rage, and almost in tears.

Withdrawal of adoration produces a rage-filled response, because the self is felt to have little value and so needs propping up by constant attention from others. Narcissists might seem suave, dressed to impress and with a capacity to inveigle themselves everywhere, but under this surface often lurks furious anger. Behind the bravado, boasting and self-promotion there is a terror of abandonment. Narcissism is the reaction to a sense of worthlessness and of being unwanted, dressed up in a kind of counterphobic reflex of self-aggrandisement. The self is fragile and insecure, anxious that if too much is demanded of it, its lack of depth will be revealed. Intimacy, the life-blood of genuine relationships, reveals an absence at the heart of narcissistic boastfulness, which is why real intimacy is avoided and other people are related to as objects to be used rather than properly engaged with.

The above deals with narcissistic individuals, but there have been times when the whole of society seems narcissistic, in the sense of encouraging self-aggrandisement and manipulative egocentrism, bragging and self-promotion. There is plenty of evidence that this happens, as a succession of recent political leaders has demonstrated, including a prime minister of the UK and a president of the US. While 'diagnosing' public figures can be a perilous activity, the self-inflating lies perpetrated by both Boris Johnson and Donald Trump, their lack of interest in or ability to process detailed information, and most of all their primary concern with appearance and adulation, fit the narcissistic framework very closely. That they also have differences, with Trump's violent attacks on antagonists and anyone suspected of disloyalty far outstripping in viciousness Johnson's vacuous obfuscations, does not reduce the recognisability of this pattern: a concern with being celebrated, even uncritically loved, that rides roughshod over any sense of responsibility or allegiance to the truth. There is also little doubt that some social arrangements (certain forms of modern capitalism, for example) promote narcissistic values as admirable, rewarding them financially and socially – as in these two cases but also in instances in which flagrantly narcissistic 'types' have achieved great success in business or in some professions.

Is this getting more pronounced? There have been many examples of narcissistic leaders in the past whose inner resources needed boosting by unadulterated admiration and who had to be protected from reality by sycophants if they were not to implode. But perhaps something about late twentieth- and twenty-first-century culture has exaggerated these narcissistic tendencies – especially in neoliberal economies premised on an ideology that rejects dependency and mutual care as 'soft' and turns 'welfare', which we might have thought was a commendable concern for others' well-being, into a term of abuse.

The vision of society as narcissistic took quite a hold throughout the late twentieth century. Perhaps the most notable example is Christopher Lasch's book, *The Culture of Narcissism*, which presents a critical vision of then-contemporary American life as all mirrors and surfaces, TV entertainment and quick fixes.[13] Lasch offers a compelling description of a narcissistic state of mind that reflects these dominant characteristics of society:

> Studies of personality disorders that occupy the borderline between neurosis and psychosis, though written for clinicians and making no claims to shed light on social or cultural issues, depict a type of personality that ought to be immediately recognisable, in a more subdued form, to observers of the contemporary cultural scene: facile at managing the impressions he gives to others, ravenous for admiration but contemptuous of those he manipulates into providing it; unappeasably hungry for emotional experiences with which to fill an inner void; terrified of ageing and death.[14]

Lasch argues that this is the ideal type for bureaucratic organisations, with narcissistic *disorders* being merely an exaggeration of the normal personality attributes that are valorised under such conditions. Narcissists thrive in an environment that rewards manipulation of others while also penalising those who prioritise intimacy and genuine care – and these conditions, he argues, are prevalent in a modern culture fixated on appearance. In a passage that seems just as applicable today, after the technological changes that have revolutionised society, Lasch writes:

> Modern life is so thoroughly mediated by electronic images that we cannot help responding to others as if their actions – and our own – were being recorded and simultaneously transmitted to an unseen audience or stored up for close scrutiny at some later time.[15]

This seems like a reversal of the influencing machine, but it is better thought of as its complement: whereas that experience was of the machine intruding into the self, the narcissistic environment is one in which the external world is treated as a set of mirrors that support the image of a self. If these mirrors fail to prop up the self, it feels depleted and lost. It is this aspect of narcissism, its core component of inner impoverishment and desperate seeking after self through reassurance and aggrandisement, that is stressed by Lasch; his attempt to link this with the broader superficiality of the American society of his time is what made this book influential.

The Culture of Narcissism was published in 1979; over forty years later, the obsession with images and surfaces seems to have multiplied, encouraged by social media and smartphone culture and the extraordinary explosion of online material that now fills every moment with activity. A word of caution: while this is often taken as evidence that 'real' relationships are on the decline, replaced by a virtual world in which no one has any depth, we should be wary of assuming that the need to find meaningful relationships has disappeared, or that the huge number of superficial personal contacts enabled by smartphone culture means that people have lost the knack for more intimate, durable and demanding connections. It certainly sometimes seems that way, as people flick from one contact to another and maintain multiple conversations simultaneously. Yet the claim that the whole of society is geared towards narcissistic fascination with images and that 'deep' relationships have been displaced by manipulative interactions in which we all seek to get what we can, is perhaps more partial and debatable, at least as a characterisation of most people's experience. For one thing, times change and with them the emotional dispositions of the cultures that surround us. From the early 1990s onwards, fuelled in the West by the AIDs crisis and by 9/11, appreciation of the realities of loss have come to the fore, and with it the shadows of sadness. Perhaps this appreciation was always lurking as a counterweight to the fantasy of omnipotence that accompanies narcissism. Most of us have spaces in our life for intimacy of a kind that is not just narcissistic; and when we lose people who matter to us, we still feel it and cannot just shrug it off, however much we might have stored about them on our phones. In fact, this is a crucial point: much of what is debated in relation to questions of how we feel real, and how real we can feel, comes under the general heading of how we respond to loss.

To experience loss, we must have valued something; otherwise, its removal might be a source of frustration but not of pain and grief. Sometimes loss might be denied, usually in one of two ways. The first is simply to claim that the lost object, whether a person or a precious artefact, or even an idea about something, such as the goodness of a person or of one's country, has not really been lost at all. The difficulty of mourning the loss of someone whose fate cannot be established, which happens in war or when someone simply disappears, is well known. Those left behind often continue restlessly to seek the lost person, wishing at least for information about what has happened to them and hoping, often against hope, that they might still return. People searching for the 'disappeared' victims of authoritarian regimes, such as those that operated in Latin

America in the second half of the twentieth century, are important examples of this. Their campaigning for information continued well after they'd accepted that their lost ones could not have survived, not as an act of denial – they knew very well what the reality of the situation was – but as a moral principle and political act, as well as to bring what is loosely called 'closure', allowing them to grieve and then move on. This is clearly a rational and ethically important process: everyone deserves to have their fate known. But sometimes there is a denial of reality when faced with unbearable loss. This is less common with a death; people whose relationships break up, however, or who are abandoned by someone they love might not accept that it has really happened, might cling to a fantasy that the loved one will return to them – making their own and often everyone else's life a misery in the process.

With a treasured idea, this phenomenon can be even more marked. The way some communists held onto an idealisation of the Soviet Union, even after the revelations about Stalin in the late 1950s, shows just how hard it can be to recognise that something one believed in was wrong. It is arguable that this is also the situation in the UK, where there is only very limited acceptance of the harms done by British imperialism, and where Britain's role in abolishing slavery is celebrated without adequate acknowledgement of the huge responsibility that Britain has for slavery itself. The failure to accept the loss of the image of a benevolent Britain produces a kind of nostalgic reaction in which, instead of facing this reality, people adopt the idea that something has been stolen from them. This has frequently been expressed in racist terms, for instance in the fantasy that Britain's greatness has been destroyed by immigrants from what were previously its colonial territories. Loss and mourning are transformed by denial into resentment, whose practical consequences are visible in anti-immigrant social policies and events such as Brexit.[16]

The second relevant type of denial is when the disappearance of a person or object or belief is acknowledged, but the significance of the loss is minimised: it becomes, in Judith Butler's words, 'a never having loved, and a never having lost'.[17] The idea here is a simple one: if it is possible to persuade yourself (and others) of the insignificance of the loss, then you do not have to mourn it. A job you fail to get? 'I never wanted it anyway.' 'Good riddance,' when someone abandons you – which may or may not be what is truly felt – or even 'it's just the way life is, people come and go.' There is an overlap here with narcissism, as this is another form of self-protection based on ensuring that commitment to others, including real intimacy with them, is avoided to protect us against the feelings stirred up by loss ('I am a rock,' as an old Simon and Garfunkel song put it). Treating people as interchangeable, so that no one means too much and we are not too dependent on any particular other, is a prime example of this kind of narcissistic state of mind: 'If I don't get close to anyone, I can't be hurt.'

But this can come back to bite us. During the First World War, Sigmund Freud wrote an article exploring the relationship between what he called 'melancholia' and mourning.[18] Melancholia is close to what we would now call chronic depression – a state of listlessness and hopelessness, in which self-blame is prevalent and the world seems drained of meaning. Freud pointed out how similar it is to mourning; the problem, he thought, was that it is a mourning process that can never be properly engaged with because the loss itself has never been fully recognised. For Freud, proper mourning is a crucial element in how we keep ourselves sane. As we lose important elements of our lives – people, objects, places, convictions – we can grieve for them by integrating them into our selves so that they continue to live on inside us. The ego, or I, he thought, is in large part made up of these lost 'objects' (a term he used for anything in which we have emotional investments, but especially people), and this gives us more substance. It makes us feel more real. If we do not accept that we have lost anything that matters, we can never absorb the losses that inevitably occur, and we end up in a perpetual state of grief in which nothing can get properly resolved. We ultimately come to hate ourselves, as the psychological energy that should be used for dealing with the loss is instead turned against the self. But more to the point, if loss is denied, then depth of feeling is too.

Of course, melancholia or depression does involve deep feeling; the problem is that it is not the kind of feeling that can be harnessed for strengthening our grasp of ourselves. It leads to what Freud referred to as 'self-beratement', a state of self-blaming that is acutely painful, yet also out of kilter with what is justified. In that sense, it leads towards more unreality: loss is denied, and we are left wondering why we feel the way we do. At its origin is an impulse towards self-protection, avoiding the full force of loss; but, like many mental defences, it leads to a kind of split in the personality that increases suffering. In blanking out the experience of loss, for fear of being hurt, we end up mystified by emotions that are demanding an outlet yet seem to make no sense. To feel real, we need to allow ourselves to risk feeling hurt and to understand that that is what is happening.

But how can we organise ourselves to feel deeply without falling apart or, on the other hand, sentimentalising things so that our apparent experience of grief is just another form of unreality? Emotional behaviour is always a kind of performance in which we show to ourselves and others what we feel inside. When the display of emotion is authentic, it is in important respects in tune with the actuality of inner feeling, even if we are not always aware of this in advance. Sometimes we do not know what we feel until we observe ourselves showing emotion. Crying, for instance, can come as a surprise to the person who cries, making them wonder what triggered the tears, especially if they seem unjustified by the ostensibly upsetting situation ('Why did I cry when she said that?'). Not uncommonly, we can be moved by things we know are meretricious or manipulative, things that shouldn't move us – a sentimental film, or an emotional appeal we recognise as cynical. Have we been duped? Surely, sometimes yes; advertising relies on this to some extent, and political rabble-rousing certainly does. But sometimes even these transparently inauthentic calls on our deeper feelings can hook into something that is real, so that when, say, we cry at the end of that sentimental film, it is not (or not only) that we have allowed ourselves to be manipulated (which, after all, might be part of the fun of it), but also that it reminds us of something that is genuinely meaningful in ourselves, or in our experience. A lost animal can bring out an emotional response in people far in excess of their actual commitment to animals; perhaps, at least on occasion, this is because it reverberates with the genuine feelings of lostness and of vulnerability that we all might have.

There are some emotions which we rely on to indicate what we are feeling and hence to make us more real to ourselves. Anxiety is the strongest of these. We often feel anxiety in an inexplicable and frustrating way, just when we most do not want to do so – stage fright, for instance, or exam anxiety, or social or sexual anxiety. What is the point of this? Why create more obstacles to dealing with the situation that confronts us by getting ourselves in a state, when remaining calm and purposeful would be so much better? There are various answers to this intriguing question. One is that anxiety is a kind of automatic signal of danger, built into our minds to alert us, even when we might not be consciously aware that something troubling is going on. The potential value of this is obvious. When it is not excessive, anxiety can help us orient ourselves to difficult situations and motivate ourselves to prepare for them; after all, it is appropriate enough to be anxious about an exam, or a job interview, or a wedding, or having a baby.

The right degree of anxiety can improve our capacity to handle these challenges. But the downside is that anxiety can also get out of control, interfering with the very response that it is meant to facilitate. In relation to feeling real, it may be better to think less about the possible *function* of anxiety than of how it operates to make us more intensely engaged with the experiences we are having. After all, people quite commonly seek out situations that make them anxious, from horror films to climbing mountains, so as to feel more excitingly alive. Perhaps few things that are worth doing do not also have their quota of anxiety attached!

Anxiety can impress on us that something matters, helping us feel more engaged with it; anxiety is an *intensifier* and if it is not too overwhelming might even be welcomed as such. *Feeling more* rather than feeling less is arguably an important human ambition, which is one reason why the thrill that comes with what might be called 'optimal' levels of anxiety (which will vary from person to person) is often welcomed. On the other hand, many people try to avoid it, preferring the security attached to relative coldness rather than the uncertainty that emotional commitment of any kind, including thrill-seeking, produces.

But anxiety can get out of hand, becoming deeply unpleasant rather than enjoyable. The thrills of dangerous sport or fairground rides are one thing, freely chosen as a way to get in touch with the excitement of physical and psychological immersion in the moment. But panic, fright and immobilisation through excess anxiety are quite another. To understand this, it is important to look beyond simple evolutionary explanations – such as that anxiety was of survival value in alerting our prehistoric ancestors to danger but is now out of tune with the societies in which we live, where the dangers have become more diffuse, less easily identifiable, and, most of the time, less dramatically life-threatening. This may be part of the story, told from a specifically biological and evolutionary perspective, but in terms of how each of us manage ourselves and what we do with our anxiety it is not a useful narrative. More to the point is a possible connection between the effects of anxiety and the depth or security of self. One way in which anxiety can operate to help us feel more real is through making a connection between the situation we face and our inner states and resources, the foundations of our psychic life. It leads us to ask, can we manage the world as it comes to meet us, how strong are we, how much confidence do we have in ourselves?

When these inner foundations are fragile, anxiety can be an escalating phenomenon. The external situation sparks anxiety, we feel inadequate to meet this, this inadequacy suggests that we could be destroyed by what we face, anxiety then increases in a vicious, escalating spiral. On the other hand, if we have sufficient resources, anxiety can mobilise them in ways that feel positive, even enjoyable. Mustering our strength, we rise to meet the challenge, testing ourselves with some degree of confidence that we will survive. Anxiety itself is not therefore the problem; it is the ways in which anxiety interacts with already-existing inner states of mind that determine whether we will be thrilled or crushed by it.

Of course, when I say resources, I do not only mean psychological resources. One issue with anxiety is whether there are also social supports that protect people and make them feel confident handling the situations that confront them. This has various dimensions, from the intimate support we might hope for from those close to us to the system of care to be found in society – how it protects us when we are ill, or in financial trouble, or physically or psychologically threatened by others. Exploring the social management of anxiety has usually been the realm of sociologists, but even some psychoanalysts, better known for their focus on the 'inner world' of the psyche, have attended closely to the environmental conditions that make people feel less or more secure.

Among the more influential of these, the mid-twentieth-century British psychoanalyst Donald Winnicott developed an account of how the conditions of infants' early care can provide them with a sense of being psychologically supported or 'held' reliably and firmly enough for them to feel safe, yet also flexibly enough for them to embrace the risky world without being immobilised by fear. Winnicott also stressed how the conditions that create security are linked to the encouragement of a sense of reality within the self. The basic idea is that infants who have their fundamental needs (for love, as well as for food and warmth) recognised and responded to in a reasonably sufficient way will gain a sense of themselves as powerful enough to have an impact on the world in accord with their own desires. Infants who are neglected or abused, or whose needs become secondary to those of their caregivers, are less likely to have this strength of self embedded in them and more likely to be conforming, eager to please, or in some way dissociated, meaning that they have an insecure sense of their ability to manage themselves.

Winnicott uses a very simple but helpful division between what he calls 'true' and 'false' selves.[19] The true self is an inborn potential for creative growth in which the personality is integrated around a strong sense of who we are and can become; the false self is a protective veneer which helps us to survive by compromising, conforming with what is required of us rather than developing our own personal agency. One example would be that of infants with a depressed parent. The infants might suspect (not consciously, of course) that if they are too demanding their parent will not be able to cope and will abandon them. The infants' 'task' then becomes that of keeping the parent alive by being interesting and entertaining or very easy and appeasing – a learned set of behaviours that become consolidated into a kind of self but that do not lead to the development of the infants' own creative ways of being, based on their own needs and desires. In the end, becoming 'real' is just too dangerous, as it seems likely to lead to rejection; the self has to guard against revealing its actual needs – a pattern that can become permanent. Think not only of the diffident person afraid to speak out when a wrong is being done to them, but also of the person whose mode of intimacy is to be constantly second-guessing their partner's wishes and never expressing their own. This can look like love and concern, and of course it contains those aspects; but it can also be a way of protecting oneself against expected rejection: 'I will do anything I can to keep you happy, just so long as you don't go away.'

This set of ideas is social, saying something about how our inner sense of reality depends on the environment in which we were brought up. It also has implications for larger social support structures and networks. Under certain conditions, insecurity is rife, and this has effects on people's psychic lives as well as on their material circumstances. Economic collapse is an obvious example, as is war. But processes within what might appear to be relatively stable societies can also systematically undermine the capacity to feel real and at ease with ourselves. An additional layer of understanding to those provided by the concepts of narcissism and melancholia is offered by readings of contemporary surveillance society that emphasise paranoid states of mind and the management of anxiety, in which everything is subject to suspicion and the search for security becomes paramount, which merely seems to fuel the feeling of being *insecure*. We are being watched all the time. Sometimes this feels straightforwardly persecutory; at others, it temporarily reassures people that they have some protection against a hostile environment; in every case, it multiplies the paranoid sense that there is no safety to be found anywhere. Under all these conditions, 'being real' is a momentous challenge.

Some people seem to thrive even under great pressure. The assumption is that the quality of their previous good experiences in their families and communities has helped them to develop the resources that allow them to do so. Their *inner* security enables them to manage situations where, objectively, the world is against them. But for many people, breakdowns in what might be called the social contract – the agreement that a society will look after its members – cause immense distress and actively interfere with their sense of belonging and their confidence in any future. Poverty, misogyny and racialised insecurity can affect people profoundly, both as children and throughout life. They militate powerfully against the establishment of a sense of security that can generate the kind of creative engagement with the world that 'being real' demands.

The notion of 'recognition' is helpful here. Just as infants seek recognition by their caregivers for what they are and what they need, so do citizens require recognition from other citizens and from state authorities. This can take different forms: economic benefits, appreciation of the nature of different communities (for instance, ethnic, religious or LGBTQI+ communities), moves towards inclusivity and against discrimination, or a more general provision of care via public health and social care resources. Through these mechanisms, a culture is created in which the security of citizens (and, for that matter, non-citizens who also inhabit state spaces) is ensured. This security allows people to feel that they have a place in the social world and are not always fighting against it. If the psychoanalytic perspective adds something here, it is to suggest that under those conditions of relative security, it will become easier for people to feel real in the sense of developing awareness of their own needs and wishes and of building strong and open connections with others. Recognition means holding in mind that other people have their own, meaningful lives, and that it is a social task to acknowledge those lives and to find a way to engage with them that treats them as significant. Yet what many people are exposed to is the opposite of this: racial hatred, gender violence, attacks on welfare. These are conditions of non-recognition, meaning that people's needs are discounted, their existence as valued social beings denied. And without being recognised, it can be hard to believe we matter, hard too to experience ourselves as real.

It is in this interlinking of personal and social concerns that the idea that being real is an *ethical* issue comes into focus. Ethics here does not need to be a very complicated notion, even though it is an often-contentious branch of philosophy. It can simply mean the concern we might have to do right, to remain aligned with a set of values that we hold to be true. This of course incites a lot of questions – for instance, how we might decide on what 'truth' means and how we might adjudicate between different versions of it. Some classic philosophical conundrums apply here: is one person's life so sacrosanct that preserving it should always be a priority, even when this puts other lives at risk? What about situations in which there are different ideologies at work, say a dispute between those in favour of absolute freedom and those who believe that regulating conduct is necessary (as in debates about the limits of free speech), and where should the lines of compromise be drawn? What about ideas some hold to be true that are abhorrent to others (for example, racist ideas)? Is ethics primarily concerned with how we deal with other people, or does it refer to a relationship with something more absolute, as some religions would suggest? In relation to the issue about being real, what kinds of 'truth' are at play and how do we know that it is, for example, better to face pain and suffering than to deny them and get on with our life?

None of these questions and the many others that connect with them are easy to resolve, which is why they keep many philosophers in business. However, the argument I made earlier about how being real involves a capacity to connect deeply with ourselves and how this is built out of conditions of security, gives us some guidance as to why 'being real' is an ethical issue. It suggests that living fully requires both an appreciation of our own desires *and* an acknowledgement of the reality of other people, in the sense of recognising that they too are desiring and needful beings with complex inner lives. Which of these come first? The French twentieth-century philosopher Emmanuel Levinas, whose writings have been very influential in this area, opposed the idea that we should engage first with existence as separate beings and that it is from the security of the sense of being fully alive that we might reach out to others.[20] Against this emphasis on 'ontogeny', he stressed an 'ethics first' philosophy, which argues that what constitutes us as specifically *human* is an ethical awareness of others as centres of consciousness – that is, we appreciate the humanity of other people, and this calls into action our responsibility for them and our human capacities for intimacy and hence for depth. Does, then, the 'subject' (the individual person) or the 'other' come first? And does this matter, if being real involves *both* self-realisation and an open encounter with others?

Some balance is probably needed here. Putting the other first at all costs may seem to be an ethical ideal, yet it is not clear that this is always helpful, and it could involve a kind of self-derogation that makes us so lacking in selfhood as to be useless to that other. Another idea of Winnicott's may clarify this.[21] He writes about how infants test the resilience of their caregivers by what might loosely be called 'aggressive' acts against them – rage, upset, demandingness. Winnicott speculates that from the infant's point of view, these aggressive acts have the potential to destroy the caregiver. If they really succeed in doing this – for instance, if the caregiver gets ill, or goes away, or retaliates in some way – the infant's aggression may have momentarily triumphed, but no more use can be made of that caregiver to help the infant come to terms with the world. If, however, the caregiver has a sufficient degree of resilience to 'survive' these attacks, so that the infant discovers that the aggression cannot destroy this valued other person, then the caregiver becomes 'useful', strong enough to support the infant's quest for survival. It is the capacity of caregivers to recognise and be attuned to infants without giving up their own selfhood, their separateness and strength of being, that enables them to be of help to the infant. Without this, they lose substance and are of no 'use', however much they may love the infant and put its needs before their own.

If a parent is not sufficiently robust to hold onto their own reality in the face of the infant's demands, it can seem as if they are an extension of the infant, rather than a separate being who can offer guidance and safe support. Similarly, if *all* a psychotherapist can do is echo patients' speech and sympathise with their suffering, worthwhile acts to some extent, they might do no more than reinforce these patients in their uncertainty about whether they can find a way to mobilise their creative resources to change. Therapists also need to be able to formulate their own views of the patient and challenge them from their position of separateness, their sense of what is possible and what is right.

The idea that we should not abase ourselves in the face of the other but should remain present is, of course, not really at odds with the idea that ethics involves understanding the needs of others and seeking to meet them. It is rather that a necessary condition for meaningfully relating to another is to have something to relate *with*, to have a depth of being that we can offer them. The process is reciprocal: we relate to others fully, this helps us strengthen a sense of our being a person with something to offer, which makes it more possible to relate more fully, and so on. The anxiety that drives us away from other people ('Will they like me or reject me?' 'Will I embarrass myself or do others damage?' 'Will I get hurt?') is the same anxiety that locks away our creative capacities, the insecurity that means we cannot risk intimacy because we may find we cannot cope with its demands. Being present for others is a crucial element in ethics because it involves recognising them so that they can flourish; it is also a practical step towards enhancing ourselves.

This is also one answer to the conundrum about 'truth'. Instead of dealing with the larger philosophical issues of what truth can mean and how it can be judged, we need to think in terms of an equally complicated but more small-scale question of how to be 'true to ourselves'. We can return here to the sense of self as a creative spark of potential that Winnicott calls the 'true self'. Each of us has needs and desires and our flourishing depends in large part on the degree to which we can recognise and enact these without harming ourselves and others. Being 'true to ourselves' means acting along the lines of these needs and desires. To the extent that we can do this, we might feel more connected with what can meaningfully be called our 'reality'. To move along this path, we need to have been given both a developmental context in which we can thrive and a current social context of support. This involves building relationships with others and drawing on social structures that are based on processes of recognition, in which what is real inside us allows us to perceive and welcome what is real in others too. The two processes, outward-looking and inward-looking, go together and depend on each other: without an interpersonal context in which the reality of others is appreciated, we cannot feel recognised because there is no one to recognise us. The ethical relationships we have with others are therefore dependent on, and vital for, the ethical relationship we might have with ourselves. This is as much a social programme as a personal, psychological one. Creating social conditions that prioritise equality and support – that, in a word, do not disdain the notion of 'welfare' for all – is an essential element in an ethical social contract.

Finally, there is the question of what it might mean to truly recognise another, something which often goes under the general heading of 'love'. Freud thought there was something contradictory about considering love a social emotion. He argued that love is essentially a feeling between two people and hence anti-social in essence, excluding all others from its embrace. He wrote,

> According to one ethical view ... [the] readiness for a universal love of mankind and the world represents the highest standpoint which man can reach. Even at this early stage of the discussion I should like to bring forward my two main objections to this view. A love that does not discriminate seems to me to forfeit a part of its own value, by doing an injustice to its object; and secondly, not all men are worthy of love.[22]

I am not sure about this, and not only because love comes in different forms. It is easy to love a spouse *and* a child, a family *and* a community, at the same time, in overlapping but distinct ways. But maybe there is even more at stake than this. For me, this is clarified by a comment made by the philosopher Rebecca Goldstein in her very moving account of her debate with her father about the place of ethics and value in philosophical and religious life.[23] Goldstein compares her own endorsement of the rational enterprise of philosophy, its purity of thought and rejection of emotion and muddled thinking, with what she sees as her father's Jewish regard for emotional entanglements. She is aware in this of how the contrast between the 'life of the mind in Western philosophy' and the densely affective context of the Judaic world may not be easy to resolve.[24] In fact, she thinks, philosophy holds 'a vision of life as pellucid with rationality as the other is thick with the ties of blood and with the heavy decisions one is asked to make between the orders of one's love'.[25] This other dimension, the one that has ties of blood and love in it, haunts her; and strikingly, it is embodied for her in the very person of her father.

> [My] father never could work up any enthusiasm for the luminous vision of the life of pure reason I tried to paint for him. I argued that it was the life that was the most consistent and thus right. He agreed with me that it was consistent, but he wouldn't agree that it was right. In fact, he thought it was all wrong. He thought it was right for human life to be subject to

contradictions, for a person to love in more than one direction, and sometimes to be torn into pieces because of his many loves.[26]

Loving 'in more than one direction' might turn out to be exactly what we need to make us real, as we struggle to appreciate and enjoy the complexity and confusion of the world and of the place that we and others have within it.

2

Recovering Childhood

When do we begin? There is much debate about when a person's life starts, some of it highly politicised and deeply antagonistic. Is it at conception? At a point during pregnancy when life outside the womb becomes viable? At birth? In some cultures, babies are not thought of as fully alive until they have survived for a while, perhaps a month, no doubt because so many of them die. On the other hand, most parents begin to feel attached to their babies well before birth and suffer greatly if for some reason they are not born alive. We might call this the baby-in-the-mind, in which case life will have begun well before birth – even before conception, if we consider the many people who wait years to have a child, if they ever do so at all. The imagined child is possibly always with us, sometimes feared (as in situations in which people are desperate *not* to get pregnant) and sometimes deeply desired.

From the point of view of the child, it is not clear when life begins. It definitely precedes birth in the important sense that events in the womb affect the foetus. If the mother is under great stress, it may have short- or long-term effects on the foetus; likewise if she is alcoholic or drug-dependent or has an accident. We simply cannot say if this is registered in some form of early consciousness, though given that babies in the womb can be observed through ultrasound to respond to stimuli of various kinds (noise, heat, movement), it seems likely that there is at least fleeting awareness of the intrauterine environment even if no memories are laid down.

Almost certainly some forms of attachment start very early. Babies have reliably been shown to recognise their mother's voice at birth, so it could be that awareness of sound is the earliest kind of conscious experience. It is also likely that the immersion in the enveloping, supportive cocoon of the womb is experienced as a fundamental tactile sensation, directly related to the comfort of being held and cuddled in early life, and in later life too. Whether this sensation is linked to a particular mother or is a general sense of being safely held is uncertain, but it hardly seems to be a great leap to speculate that something engrained from the experience of being in the womb comes with us into life and starts us off on the path to become fully ourselves. Whatever that means.

The link between these two issues, the baby-in-the-mind of the parent and the baby's experience of the early environment, is perhaps one of the more important points to arise from this. Perhaps we can agree that both things are genuine, that babies are imagined before they are born – sometimes years before – and that the conditions of their conception, gestation, birth and early life are registered in some way by babies, increasingly consciously but also as 'unconscious' patterns of being and expectation about how the world works and what their place is in it. The link is then that the baby-in-the-mind of the 'other' is a highly significant feature of babies' sense of *themselves* as they emerge into life. I use the term 'other' here to mark that we are not just talking about mothers or parents, but also about extended systems of relations and communities, even of society as a whole. These systems will vary with people's circumstances, but the key point is that babies are born into a world that is already intent on positioning them in webs of fantasy and expectation, anxiety and hope. What name shall we give the child, or after whom might the child be called? Who do we wish them to be like, whose loss are they making up for, what disappointments are they due to remedy, what ambitions to fulfil? Will they help solder together a frail relationship between their parents, or are they seen as the fruition and presentation to the world of the richness of that relationship? Are they meant to complement already-born siblings ('two boys, now a girl'), 'completing' a family? In a community, are religious or social expectations already placed upon them, even, for example through circumcision, literally inscribed on their bodies? In the wider social environment, what privileges or handicaps relate to their social class, ethnic origin, physical state or gender? The possibilities here are varied and have different effects, but the overall point is clear: babies are already part of the social world when they are born, already subjected to material inequalities, already placed into a network of fantasies held by others about them; and these inequalities and fantasies themselves may have long histories, stretching back over many generations.

The impact of these social influences on how children develop is considerable, but it is worth pausing for a moment to think about whether this means that children are wholly determined by them. Do we come into the world with no inner reality of our own, just waiting to be shaped by the forces that surround us?

These forces are crucial, and newborns are at their mercy. No babies can survive on their own, and this vulnerability may be the ground for what is genuinely our reality as human beings. But it would not be fair to discount the agency of babies themselves – their immediate impact on their environment, their own capacity to affect the world in which they live. I think it unlikely that any parent would say that their children turned out exactly as they had imagined; and for many the reality of their child is radically different from what they had expected – for better or worse. From the start of life, any fantasy of having a compliant, quiet baby who simply responds happily to the ministrations of a loving parent (a kind of 'madonna and child' fantasy) is liable to be quickly dispelled by the presence of a demanding, sometimes bawling, unsettled creature that refuses to be easily managed and that takes several weeks or months to show any appreciation of their carers' hard work, if they ever do at all!

Some babies are much easier than others, presumably owing to the conditions into which they are born (happy, stable parents with enough emotional, financial and social resources to feel well supported) but also connected with their own genetically and constitutionally produced temperament. But most babies are demanding not just because of their biological needs, which don't necessarily fit with their carers' clocks, but also because of their always-existing *originality*, which we might call their character, even though it is not by any means yet fully formed. Despite being the most dependent of all human creatures, matched only by the neediness of those who are dying, young infants are also remarkably *independent* in terms of what they ask of their carers. 'It's your job to look after me properly,' they seem to say, 'and if you don't, I will complain and make you feel my rage!' This can lead to quite a divergence between what was imagined and the reality, at least for a first child. Of course, most people will recognise that to have too 'easy' a baby would be quite worrying. An infant who is passive, who needs to be woken up all the time, or young children who always do exactly what they're told without demur – these are likely to be signs of something wrong, a lack of liveliness that indicates something blocked, psychically and emotionally, and possibly physically too.

Healthy infants, then, are born with a strong impulse towards liveliness. Their demandingness, what some have called the aggression with which they encounter the world, is the outward expression of this inner impulse to be real. When this goes well, the liveliness of the child meets with a responsive environment in the form of carers who can tolerate the demands and even enjoy them as signs of an emergent personality. This is what it might mean to survive in the presence of your infant: to know that what feels like an attack, a bombardment of your ease and personal space, is also what you want for this creature – that children should find a way to develop *as themselves*, not just as compliant copies of their parents or anyone else. Of course, a little compliance would be welcome and is not always forthcoming. But the difference between the 'true' and 'false' selves proposed by Donald Winnicott is evident to most people when they see their children in action. The conformist false self is taken on as a protection when things feel unsafe; the true self is marked by alertness, creativity and a kind of freedom that may at times be wearing but is part of being alive.

If children are born lively, programmed to be curious about the world, eager to have an impact on their physical surroundings, primed to form relationships and to respond to their carers – in a word, if they are born *real* – then why and how does it so often go wrong? What is it that gets in the way of flourishing – that chooses a false self over a true one – as a child grows older? This is not to say that such a withering away of the life force is what happens to everyone, a point I will come back to when considering the 'childishness' of creativity. Yet it seems inarguable that most of us operate in ways that become more constrained with time, that our level of alienation from the liveliness with which we began grows more and more pronounced. Some of these constraints are undoubtedly necessary: the selfishness of infants, their ruthlessness, is not a great basis for a good society, though it often seems to be enacted in an extreme way by many adults. Some degree of modification of the Life Drive (as psychoanalysts call it) is necessary for getting by in a peopled society, some agreement that there are rules by which we conduct ourselves in relation to others and to the natural world.

This is not really the issue, however, because such constraints can be taken on willingly and not even be experienced as constraints, but rather as channels through which mutual fulfilment at interpersonal and social levels can be achieved. The problem comes when the forces that operate on people are so destructive and drive such a profound wedge between the person's inner liveliness and the demands made on them that the former dries up. It is as though, when it is not possible to survive as a fully alive being, the sources of liveliness have to be protected by the formation of a shell that is as impenetrable as possible. This kind of alienation, which can be produced by the social forms of alienation written about by many social theorists, smothers the healthy aggression with which children are born. It is as if what has been communicated to infants is that they are not safe to 'become themselves', that they must comply with what is required of them or they will die.

This is in large part a question of balance. Infants need care; indeed, everyone needs care, taking different forms across the life cycle but always to a considerable degree indispensable to human well-being. At the simplest level, to keep alive we need a social infrastructure. In early infancy this is the (hopefully loving) ministrations of parents and other carers, but later it is a physical and social surround that allows us to proceed with our lives, sometimes with scant recognition of the existence of this caring or holding environment (how many of us think about the planning and work that has gone into the physical infrastructure of our cities, for instance, when we navigate our everyday relations with water, sewage, electricity and so on?).

In early life, the need to be held is literal and immediately obvious, so that when it is endangered it produces quite desperate responses in children to increase their chances of survival. Later, we might say, the same is true but sometimes in a more hidden way. An influential account of this is given in attachment theory, which was invented by John Bowlby in the 1950s and 1960s and developed by many other researchers since. Attachment theory claims that there is an inborn, biologically given, evolutionarily derived tendency for humans to seek closeness to others.[1] They do so, it is argued, because of the dangers of the external world and the need for protection and succour. Infants want to maintain proximity to their caretakers; young animals do so by moving towards them and clinging to them, while young humans, who are less mobile, cry and demand, eliciting responses from mothers and others who then come to look after them. Attachments protect children, who could not otherwise survive on their own, and the quality of these attachments – whether they are 'secure' or 'insecure' in various ways (for instance as 'avoidant', 'resistant' or 'disorganised') – is crucial for development.[2]

Attachments do not only have physical effects; they also fulfil emotional needs, making it possible for infants to become capable of reflecting on their situation and, importantly, of understanding the emotional states of others.[3] As is often said by those using attachment theory, children who are secure in the knowledge that there is someone watching over them are much more likely to be able to separate from that person and experience the outside world – including the world of other people – with greater curiosity and enjoyment, precisely because they know they will be rescued if something goes wrong. In a slightly different register, we can draw on another perception of Winnicott's, that what he called 'the capacity to be alone' depends on having, and having internalised, the experience of being in the presence of someone who can hold us in mind.[4] In order to think freely and creatively, we need the sensation of having been thought about. Without this inner conviction of being cared for, of registering as a person in the minds of others, it is very hard indeed to feel confident about our own existence and resilience in the world. It is hard, in fact, to feel real.

This all means that we mostly get our sense of being present in the world as a person through the concern of others, their capacity to see what it is that a child might need, what children might be expressing even if they do not have the words to communicate clearly, or the reflective ability to know what it is they want or what is troubling them. It is in fact remarkable how often parents and carers seem to get this right, considering how confusing a young infant's cries might be (are they cold, tired, in pain, hungry or even angry?).

As children get older, they become clearer about what they are feeling, but also can be more hidden, more careful about expressing it, more troubled or just more complicated and harder to manage. Much of the time, the people who look after them seem to be remarkably adept at learning about each individual and the different ways in which different children express themselves. They can be said to *recognise* the child, in the sense of being reasonably attuned to that child's needs, making mistakes, of course, and relying on trial and error to get things roughly right, but still being helpful and conveying to children that they are cared for and thought about and that they have an important place in the life, affection and mind of their carers.

There is clearly a process of moulding going on, in which parents start to 'socialise' their children by the way they react to them, showing enthusiasm about their behaviour when it fits the parents' desires and perhaps the acceptable norms of the social environment. This could be when the child is friendly to other young children, or charmingly responsive to adults, but also when children just fit in with expectations such as gender norms. Parental and social approval is a very powerful route through which social values are communicated and traditions passed on, as well as through which children learn about what will make their lives smoother, what is permissible and what is deprecated or even forbidden. But this moulding is not only in one direction. There is also a process of what might be called 'mapping' or, as it is often named, 'attunement'. Child and parent come together in a kind of dance in which each gets to know the other, working out each other's idiom or basic way of being and behaving, each of them adapting to the way in which the other relates to them in what is usually, and largely, a benevolent cycle. Whatever the parents' pre-existing expectations and hopes, they (generally speaking) find their child attractive and start to enjoy the child's specific nature, and the feedback from this leads them to adapt those preconceptions to better correspond with the child's emerging selfhood.

In addition, many parents feel that something new is drawn out of them by their children, something they did not necessarily know about themselves. This could be a long-forgotten aspect of their own childhood experience, for good or ill (loving elements, or inhibitory or destructive ones that stem from past resentments and unhappiness). It could also be something creative inside themselves that has never yet had the opportunity to find expression. For example, a child's playfulness might release something playful in a parent; a child's vulnerability might provoke a loving gentleness and altruism not usually shown; a child's active engagement with the world might spark a parent's own curiosity and enjoyment of what is around them. These are common moments in ordinary parenting, yet precious in the becoming-real of parents themselves.

From the perspective of the child, the process is at least as powerful and probably even more important. The learning of social and interpersonal norms that I mentioned above is an aspect of what children absorb from professional carers such as nursery workers and schoolteachers as well as parents. This is often taken to be a simple matter of instruction, yet it is a complex process involving identifying with the carer (wanting to be like them) as well as wanting to be approved of and loved. It can also be resisted by children, sometimes for good reason. The clash between the relative freedom of the home and the constraints of public spaces, especially educational ones, is sometimes too much for a child to bear and usually involves some level of unhappiness. When those spaces are good, however, this can be combined with what is experienced by the child as an exciting channelling of their energies into new directions, made safe by the continued presence of carers of one kind or another.

Children also, of course, pick up norms from what they see of the outside world and what penetrates from there into their domestic sphere through TV programmes, computer games and so on. Holding onto a sense of what the child needs and wants in the face of these very powerful forces of persuasion is not an easy task, for child or adult. Yet it is also true that children will develop their own ways of selecting what is and is not meaningful for them from the offerings that the culture makes, what they agree with and what they reject, sometimes in accord with their parents' values but quite frequently not. The latter is often playful, in the sense that children and young people try out ways of being to see what will fit for them given their skills and attributes; but sometimes it is principled and can genuinely be called resistance. Children rapidly develop a sense of what is good and bad, enjoyable and painful, right and wrong, indicating that they are by no means passive receivers of values imposed upon them.

Much of this depends, again, on the processes of recognition that they experience. A fundamentally benevolent context, in which carers genuinely do their best to notice and acknowledge what a child needs and is feeling, will communicate to children that they matter, that their impulses are legitimate and that their emerging selves have value and can be appreciated, enjoyed and loved by others. The surrounding environment's capacity to adapt to the child is in this sense a precondition for the child to feel secure enough to adapt to the world and, as noted just now, to resist it when that feels like the right thing to do. The 'genuineness' of children's responses to what they experience is often very attractive, as they see things for the first time and react without inhibition, sometimes saying and doing things that adults would like to say and do, but have lost the courage, conviction or intuition that would allow them to. When recognition of the child and not just imposition of the adult's view is primary, we have a situation in which children are supported to develop their own sense of reality, however much that might rub up against parents' wishes and society's demands. Whatever constraint might have to be put on a child's behaviour (look out for the traffic!), if it comes from this fundamental position of recognition, it can potentially serve as a source of creative growth.

But things can go horribly wrong. Much of the psychological literature is concerned with what happens when the environment in which a child is developing fails to provide the kinds of conditions of safety that I have just been describing. These may be extreme situations or abusive settings. Children growing up in war zones, for example, or where 'natural' disasters strike, or in significant poverty, or under conditions of persecution, will need to possess exceptional resilience to preserve their creative potential and to flourish. The damage done to children in these circumstances is rightly regarded as among their worst effects, not only putting children's lives at risk but also stunting their prospects for growth. Similarly, children who are exposed to significant antagonism between their carers, including domestic violence, who undergo neglect or abuse or who suffer early bereavement of their parents are much less likely than other children to feel secure enough to push the boundaries of their world through their curiosity and challenge. Their natural 'aggression', in which they test out their own capacities and the boundaries of acceptability and possibility in their social world, is at risk of transmuting into frustration and destructive violence, or into passive acceptance and self-protection.

Many years ago, before I trained as a clinical psychologist, I was working as a houseparent in what was then known as a school for 'maladjusted' children, isolated in the English countryside. Children were sent there from a city fifty miles away when it was decided that they could no longer live at home and could not be contained in local schools. The term 'maladjusted' says a lot about the times (the 1970s) and the attitude towards these children; presumably it implied that our task was to 'adjust' them, although even then that was not the way we looked at things. As a staff group, we aimed to provide a healing environment in which children who had nothing going for them at home – or no homes to go to – would feel safe and be able to develop freely. The problem was that this often clashed with the need to look after very angry and aggressive children, with staff members who like myself were young, naïve and ill-trained. Just being 'nice' did not work too well and was hard to sustain.

Among the children who stand out in my memory are a pair of twin boys who came to us aged seven, after being discovered at home tethered to a playpen. That had basically been their life up to the previous year: they had never been outside, never seen other children, and barely interacted with their parents or anyone else. Taken into the care of the local authority, they were very difficult to manage and could not tolerate the social demands of school. Their relationship with each other was tense, rivalrous and at times violent, yet they clung to one another and rejected other people, children as well as adults. Most graphically, they had developed their own language, a version of English that only the two of them could understand.

Over time, the boys formed some relationships with other children and became very attached to some members of staff, in an erratic way that was highly possessive and demanding. Their language improved, though their schoolwork remained rudimentary and their attention span extremely short. They never spoke about their experiences prior to coming to the school; it was not clear to me, then or now, whether this was because they refused to think about them or simply could not remember. Perhaps the delay in their language development had also robbed them of the capacity to symbolise and develop their memories, or maybe those early years were just too painful to recall. The damage from this period was only partly remediable. Research on children like these has shown that they can recover intellectually from such environments, though these twins did not fully do so, but that extremely deprived children's social and emotional relationships may always be impoverished and difficult.[5] It is certainly the case that even with the supportive, if sometimes chaotic, environment of the school and with a genuine effort to provide loving care, these boys looked likely to always need help and to struggle with intimacy and trust.

Later, I discovered that one of the boys was killed in a road accident in his teens. The fate of the other I do not know. The school closed, and its buildings have now been converted into an upmarket hotel.

Sometimes the hardship that children face is obvious, as in my example above. But it can also be quite subtle. For example, an idea that derives from early family therapy studies is that some children might become 'parentified' – that is, forced to take up a parental-style relationship with regard to their siblings and even to their actual parents, looking after them psychologically (and on occasions physically) in a kind of role reversal.[6] A more extreme version of this was named by the French psychoanalyst André Green as 'dead mother syndrome'.[7] We must be careful here about the potential for mother-blaming that can be found in much of this literature, but it is still useful to think about Green's general idea, namely, that a depressed or ill or neglectful parent might be experienced by a child as unavailable for recognition of their needs and so might require 'waking up' or bringing back to life. This can lead to children adopting a kind of false self, in which they unconsciously perceive their role as activating the parent through their own efforts by being exceptionally lively and entertaining or, conversely, unusually passive and 'good', so that the parent will not collapse and abandon them.

It is worth imagining this again for a moment. Children need the parent or carer to be resilient and real enough to look after them but may be faced with a parent who is lacking, absent or vulnerable, themselves in need of care. The child cannot ignore this, because being cared for is essential for survival: children are dependent beings who cannot manage on their own. Under such circumstances, children might rapidly learn not to make the kinds of demands that could 'destroy' their parents but instead to 'prop them up' by being docile.

We can understand this kind of response as the formation of a shell in which children under duress protect their incipient liveliness for fear that it will either be destroyed by the violence they perceive outside themselves, or that they themselves will destroy this world (the world of their parents, for example) through being too demanding and aggressive. This is also seen in adults, and in such cases can often be traced back to the kinds of childhood circumstances that I am describing. Take a not uncommon situation in psychotherapy in which a patient appears to feel they will be too dull for the therapist and need to entertain that therapist to keep them engaged and awake (it doesn't help, of course, if the therapist actually falls asleep or looks bored). Such patients produce stories, dreams, jokes and questions and sometimes seem insightful about themselves, but they tend not to manage to be reflective or to absorb what is happening in a thoughtful way that allows the therapy to develop. They seem, instead, manic, moving too quickly from one thing to another and being too keen to produce the kinds of material that they imagine the therapist might be looking for.

There could be several things going on in such a situation, but one scenario is that the patient has never felt fully valued for themselves – supportively 'recognised', in the language I have been using – and instead thinks that the therapist, like the parent in their early life, must be kept awake or else will disappear, abandoning the patient to their own insufficient resources. If the patient needs the therapist yet does not believe that the therapist can cope with exposure to their reality – a lack of faith based on their earlier experience of parents who seemed unable so to cope – the work they do in therapy might be geared towards protecting the therapist rather than examining and somehow 'releasing' themselves. Progress in such a therapeutic encounter might involve patients becoming *more* demanding or perhaps slowing down in the session, taking more risks about not being interesting, but rather accepting that the obsession with being entertaining is a defence against acknowledging their neediness, with the imagined risk of driving the therapist away.

Children who are put in the position of not being secure enough to allow themselves to take risks, to be difficult or demanding as well as loving and responsive, are a kind of paradigm for the difficulties many of us face throughout our lives in having the confidence to assert ourselves without being overly anxious or converting such assertiveness into aggression. Trusting that the surrounding social environment is resilient enough to receive and recognise our needs and to provide a safe space for the discovery and expression of our personality is not easy in settings where the environment is genuinely hostile or neglectful and inadequate, poverty being a key circumstance of this kind.

The intergenerational consequences of this can be profound, as the person who struggled with non-recognition in their own development finds it hard to bear the demands of their children, potentially repeating the pattern. However, we should also note how the situation can be reversible. Often this is because of other relationships people have managed to form that instil in them sources of value and trust (teachers may be important here, but grandparents are also commonly referenced, and sometimes it is friends or later partners who help most). Battling towards being real is nevertheless something many of us struggle with. Pushing boundaries, challenging norms, becoming creative – these are risky undertakings, which require an inner sense that we have something of value to offer and that there are others around us who can respond to this. This is hard work, but it is also, in an important sense, play.

Play is something recognised by most people as essential to development for humans, and for many animals too. It might be partially defined as 'risk-taking without (too much) risk': trying out ways of being that stretch the boundaries of selfhood without the negative consequences that can arise if there is too much insistence on reality. When children imagine themselves as explorers or warriors, put themselves in the place of a parent, or embrace physical challenges in a safe environment, they are making forays out from the reality of a dependent, vulnerable self to see what might be possible, made safe by the limitations of the child's actual situation, by the use of toys in place of people or valuable objects, and by the watchfulness of adult carers. In adolescence, play also means young people extending the range of their development and exploring possible states of mind, identities and sexualities – what the psychoanalyst Alessandra Lemma has termed 'omnipotentiality'.[8] She describes this as 'the developmentally appropriate experimentation through the extension of one's possibilities and limits (mental and physical): it is a "trying on for size" of different versions of one's self that is commonly observed post puberty'.[9] All this shows just how important play can be. It makes possible an expansion of the self under relatively secure circumstances. Without it, not only can life be drab, but also it becomes dominated by fearfulness, by the sense that if the child does something wrong, catastrophe will ensue. If the wrong turn is taken in play, however, nothing is likely to be severely damaged, and children – and indeed people in general – can relatively safely calibrate what they are capable of doing, and perhaps what they would most like to do as well.

The kind of play I am referring to is not so much organised games, which can indeed be playful but which in their institutionalised forms can give priority to competitiveness, force and the kind of discipline that many children find oppressive. It is rather play that lets the imagination loose and fuels the possibility of thinking, doing and making new things, investing energy in them without too much worry about consequences. This does not mean being totally unconcerned about the damage we might do by enacting our wishes, which is always a real danger. It is rather a description of a certain kind of energetic investment that a child might have in the world, an investment which when carried forward gives rise to more adult forms of creativity and, dare one say it, love.

Some psychoanalysts call this the 'Life Drive' or 'Eros', signalling a tendency to bring things together with enthusiasm (to bang them together in infancy!), to make life more complicated, to do unnecessary things and think unnecessary thoughts, and most of all to invest ourselves in people and activities. For Freud, the opposite of this is the 'Death Drive', which tends towards negation and subsiding into passivity or, as later psychoanalysts proposed, is expressed in destructive violence and envy. We will come back to this in a later chapter. But here it is the Life Drive and its expression or inhibition that is at stake: how can we hold onto it as we grow, drawing sustenance from it in the face of the various constraints which the 'reality' of the social and natural world place upon us?

In the broadest sense, this version of the Life Drive might be called 'eroticism'. This is different from understanding the erotic as purely sexual, though sexuality is certainly infused with it. Rather, eroticism refers to the excitement and enjoyment that might be invested in something, the capacity to generate imaginative engagement that is as much intellectual as sensual, if it is possible to differentiate these two modes of experience. In fact, this already points to an issue of importance: the separation of the intellectual from the sensual is part of the process of clamping down on enjoyment that turns learning too often into drudgery. Infants' fundamental, one might say 'natural', curiosity does not make this distinction. Finding things out, for example about the mother's body or their own, or about the way in which light shines or wind makes things move, or about loud or soothing noises, is a matter of excitement that is felt in the body and forms the mind as a single process. The same is often true for adults, although it is equally often denied: we need only think of the bodily impact that horror films can have, or about how certain ideas can create embarrassment and make us blush or stammer, or indeed about the bodily effects of fear. Sensuality, eroticism, is a part of any full engagement with life.

In much debate about the sources of our behaviour an opposition is made between nature and society, or between biology and psychology. This suggests that these are separate entities, that it is possible to think about nature without considering how society structures it, and vice versa. Yet it is obvious that the two are interlocked. The urban landscape, for instance, produces certain natural environments, and socially produced climate change has enormous impact through famine and drought, submergence of low-lying areas and wars based on scrambling for resources, as well as inciting migrations that themselves have massive political effects.

At the macro level, it makes no sense to think about either nature or society in isolation: they construct each other, determine what is possible and what is not, and show the effects of each other in everything that happens. Something similar applies at the level of the person. Our bodies make some things possible and constrain others; they are implicated in everything we do; but they also respond to our psychological states (anxiety, pleasure, depression, joy, and so on) and to our social connections. Preferred body shapes and the experience of desiring and being desirable are examples of just how strongly the physical and the social entwine. Eating disorders from anorexia to obesity are clearly cultural phenomena that nevertheless have physical and psychological sources and effects. All this is to say that when we consider how development can act in the service of 'being real', of connecting as deeply as possible with the actual conditions of our social and psychological environment, we need to think about ourselves as embodied beings – without imagining either that we are determined in all that we do and feel by a pre-given biological (including genetic) structure, or that we can somehow escape from the physicality of our bodily states. We need only think about illness or ageing to realise this. The body matters, but it has its effects in specific psychological, relational and social contexts (for example, the quality of care offered to the elderly will greatly affect their ability to manage bodily frailty; the design of the built environment will make independent living more or less possible for people with physical disabilities), and these in turn establish what the body means.

This point is crucial for understanding the nature of embodiment. The body into which we are born is, to a considerable extent, 'given', and many aspects of its adult outward form (height, mass, hair, skin colour, anatomical sex, propensity to illness) are already programmed-in at or before birth. Events also matter: birth accidents, nutrition, injuries, viruses, cultural practices, grooming and deliberate work on the body (prosthetics, tattoos, self-harm). Crucially, the way in which we relate to our bodies develops over time. While the point about the inextricability of body and psyche remains valid, we also take up both conscious and unconscious positions in relation to the given body. Indeed, this is very often a central issue for us throughout life, changing at different stages of development. Do we like what we see in the mirror? How do we feel about the way other people look at us, or the way we imagine they do? Are we comfortable with the bodily desires we have, especially around sexuality and other appetites, such as for food, but also when we feel driven towards addictive substances? What about race – do we feel harassed because of our racialised appearance, or at ease with it and with how others treat us because of it? And what about the sexed body: how does it feel to be placed on one side of what is usually taken as an absolute divide, between male and female?

This last question is proving to be immensely aggravating and potent in the so-called culture wars. Strong opinions are frequently expressed about the reality of transgender – or trans*, with an asterisk to indicate both the complexity of the field (especially the uncertain distinction between different terms such as 'transgender', 'transsexual', 'non-binary' and 'genderfluid') and the multiplicity of different experiences. For some, a declaration by somebody, especially a young person, that they find themselves in the wrong-gendered body is an indication of psychopathology, or that they are the victim of suggestion and propaganda on the part of a pro-trans* community. For others, such statements must always be accepted or 'affirmed', so that gender becomes a matter of self-actualisation and choice rather than an identity that follows from anatomical structures.

The intensity of this debate has itself been problematic, as a major report into gender identity and young people in the UK has recently demonstrated.[10] People on both sides feel pilloried, and this has created what has been described as a highly toxic environment for those – including many trans* people – trying to work out what is going on for them and what support they need. I am not going to venture too far into this discussion; among all the polemics there are now some very good and accessible texts available.[11] Here I want merely to reflect briefly on how the trans* experience relates to the question of feeling real in the body. If feeling real involves an exploratory, playful engagement with the world and with oneself, it also entails finding a way to develop a relationship with the body, to become 'personalised' within it, so that embodiment can be taken for granted. This does not of course mean that we are never dissatisfied with how our bodies feel or look; most of us at various times yearn for our bodies to change – to put on or lose weight, to look 'better' or younger, or for aches and pains to go away. Yet this can all still come about within a context in which we accept that this is 'our' body and feel like we belong to it, the 'we' here being something like 'our conscious and unconscious selves'. It can therefore come as a shock to discover, either in ourselves or others, that there are people for whom something as supposedly fundamental as their sex is experienced as *not real*. The 'meaning' of their embodiment is for them a kind of lie; they draw a distinction between the truth of their gendered experience and the false shell in which they feel themselves to be trapped.

This draws attention to the way in which embodiment is not automatic, but something that develops over time and through the numerous forces acting upon it. For those who pathologise trans*, these forces include hormonal variations, physical accidents, cultural mores, psychological disturbances due to other factors, 'narcissism', 'psychosis', and failures of recognition by carers, which can involve children internalising the wish that their parents may have had for a child of the other sex. This long list should itself make it apparent that different trans*-identified people might be very different from one another, and that we should be more wary than is often the case about generalising across a whole group defined only by their discomfort with their given bodily sex. It also draws attention to the energy that has gone into developing theories to fit trans* experiences into a pathological framework.

As a social discourse, this certainly contributes to the difficulties trans* people have, highlighting the vital importance of positive versions of trans* embodiment. What is beyond doubt, however, is that there are people who declare themselves trans* for whom it is a matter of life and death to be recognised as wrongly embodied and to be helped with this, sometimes to the extent of having major surgery. Despite occasional celebrations of the playfulness of trans* in some of its forms, for those people who follow through with their sense of gender-incongruity – pursuing outcomes they believe will make their lives more meaningful – the 'choice' to be trans* is without doubt a serious one, with huge, lifelong consequences.

This demonstrates just how important, but also how complex, the process of embodiment might be. As Alessandra

Lemma writes, in her fine introduction to issues involving transgender and psychoanalysis: ' "Arriving at the body" is a core aim in work with transgender individuals, but this work requires that we also keep in mind that embodiment is always precarious and evolving.'[12] At the very least, it shows how people ache to feel at one with themselves, in whatever ways this might be possible, to be recognised by others, and to feel that they are, in their embodied selves, real.

There is much to inhibit active, playful creativity and much work goes into draining the life out of experience. Sometimes it is due to privation, to horrible conditions that make it impossible to enjoy anything but instead produce constant anxiety and fear. War is the largest of these, as the many (too many) images of children in war zones, searching for lost parents, hunting for food, parenting their siblings or dealing with their own injuries dramatically reveal. But it can also be true at the domestic level as well as through cultural and religious oppression, especially around gender and sexuality. If it is too dangerous to take risks, then people learn quite quickly not to do so; if lively investment in the world and loving commitment to others is likely to bring grief, then withdrawal is the obvious adaptive response, hard to counteract. But the resilience and creativity of people is often extraordinary. It is evidenced by those in terrible situations who remain attuned to their own liveliness, to what they can give to and receive from others, and at times to what they can make, ranging from makeshift homes in disaster conditions through to artworks (music, literature, drama, visual arts) that speak to others about their experiences.

A fascinating and famous example about survival in the face of extraordinary early deprivation comes from an article published in 1951 by Sigmund Freud's daughter Anna, herself a distinguished psychoanalyst. This article, 'An Experiment in Group Upbringing', described the work carried out under Anna

Freud's guidance by her co-author, Sophie Dann and others with a group of six child survivors of the Holocaust.[13] It is worth quoting the first paragraph in full, as it presents graphically but succinctly the background story of these children.

> The experiment to which the following notes refer is not the outcome of an artificial and deliberate laboratory setup but of a combination of fateful outside circumstances. The six young children who are involved in it are German-Jewish orphans, victims of the Hitler regime, whose parents, soon after their birth, were deported to Poland and killed in the gas chambers. During their first year of life, the children's experiences differed; they were handed on from one refuge to another, until they arrived individually, at ages varying from approximately six to twelve months, in the concentration camp of Tereszin [Theresienstadt]. There they became inmates of the Ward for Motherless Children, were conscientiously cared for and medically supervised, within the limits of the current restrictions of food and living space. They had no toys and their only facility for outdoor life was a bare yard. The Ward was staffed by nurses and helpers, themselves inmates of the concentration camp and, as such, undernourished and overworked. Since Tereszin was a transit camp, deportations were frequent. Approximately two to three years after arrival, in the spring of 1945, when liberated by the Russians, the six children, with others, were taken to a Czech castle where they were given special care and were lavishly fed. After one month's stay, the 6 were included in a transport of 300 older children and adolescents, all of them survivors from concentration camps, the first of 1000 children for whom the British Home Office had granted permits of entry. They were flown to England in bombers and arrived in August 1945 in a carefully set-up reception camp in Windermere, Westmoreland, where they remained for two months. When this reception camp was cleared and the older children distributed to various hostels and training places, it was thought wise to leave the six

youngest together, to remove them from the commotion which is inseparable from the life of a large children's community and to provide them with peaceful, quiet surroundings where, for a year at least, they could adapt themselves gradually to a new country, a new language, and the altered circumstances of their lives.[14]

A supporter of Anna Freud offered the children a year's tenancy of a large house in Sussex named Bulldogs Bank, so the children have become known as the 'Bulldogs Bank children'. At that time they were all about three to four years old. The house was staffed by Sophie Dann and her sister Gertrude, who had worked with Anna Freud at the wartime nursery she had set up in Hampstead. Anna Freud notes some 'relevant facts concerning the early history of this group of children':

> i) that four of them (Ruth, Leah, Miriam, Peter) lost their mothers at birth or immediately afterward; one (Paul) before the age of twelve months, one (John) at an unspecified date;
> ii) that after the loss of their mothers all the children wandered for some time from one place to another, with several complete changes of adult environment. (Bulldogs Bank was the sixth station in life for Peter, the fifth for Miriam, etc. John's and Leah's and Paul's wanderings before arrival in Tereszin are not recorded);
> iii) that none of the children had known any other circumstances of life than those of a group setting. They were ignorant of the meaning of a 'family';
> iv) that none of the children had experience of normal life outside a camp or big institution.[15]

Anna Freud describes in moving terms, made if anything all the more poignant by her objective, 'scientific' style of writing, the very difficult behaviour of the children, how they 'showed no pleasure in the arrangements which had been made for them and behaved in a wild, restless, and uncontrollably noisy manner'.[16] They were destructive towards toys and equipment and responded to their adult carers with either indifference or hostility. Most noticeably, they clung together as a group:

> The children's positive feelings were centered exclusively in their own group. It was evident that they cared greatly for each other and not at all for anybody or anything else. They had no other wish than to be together and became upset when they were separated from each other, even for short moments. No child would consent to remain upstairs while the others were downstairs, or vice versa, and no child would be taken for a walk or on an errand without the others. If anything of the kind happened, the single child would constantly ask for the other children while the group would fret for the missing child.[17]

All the children looked out for each other and were sensitive to any threat to any of them or any separation. Strikingly, there was no one leader in the group, but all the children had equal status, even if one or other might take a leading role at different times and in different contexts. In contrast to their difficult behaviour towards adults, the children were immensely supportive of and collaborative with each other, although one of them (Ruth) showed occasional rivalry (Anna Freud suggests this might be because she was the only member of the group to have formed a prior attachment to a mother-substitute). Anna Freud remarks on the 'almost complete absence of jealousy, rivalry and competition, such as normally develop between brothers and sisters or in a group of contemporaries who come from normal families'.[18] The paper describes how the children looked after each other, comforted each other when upset, shared food and toys without demur, and displayed a highly developed sense of each other's needs and emotional states.

Over time, as we might expect, the children's behaviour and emotional relations shifted. They began to include adults in their group. Later, they did begin to form individual attachments to adults, though these were never as strong as their ties to one another, and according to Anna Freud, were much less passionate than other young children's relationships to their parents. The paper goes on to describe in detail the children's auto-erotic activities (thumb-sucking, masturbation), their complicated relationship to food, their toileting and other activities, all of which were different from 'the norm' and in some cases showed delayed development. Their fears were many and strong; Anna Freud explains this as linked to the terrible precariousness of life in Theresienstadt, where being taken away to death camps was a daily reality, and loss and fear were all around.

Anna Freud concludes her article with some thoughts on the significance of the Bulldogs Bank children for psychoanalytic theory, without writing much about their therapy. However, it seems that the children made great progress over the course of the year. Anna Freud's biographer, Elisabeth Young-Bruehl, emphasises the importance of 'providing the children with a staff member substitute mother', a lesson that Anna Freud had taken forward from her work in the wartime Hampstead nurseries.[19] Perhaps what is most striking, however, is the resilience of these children in the face of extraordinarily deprived early childhoods (albeit moderated slightly by the care given them by adult inmates of Theresienstadt). Clinging together, they offered each other support and love, doing their best to make up for the absence of bonds with benevolent adults. Afterwards, they remained in contact and seem from reports to have built healthy lives for themselves. We might think of this as the Life Drive finding its way through the 're-routing' it took in the intensely supportive peer/sibling relationship that these immensely deprived children managed to create with one another.

The remarkable thing about this kind of life force is how it can hold onto a sense of creativity even in the worst of circumstances. This does not mean it is easy to do so, of course – better circumstances would enhance liveliness less effortfully – but it does demonstrate how fundamental the impulse and need for self-expression may be. Imaginative investment in our encounters with the world, sustaining bonds with others, wrenching reality into some kind of meaningful form that can be related to and acted upon, reclaiming agency even when it is being wrested away from us, are all important aspects of resistance to oppressive circumstances as well as ways of celebrating more comfortable lives.

So how can we retain childish playfulness and the erotic charge of loving creativeness in later life? I have already discussed some of the necessary conditions for healthy growth: recognition, some form of secure acknowledgement of a child's needs, circumstances in which safe exploration can take place, and an environment in which the assertive curiosity of the child is welcomed rather than treated as a disturbance or a nuisance. Later, the kind of schooling that is important promotes imagination and does not prescribe competitive individualism with its basis in fear of failure, as it is precisely this fear that inhibits constructive risk-taking. A wider culture that values relationality over narcissistic manipulativeness and that has broadly humanitarian rather than bellicose values will make a difference. But there may be something else too, more subtle.

I have stressed much of the literature on 'security' as basic to growth, and this certainly is important. However, security can only be a relative thing. There is something fundamentally *insecure* about the human condition, especially in early life where dependency is primary but also later, when our vulnerabilities are only too obvious as we face (as Freud put it) the power of nature and society, and the frailty of our ageing bodies. We might seek absolute security, but it can never be found. As we try to make ourselves more secure in a practical sense, by building walls or installing surveillance cameras or making borders more hostile or hiring security guards to protect schools and places of worship, so we also produce invitations to find new ways to breach this security and, more significantly, increase the risk of feeling insecure. If we need so much protection, the world must be a dark and hostile place; if we have CCTV monitoring us all the time, we must be expecting disaster at any moment. You might even claim that it is the obsession with security that makes us insecure, producing a vicious cycle in which more security is sought, less risks are taken, more insecurity is felt, and so on until we are prisoners in our homes and minds.

The Life Drive involves an engagement with inherent insecurity, with recognising that the genuine vulnerability that characterises life, including human life, is inescapable. This is not a justification for morbid pessimism and withdrawal from the world – this will not make anyone feel safer – but rather an injunction to notice how shared insecurity demands mutual recognition of vulnerability across different groups. It also means that hiding within our shell is not a recipe for survival. We are vulnerable, and our vulnerability in large part defines our being; recognising this is the first step towards building on that very vulnerability by reaching out to others, who are equally vulnerable. That is to say, the walls we raise up drain life out of us; the breaches that we allow in these walls make it possible to feel connected and real.

3

Hate

It can be argued that hatred is the original emotion. This might sound counter-intuitive when we observe newborn babies and young infants. Aren't the key issues for them, first, survival, and then love, affection and attachment towards, and received from, their caregivers? Don't they learn fast to reach out to their parents, smiling at them and gurgling with pleasure when they are attended to? Yet much thinking about the experiences of young infants, especially from psychoanalytic perspectives, focuses on how they discriminate between aspects of the world by repudiating those that produce pain, adopting an attitude of hate towards them, as well as internalising those that advance pleasure. For Freud, getting rid of unwanted, hurtful sensations by mentally pushing them out of the self was a vital mechanism for developing the capacity to discriminate between good and bad.

Melanie Klein saw the situation even more starkly.[1] Her rather Gothic theory is full of embellishments and excesses but also evokes something about the turmoil and confusion of early childhood. For Klein, infants are born preoccupied with managing their internal Life and Death Drives, particularly the latter. By this she meant the psychobiological forces, assumed to be inborn, that drive the infant forwards towards either love or hate. She was impressed by the intensity of these basic feelings, and indeed if we try to do what she did, to speculate about what it might feel like to *be* a baby, it is possible to see why she might have put so much emphasis upon them.

The Life Drive refers to those aspects of the infant that seek survival, enjoyment and connection with others; the Death

Drive refers to those that aim towards quiescence, retreating from the booming confusion of things, and when this is not possible, to violent fantasies about destroying the world. Given how small and helpless newborn babies are, how much at the mercy of the environment, which even at the best of times is likely to fail them (too hot, too cold, too noisy, too slow to respond, too painful), it does not require too great a leap of the imagination to think that they could feel more hatred than love. Infantile dependence is not a comfortable state to be in, as adults realise when they become ill or needy; and railing against it might be an understandable response. From there to hatred may not be such a huge step.

Kleinian infants are fragile and easily fragmented, overwhelmed with the anxiety of possible dissolution of their precarious sense of self by their own pulsating and uncontrollable needs, and at the mercy of an environment that may or may not be benevolent – and even when it is, may not feel that way. Internal strife dominates the infant's early psychic world. There is a battle between a destructive force that Kleinians call 'envy' and a set of defensive strategies that seek to preserve the infant's mind and indeed the environment needed to sustain it. These strategies are built out of loving impulses, sometimes coded as the Life Drive or, in a more everyday terminology also used by Klein (though not always in an everyday manner), 'gratitude'. What makes the destructive drive so strong is that it arises naturally from the experience of birth, of being wrenched from the maternal cocoon in which the baby's needs had been met without any effort or negotiation. Life as a separate being starts with the loss of this paradisial environment, a loss that is resented and provokes rage-filled vulnerability. These 'bad' feelings (painful sensations, anxious emotions) are dealt with by pushing them out so that they are no longer an inner threat. This brings some relief to the child, but at the price of filling the external world with badness and consequently making it persecutory.

The template here is the infant's relationship to the mother's feeding breast. If that breast is experienced as reluctant or rejecting, the infant's inborn envy is increased and becomes aimed at the breast, because it holds gifts it refuses to give. But even if the breast is nurturing and generous, envy is activated. This is because the giving breast is resented for its ownership of good things that the infant wants and needs. The unformulated but motivating question for such infants is why they should have to be dependent on this external thing that possesses what they desire and cannot find in themselves. Either way, the Death Drive wins: either infants hate the breast that denies them what they need (the 'bad breast') or they hate the breast that owns the means of gratification (the 'good breast'). The best that can be hoped for is the abatement of envy through actual experiences of loving care (which means that it matters whether the breast is *in reality* giving or withholding), allowing the infant to mitigate hatred through a formula that runs something like, 'There is love in the world and it is directed at me, so my hatred of everything needs to be balanced by gratitude for what I am being given.'

Klein's account of infantile hatred then gets very elaborate. In outline, she argues that this early envy can only be managed by a process of *projection*, where the feelings and fantasies involved are externalised so that they no longer seem to come from inside (and hence are inescapable) but instead are experienced as properties of the world that can be resisted or avoided (the breast is felt as bad and persecutory, though also, when things are going well, good and benevolent). Over time, if the goodness of the external environment outweighs its failings, and as children become more able to appreciate the care they are receiving and feel less paranoid and less internally persecuted by their envy, they become capable of drawing together the loving and hating elements both of their 'inner worlds' – their minds – and of external reality. Now the core issue becomes that of managing *ambivalence*, or the integration of love and hate so that neither fully dominates the other. Hate is still needed, to differentiate what are genuinely hateful sources of pain and deprivation – an important point for consideration of how we might deal with abusive and oppressive circumstances. But if there is sufficient resilient care in the world for children to feel that their hate (and hatefulness) can be managed and survived, loving tendencies can be brought into play in a beneficial cycle that does not deny envy but allows it a place alongside love and gratitude. The result is a more realistic state of mind in which different emotional states can be faced without the fear that the more negative ones will make positive feelings unobtainable.

This remarkable account of how hatred is central to early experience and how the management of hate is crucial for the psychological well-being of infants, has proved surprisingly influential. What is odd about it is the idea that infants, who we might imagine would be primed towards attachment and loving responses to others, are in fact bundles of envy and rage that have to be survived and 'contained' by their caregivers if they are to develop a full capacity for love and gratitude. Many writers, including psychoanalysts of the 'object relations' school, have argued that the situation works the other way around: rather than it being hate that is primary and must be dealt with in this way before love can arise, the child starts life full of loving expectation and only turns to hate when things go wrong.[2] Babies are born from a womb in which their needs have automatically been met; they meet a mother who in important ways is already known and who is primed by her wishes and possibly by some biological mechanism to love her child; and if things are reasonably all right they arrive in a broader social world that welcomes them. What is there not to like? Why prioritise the presence of hatred, even if it is clear that babies are not always happy, that they feel pain and early forms of anxiety, and that much of the time they have no idea what is happening to them and no control over it? Surely when babies cry and appear to rage it is because they have immediate needs that must be met and they are simply communicating this to their caregivers? Continued rage would then be a response to deprivation, and perhaps later hatred is itself a signal that something has been denied that person; that frustration of their fundamental needs – either for material support or for psychological recognition – breeds hatred, which otherwise would be minimal or non-existent. Hatred is a signal that something has gone wrong, not a primal feeling in itself.

There are arguments either way on this. In favour of the claim that the primary human emotion is love and that hatred only appears when this is thwarted is the observation that babies seem to be born with a capacity for recognition of their mothers and an impulse to make contact with them. The powerful social orientation of most babies is often what makes them very rewarding to their caregivers, even when looking after them is also exhausting work. Biologically, babies are utterly dependent creatures. It would not make much sense for them to be pre-programmed to hate those who offer them that service.

Psychotherapists who work with very difficult children often understand the aggression and hatred evinced by their young patients to be a response to the harshness of their surroundings and especially to parental care that has been far from optimal. The focus of such therapeutic work is on recovering children's capacity to find sources of love inside themselves in the context of a more benign relationship that nevertheless does not hide from the reality of their situation and the intensity of their feelings of disappointment, abandonment or hate. Such work is delicate and difficult, as every 'failure' on the part of the therapist to get a response exactly right can be felt by the child as another confirmation of rejection. A vulnerable child whose hopes of reliable care are raised by regular, tolerant therapy can feel devastated by something quite simple, such as the therapist getting ill and cancelling a few sessions. This can reawaken a sense of abandonment that was anyway close to the surface and might even feel worse than the original hurt, precisely because hopes of something different have been raised. But the work is possible nevertheless, and this seems to confirm that such children's often very demanding or aggressive behaviour is caused by the way they have been let down – sometimes horrifically – by the conditions in which they have found themselves. Proposing that they were somehow born with hatred in their hearts is neither helpful under such circumstances nor especially convincing as an explanation of their behaviour and the feelings that give rise to it.

On the other hand, hatred is a powerful emotion, and while it is sometimes attuned to reality – some things *are* hateful – it is also often excessive to the situation that calls it forth. Much creative literature deals with this question of whether there is such a thing as fundamental evil reflected in the hate and envy that certain characters carry around inside them. Shakespeare's Iago is usually quoted as the paradigmatic example. But we do not need to look far or invoke extreme cases to find instances of hate that seem to overspill their origins (if that is what they are) in deprivation and injustice. Racism, antisemitism, misogyny and homophobia, which are often hate-filled and always irrational, are social examples of this. They seem to be full of intensity, out of touch with reality, and while they might appear explicable at times by external conditions such as economic crisis, the degree of emotional investment in them is almost always disproportionate to those conditions. What is it that energises these hate-filled states of mind? If we grant that it is unlikely that they are simply innate, that they can be fully explained by a possibly constitutional fear of strangers, let alone a biological Death Drive, then what is it that engenders such hatreds and turns everything so sour?

The idea of 'enjoyment' comes into play here. This does not mean 'fun', although in some ways it contains that sense. It has rather more to do with *excitement*, which is why it is relevant to the question of being real, and specifically to how hating can make people feel more alive, even if we might want to consider hate as a deadening emotion. Maybe both things are true. Living full of hate is a corrosive state to be in, as many people have described. Hate can take us over, destroy the connections we have with others, make us feel stained and putrid inside so that the potential sources of goodness and succour in the world are spoiled. If someone is full of hate, they are unlikely to feel refreshed and healthily 'fed' by the elements in their surroundings (people, objects, ideas) that could offer them sustenance. It is instead more likely that these 'good breasts' become infected by the person's hatefulness, become tarnished and corrupt. Among other things, there is a close relationship between hate and cynicism: hate drains the world of innocence and encourages an attitude in which nothing is held to have value. If we are full of hate, we approach others 'knowing' that they cannot be trusted, that their supposed good intentions and generous acts are in fact motivated by greed and malice. Everything is spoilt. The person who is governed by hate is therefore in thrall to death.

Yet there is another side to this. At times, hate itself can be enlivening. Hate can be a social emotion, one that is shared and generated by connection with others. From football crowds to mass rallies, from street protests to the 6 January 2021 attack by Trump supporters on the Capitol Building in Washington, perhaps even extending to online 'communities' of conspiracy theorists and other bigots, expressions of hatred can draw people together, making them feel part of something meaningful and arousing. 'Getting off' on hate is a recognisable phenomenon: participating in murderous acts, in which the usual boundaries of acceptable behaviour are crossed and a kind of exhilaration in destructiveness is cultivated, is one extreme version of this. Perhaps the most compelling literary example comes from near the beginning of George Orwell's dystopian novel *Nineteen Eighty-Four*, when Winston Smith is watching the daily Two Minutes Hate. This orchestrated hate centres on the figure of Emmanuel Goldstein, identified as the 'Enemy of the People'. Orwell describes how the figure of Goldstein is used to generate a mixture of fear and violent antagonism, building up to a crescendo:

> The horrible thing about the Two Minutes Hate was not that one was obliged to act a part, but, on the contrary, that it was impossible to avoid joining in. Within thirty seconds any pretence was always unnecessary. A hideous ecstasy of fear and vindictiveness, a desire to kill, to torture, to smash faces in with a sledge-hammer, seemed to flow through the whole group of people like an electric current, turning one even against one's will into a grimacing, screaming lunatic.[3]

The thrill of violence, the joy of hatred – these are emotions that wake people up and may make them feel more powerful, more present to themselves, sometimes as part of a crowd or in what is usually called 'sadistic' states of mind, often though not necessarily linked to sexuality. It has long been argued, for example, that antisemitism thrives in contexts where people under pressure and filled with an inchoate rage that cannot locate its object because it cannot make sense of the complexity of the situation, turn (and can be turned) against Jews as a well-worn receptacle for this rage, making them an object of hatred that is often legitimised by social and political interest groups. That Emmanuel Goldstein (modelled on the Russian revolutionary Trotsky), the arch-enemy of society in *Nineteen Eighty-Four*, should be Jewish, is no accident on Orwell's part. The engulfment of much of Vienna in anti-Jewish violence that followed immediately on the *Anschluss*, the absorption of Austria into the German Reich in 1938, is another instance. Even the German Nazis seem to have been shocked by the alacrity with which Austrians turned on their Jewish neighbours. In his biography of Freud, the historian Peter Gay describes some of the scenes that eventually persuaded the founder of psychoanalysis to flee Vienna for London. He comments,

> The mobs ransacking Jewish apartments and terrorizing Jewish shopkeepers did so without official orders and thoroughly enjoyed their work ... Incidents in the streets of Austrian cities and villages right after the German invasion were more outrageous than those Hitler's Reich had yet witnessed.[4]

And emphasising the point about the 'fun' of explosive hatred:

> What struck all the journalists reporting from Austria during these days was the general mood of celebration. 'VIENNESE GO WILD; JAM NOISY STREETS,' ran one headline on March 14. 'Yelling, Singing, Flag-Waving Throngs Surge Through City, Giving Nazi "Sieg Heil!"/YOUTHS ON THE MARCH/ German Martial Airs Replace Waltzes in Coffee Houses – No Opposition Visible.' For a time, as the German Nazis imported the stagy mass manipulation that had worked so well in their own country, Austria was on holiday.[5]

The violence obviously had its roots in longstanding Austrian antisemitism, and of course there were Viennese who resisted, or tried to do so; but what is worth noting in the account Gay draws on is the carnivalesque nature of this outpouring of hatred among so many of Vienna's inhabitants.[6] People lost their inhibitions and were carried away by the thrill of destruction, made legitimate by the Nazi takeover and the permission this gave them to act in the most transgressive way. It is as if all the repressions and disgruntlements, the agitation of the previous years (which had been highly fraught in Austria as in much of Europe) came together with a long history of antisemitism in an eruption of joyous rage. Hatred of this kind is societally sponsored but can become integral to people's personality, invigorating them and filling in the mental spaces vacated by insecurity, anxiety and even terror. 'Enjoyment' here signifies a kind of loss of selfhood that makes up for that loss by providing excitement and a sense of belonging; it can also be fuelled by the paranoid way in which the world now makes sense.

Conspiracy theories are another good example. A full engagement with the world, in all its difficulty, is displaced by a simple binary: them and us, those who perpetrate falsehood and those who know the truth, baddies and goodies. Dividing things up in this way is reassuring and has various benefits. It makes us belong to a club of the elite who can see what is 'really' happening and who is to blame. The recent 'QAnon' phenomenon is a particularly disturbing instance, recycling old antisemitic tropes of a worldwide conspiracy centred on the Rothschild banking family and integrating them into a fantasy of satanic rings of paedophiles that operate a 'deep state'. For its adepts, Donald Trump is the saviour, the chosen one who will destroy the evildoers. The QAnon movement, like other 'denialists' such as those who reject the reality of Covid, or indeed of the Holocaust, relies not only on the expression of hatred, but also on perpetrating the idea that they have knowledge of the truth – that they are the ones who can see through the machinations that befuddle most people. Yet this is of course a way of *avoiding* reality, of dodging the complexity of truth in favour of a simplistic interpretation of the world that allows inner frustration and hatred to be channelled away from believers' own psyche and into others. The hold on reality becomes more precarious as this process continues, which leads to further exaggeration; the paranoia underpinning conspiracy fantasies thrives on resistance and opposition, all of which can become grist to its mill. Recovering a sense of reality becomes exceptionally difficult under these conditions, as the self is increasingly depleted through projection of its own hateful impulses out into others, now fantasised as poised to attack.

The rather moralistic version of things in which hatred is seen as always deadening needs to contend with the fact that for many people, at least some of the time, expressing hatred may be what makes them feel real. Hate is not necessarily deadening, and it is not usually kept inside oneself. It often bursts out in frenzied activity, sometimes patently self-destructive yet also addictive; once started, it can be hard to stop it escalating. Can we understand this as *solely* a revolt of the psyche against the kinds of infractions and disappointments described earlier, in which our fundamental need for recognition and loving nurture is denied? Such circumstances lead to the withering of creative developmental possibilities for the self, resulting in it feeling empty and tired; filling this space with hate at least has the virtue of re-engaging with some kind of intense feeling, as well as offering a route towards revenge. If, as Kleinian psychoanalysts argue, a wellspring of hatred is already wired into human psychology, then there is an odd and slightly confusing way in which hatred becomes an expression of the *Life* Drive under these conditions. What this means is that the drying up of loving resources leaves the psyche de-energised and lost; at least hatred reminds us that we are alive and have some kind of psychological force available to us. So, the possibility of hatred might arise from the Death Drive, but its expression could actually be in the service of staying alive. There is also the issue of what to make of situations that are truly *hateful*, which engender hate because they deserve it. To return to the point raised in passing above, about those who managed to resist Nazism even in the face of genuine, life-threatening terror plus the coercive power of social conformity: the capacity of such people to resist can perhaps be understood as a way of holding onto and mobilising their hatred of patent evil. More such hatred, if that is what it was, would be important to sustain. Such *constructive* deployment of hate surely signals a life-enhancing healthiness. But perhaps here we are not talking of hate at all, but of an assertion of a capacity to discriminate between truthfulness and lies, and an anti-destructive, which is to say loving, impulse.

Maybe some of this is too sympathetic to hatred, suggesting that it has value in preserving feelings of reality and should not necessarily be anathemised. Yet arguing that hatred has functional value in helping to preserve the psyche from annihilation does not mean that it is justifiable. In part, this calls for us to make the familiar, but important and often neglected, distinction between explaining something and justifying it. We might, for instance, understand that an explosive act of violence has arisen out of a situation that feels intolerable, or that reminds someone of traumatic past events, while still finding the violence itself unacceptable and culpable. Our own suffering does not legitimise making others suffer; there is always something else that could be done, and there are plenty of examples of people whose suffering motivates them to protect others from having the same experiences.

Understanding hatred could be a better way to combat it than to accept it as necessary. The problem with this, however, is that much of the time the opposite occurs: hatred and suffering feed further hatred, both at the individual level and in the social and political realm – and even, at times, between nations. Cynicism seems more attractive than 'naïve' optimism; aggression towards others more fulfilling than care for them. It can seem that the springs of concern are easily blocked, leaving room only for the overpowering river of hate; and that if we want to stay real, we must allow ourselves to be carried along in its wild flow.

This is the sense in which I am using the term 'enjoyment': a lively state of mind in which excitement dominates. The thrill of it can make us feel real – though whether this is a lasting sense, producing sustained satisfaction, or whether it has to be continuously replenished by further thrill-seeking aggression, is a moot point. Is hatred a drug that must keep on being taken to stop its effects wearing off, to maintain the 'high', or can it be a driving force towards something more enduring; and if the latter, how do we harness it so that the end result is not destruction of the self and others? What is clear is that hatred cannot be wished away, and that its capacity to twist and thwart creative growth is only part of the story.

The enjoyment of hatred is central to its perpetuation: there is something attractive about smashing the world to pieces, either as an act of desperation (taking everything down with us) or as an assertion of our own liveliness. Hatred can be an expression of nihilism or of power. But perhaps something is being overlooked here. Hatred is, generally speaking, an antisocial state of mind, and hateful acts are socially destructive. Hatred breeds contempt and cynicism about others and it wilfully acts to damage them. Societies governed by hate are oppressive societies, which may serve some people's interests but tend to have dismaying effects on their populations – indeed, they are always oriented towards war. This socially destructive aspect of hatred speaks volumes about it. It announces that while hatred may be felt as a personal emotion, located within the self, it is also a deeply social phenomenon.

It is not only that the *effects* of hatred are social; hatred is directed towards other people (or sometimes towards oneself, taken as an 'object') and arises in a context of antagonistic social relationships. Even if the Kleinians are right and there is some predisposition towards hatred, its sources lie mostly in the way people have been treated by others and in how they respond to this treatment, and in the channels that societies make available for the expression of the resulting feelings. It finds its place under certain social conditions, whether at the level of family interactions or of broader societal processes. We are all embedded in such conditions, but not everyone becomes consumed by hate as a result. This is why accounts of vulnerability and of relationships with others become critical in trying to understand and reduce hatred.

Human life is vulnerable from the start. As I flagged up at the end of the previous chapter, the search for total security will always be futile: something might happen at any time, whatever the precautions we take. In early life, vulnerability is the fundamental state of the infant. Unable to do anything for themselves, infants rely on dependable surroundings of care by which they are protected and supported. When infants get ill, as they regularly do, they need proper looking after; when they are cold they need warming; when they are hungry they need feeding. This is bound to go wrong. Even with the most perfect situation, there will be times of mismatch between a baby's needs and demands and the response from caregivers – misinterpretations (the baby's hunger is understood as tiredness, for example), minor or more extended separations, moments in which a baby is psychologically 'dropped' from the caregiver's attention. At the extreme, infants' vulnerability can be life-threatening, as we see regularly when they are born during war or in other very deprived and unstable circumstances.

And this precarity continues: our lives are impinged on by all sorts of threats and discomforts, by the potential for violence from other people, by so-called natural disasters, by the gradual decline of our own bodies. For Freud, these were the reasons why people cluster together in groups, gaining mutual protection under the aegis of what he called 'civilisation'.[7] Such is the social contract we might have: society protects us in exchange for our loyalty and commitment to support others. This contract is frequently reneged upon, honoured in the breach, as different social groups turn on one another. As Freud also noticed, 'civilisation' can cause less happiness than it does pain.

There is no early idyll, a personal or social Eden, that might offer a rock-hard foundation for life, even though people try to imagine it, religions promote it, and demagogues claim it ('make our country great *again*'). One idea, derived from the theories of the French psychoanalyst Jacques Lacan, posits a racist dynamic in which the racist imagines that the despised other has 'stolen' something from them.[8] This 'something' is further coded as their 'enjoyment'; that is, an enjoyment to which they are entitled has been robbed from them by the racialised other. So, for example, migrants have supposedly stolen homes and jobs; Jews have gathered up all the money and influence; Indians have a monopoly on close communities and family lives; and black people have an embodied sensuality and style denied to the white person. This is a misattribution of responsibility for feelings of inadequacy and the possible realities of material disappointment and hardship, shifted away from the societal dysfunctions that produce inequality and onto minoritised groups. Of course, this 'misattribution' is not accidental. It derives in large part from the intentions of politicians and powerful groups to displace responsibility by mobilising what are often age-old tropes, and are certainly contemporary anxieties, in the service of perpetuating their own privilege. Racism works by nominating certain groups (blacks, Jews, Muslims, migrants) as convenient receptacles for this intentional misattribution, as repositories of blame. In this way the fantasy that something we are entitled to has been stolen serves social functions, by obscuring the actual causes of suffering.

To this, psychoanalysis adds the idea that this process is intensely affectively laden, fuelled by emotion that in turn derives from a set of unconscious impulses in which confusion and suffering is defended against by projecting it outwards into the denigrated other. Dealing with our own vulnerability, especially in conditions of heightened precarity, by imagining that others have stolen the 'goods' from us focuses attention on an identifiable culprit, thus reinforcing the self's psychic defences. It is also psychologically useful, but corrupting, in helping us avoid acknowledging how vulnerability and insecurity are fundamental to our lives. Paradise has not been snatched from us: we never had it in the first place. From the start of life, even in the womb where maternal anxiety or illness or genetic disruptions can have their effects, something impinges on us to cause different kinds of hurt. And societies too, have their origins in violence, as inspection of their myths and their histories shows. Some of our most profound religious stories support this: in the Biblical Book of Genesis, Adam and Eve's stay in Eden lasted no more than a day, and it did not take long for Abel to be slain by Cain.

The consequence of this inborn and continuing vulnerability is that people are hurt, subjected to what in the broadest terms can be called the violence of others' demands and actions. From minor to major infractions, from momentary lapses to all-out war, people suffer. Wishing for a return to a prelapsarian state of bliss might be understandable, but it is an escape from reality rather than an engagement with it, and at times (such as when states go to war over 'stolen' territory which they imagine was once theirs) can be actively destructive. Indeed, this wish can be understood as one of an array of possible responses to the realisation of our actual vulnerability: basically, wishing it away by recasting it as a fall from grace, as something that has gone wrong or been done to us and can be put right. The more this fantasy prevails – the more strongly we believe that relief from precarity is fully possible or that we can ever be totally secure in our lives – the more likely it is that further precarity will be produced, in ourselves as well as in others, by the desperate and often violent attempt to obtain security by force.

The more constructive response is surely to recognise the inevitability of vulnerability and to consider how we might deal with it. Here, there are really only two possibilities. The first is to function on an 'all against all' basis in the sense that our own vulnerability, and the hurt we experience as a result, provokes us to act in a retaliatory way against others. The principle here is, at its crudest, a kind of playground tit-for-tat: 'because I have been hurt, you will be too.' More subtly, it is expressed in a 'mutually assured destruction' scenario: 'the only way to protect myself is to have a bigger armoury than you,' either literally or in the way in which we treat other people.

Sometimes this is a type of traumatised response, in which hurt is responded to with fury. We can see this in the obliterative military actions that follow terrorist attacks, for example after 9/11 in America or the October 2023 slaughter in Israel. The initial reaction to these atrocities was perhaps understandable, but had all the attributes of a violent acting-out in which the prime motive is to destroy as much as possible of the other, in order both to wreak brutal revenge and to make the victim states feel more powerful and secure. Translated into relational terms that are not quite appropriate, but nevertheless capture something about the psychological dynamics of the situation, this response says: 'If you do this to me, I will do it to you back, but so much more severely that you will never do it again.' Among the many problems with this attitude is its ineffectiveness. It destroys everything, for sure, but as events in Iraq after the 'war on terror' and in Gaza have shown, it also prolongs hatred, offering no way forward towards reconciliation. At best, people are kept in their place by fear, until the next time their resentment breaks through.

The dynamic of 'if you hit me I will hit you harder' and its traumatised sibling 'you have made me uncontrollably angry' can be reproduced later in small aggressions, pinches of hurtfulness, recriminations and hostility of one form or another towards those close to us. It is not easily opposed. This is because this dynamic allows us to channel hatred in a seemingly justifiable way. Whatever the truth of these claims at various times ('they' may indeed have started it; states have a genuine responsibility to ensure their citizens are safe), they also foster the expression of powerful emotions that might draw social groups together or allow individuals to feel that their pent-up aggression can be let out. 'I have been hurt so I will hurt others' is a very potent underlying idea, not usually stated as such but frequently observable in individuals and social groups, and seeming to indicate that there is a base level of fury at 'being hurt' that has been waiting for an object to attach itself to. The Death Drive finds its way in again here, not necessarily as a real force, but as a metaphor for the constant pressure towards aggression and hatred that is always waiting in the wings, ready for its starring part in the play.

The alternative way of responding to basic vulnerability suffers from being caught up with a moralism that can seem to be at odds with reality. This is not necessarily Christianity's 'turning the other cheek', which is frequently at variance with Christians' actual behaviour, suggesting that it is an unsustainable ideal. It is rather an attitude to vulnerability that recognises that everyone is vulnerable, and tries to respond to personal and social insecurity through actions that remedy rather than replicate it. For some writers, such as the American philosopher Judith Butler, this is linked to a forceful approach to what they call 'nonviolence', in which nonviolence is seen as a *struggle* rather than as an attitude that we can simply adopt at will.[9] The reason for emphasising the degree of struggle involved is that the temptation towards violence, towards retribution as well as outright aggression, is very strong. Opposing it without being self-demeaning and inviting more violence from others is not a passive approach to life. It is instead radically assertive, taking on the temptation and converting it into something else. Nonviolence is not withdrawal, but a form of active engagement with the conditions and realities of violence; sometimes itself involving certain kinds of violence.

Nonviolent violence sounds like a contradiction in terms, which of course it is, but in certain situations it makes sense. It is the rationale of peace-keeping forces as well as of consensual policing, which are backed by the threat of force yet do not actually use it. Nonviolence acknowledges the ubiquity of the temptation towards violence and tries not to give into it, tries instead to respond to hurt differently from just lashing out.

Responding in this way is challenging. First, it requires full awareness of the hurt we might have suffered and of how this is connected to the universal vulnerability of humans. Then it involves what we might call the 'de-objectivising' of other people, reversing the common tendency to treat them as *objects* rather than subjects of their own lives.

This needs some unpacking. It relies first on the idea that each of us is a human 'subject' in a variety of senses, the most important of which for current purposes is that we have our own consciousness, our own centre of selfhood and subjective – that is, internal – life. The foundation of an ethical relationship to other people is precisely the realisation that just as we have unique access to our own subjective experience, our 'inner lives', other people also do to theirs. If each of us is precious to ourselves because we are aware that we have such inner reality, if in important ways we know we exist precisely because of this awareness, then the same must be true for others. However, holding onto this knowledge is in a way an act of imagination: we know of others only what they show or tell us about themselves, and must take it on trust that they too exist as subjects of their own worlds. The tendency, especially when we are at odds with these others, is to treat them not as subjects like ourselves but as objects in our world, upon which we act and which act on us to give pleasure or pain, satisfaction or frustration, comfort or antagonism. This removal of subjecthood from others, in which we fail to comprehend them as centres of meaning or as equally human to ourselves, is possibly a tendency in all our relationships. But it is especially the case among those whom we 'other', pushing them away, acting and feeling towards them as if they were radically distinct from ourselves.

It is easier to imagine the inner worlds of those with whom we are intimate. These people make demands on us, share views, tell us about their thoughts and feelings, challenge us with their different responses, ask us to react to them in a manner that respects and validates their ways of being. Regular exposure to such intimacies makes it easier to understand the substantial nature of these people's presence. We are more likely to feel them to be kindred 'subjects', like us in their human constitution. It also means that we can become aware of their vulnerabilities much as we are aware of our own: they too can be hurt, and we can imagine what that is like, and if we care about them we also care about that. These relationships are of course very challenging, precisely because they cannot be dismissed or 'objectified'. Those we are close to make demands that we might find hard to respond to; their own vulnerabilities might elicit ours, and we might react defensively to this, withdrawing if we find it difficult to deal with lacks or losses in ourselves. We might even find such intimacy so burdensome that we come to hate those we are close to more than we love them. Yet even under these circumstances, it is harder to dismiss people we are intimate with as somehow not real people, harder to reduce them to objects who do not matter.

Human ethics perhaps starts from here: other people matter, because they are human subjects, putting them on a par with ourselves. As some philosophers argue, ethics of this kind is 'first philosophy', in the sense of being the foundation from which all else flows. I mentioned in Chapter 1 how the philosopher Emmanuel Levinas has influentially asserted this view. For Levinas, it is not the case that we are formed as individuals – or rather, constituted as 'human' – and then find ways to relate ethically to others; rather, ethics is the defining feature of subjectivity itself. Responsibility towards the other comes first and is what defines us as human. Levinas writes, 'I understand responsibility as responsibility for the Other, thus as responsibility for what is not my deed, or for what does not even matter to me; or which precisely does matter to me, is met by me as face.'[10] Levinas insists that responsibility for the other comes before the subject can even know what the other is; it is, consequently, an absolute given and does not depend on what that other person is like: the 'face' of the other makes a demand on us to which we are called to respond. Knowledge of what the other might be, what use or reciprocity might derive from them, is irrelevant. Rendering the other as 'like us' is also not the point, for this is a form of colonisation, reducing the other to being the same as the self. In the Levinasian scheme, by contrast, the otherness of the other is always maintained. Yet across this constitutional difference, there is always something that links one person to others – a recognition that we are essentially bound up together, facing similar vulnerabilities and immersed in the same conditions of human frailty that make it crucial that we take responsibility for one another's well-being.

The very forceful, even austere, position taken by Levinas can be debated, as it raises the question of whether it is necessary to form a solid self before being able to reach out to others, and it also seems to risk promoting a kind of 'self-beratement' in which the other takes precedence over oneself even if that other is antagonistic – a point discussed a little more fully below. But if there is anything in Levinas's promotion of ethics as the core of human subjecthood, then being real involves sustaining a sense of the reality of other people and recognising that their essential responses to the world will have similarities to our own, however different they might be in terms of culture, background or other features that differentiate between individuals and groups. This is true of their vulnerabilities as well, bringing us back to the question of violence and hatred.

As I described earlier, the great temptation is to react to the hurt that comes from being vulnerable by retaliating, sometimes even pre-emptively – we strike first out of fear of what the other is likely to do. This process is aided by objectifying others so that their human vulnerability becomes less clear, less visible to us. As 'others' they are no longer quite the same; at the extreme they can cease to matter at all. We see this in war situations where the suffering of our own side is attended to and marked, for example in elaborate funeral ceremonies and the naming of victims and reciting of their life stories; whereas the suffering of the other side is barely registered, chalked up as a count of dead bodies or only sketchily reported. As Judith Butler describes in a hard-hitting chapter of their book *Precarious Life*, there are many examples of this. In relation to the Gulf War of the early 2000s, Butler shows how the process of 'humanisation' determined who was recognised as having a life important enough to grieve when it was lost, and who was not. 'If 200,000 Iraqi children were killed during the Gulf War and its aftermath,' Butler writes, 'do we have an image, a frame for any of those lives, singly or collectively? ... Are there names attached to those children?'[11] In the more recent horrific brutality in Israel and Gaza, the fate of Israeli hostages is tracked and highlighted, as it should be, with names and biographies attached; but the tens of thousands of Gazans killed are far less individualised.

We see this dehumanisation reflected in genocidal acts, in the turning of groups on one another, and in the construction of versions of society that include some people but not others. In her meticulous examination of the formation of what she calls 'bystander society' in the Germany of the 1930s, Mary Fulbrook documents how the process of exclusion perpetrated by the Nazi authorities particularly against Jews, as well as other minoritised groups, paved the way for the majority of Germans to accept the murderous oppression of those who had been their fellow citizens. Describing the situation quite early on in Nazi times, Fulbrook notes how the isolation of Jews made it increasingly easy for other Germans to ignore what was happening to them – and to participate in it:

> By 1934, insidious changes had taken place in everyday social relations. As 'Aryan' Germans were energized by a sense of national regeneration, and as they dropped social contacts with Jews and snubbed any they met on the street, so they increasingly lost touch with the lives of the outcast. The growing social and spatial difference made it easier, too, no longer to care about those with whom they were no longer in contact: indifference

grew more easily if one simply did not know, or chose to ignore, the fates of the excluded.[12]

Similarly, the separation of black and white lives in apartheid South Africa, or of Palestinians from Israelis in Israel–Palestine, makes the exclusion of the derogated other much easier to accomplish. Fulbrook refers to this as the creation of certain 'ethical communities' that mark boundaries between who matters more, and who matters less.

For Judith Butler this comes under the term of 'grievability', or the question of whether someone's life is valued enough for its loss to be a source of grief.[13] Would it matter if they were gone? For everyone, the answer should be 'yes'; for many people in the eyes of others – even if it is not admitted to as such – the answer is 'no'. When, for instance, refugees and migrants in fragile boats are allowed to sink into the sea, their lives are not being treated as grievable. When black people are systematically more likely to be killed by the police, demonstrators are fired upon, or misogynistic violence is normalised, then the lives concerned are not being seen as of sufficient value to make the mark they should. When racism, antisemitism and Islamophobia are mainstreamed and played on by political manipulators, then grievability for all human lives is lost. The point here is more than rhetorical: everyone is degraded when the vulnerability and grievability of the lives of others is denied.

Sustaining a sense of the grievability of all lives is as much a challenge as is the general attitude towards nonviolence that is connected to it. The vulnerability we all feel makes reaching out to others risky; there is little guarantee, after all, that they will respond in the way we might hope. For some, like Levinas, this is precisely the 'call' that constitutes the ultimate human demand.[14] Even what he labels the 'face of the torturer' requires of us an ethical response, which he describes as 'putting the other first.' Few of us, including at times Levinas himself, can manage this fully, not least because we cannot completely leave aside the question of whether the 'torturer' should be regarded as having given up his claim to grievability – a question that is closely tied to perennial arguments regarding the nature of evil, many of which emerge in reflections on Nazism. Forgetting, forgiveness and putting the other first are ethical principles that are left extremely stretched by the reality of horrific acts. Nevertheless, as a statement of what we might seek to achieve, the nonviolence that demands we assume the grievability of all lives is a useful yardstick, an ideal for sure, but still something to be aspired to. We might desist from it under circumstances where hate of the hateful is justified – the actual torturer, to use the shorthand – but still use it as the default position. Others deserve a response from us that reflects what we know about human needs; and our own vulnerability is part of the evidence for that, not an excuse for reneging on our ethical responsibilities. Hard work indeed, and observed in the breach most of the time, but surely crucial to the task of moving away from the violence that threatens us all.

The objectification of other people can be understood as a process of 'othering' them, of making them different so that their claims to equal treatment, to forms of grievability, can be ignored. The question of how to relate to others is significant here, both in the way just discussed (making others grievable, valuing their lives) and in the broader sense of how to see them not so much in terms of their 'otherness', their difference, but in terms of their similarities to those classified as 'us'. The motivation here is certainly recognisably ethical, asking about how borders can be crossed, oppositions reduced and bridges between people forged over what on the face of it are important distinctions between them – class, culture, ethnicity, gender, religion and so on. Yet it is arguable that the very vocabulary of 'us' and 'them', self and other, is objectifying, producing the differences that it also tries to overcome. The other is other to the same; the same is the starting point, the assumed norm, at best exoticising the other and at worst excluding and demonising them. While we might legitimately suggest that this recognises reality rather than backs away from it, that we need to make the self–other distinction so that we can think about how to bridge it, it also reinforces the problematic of othering, of turning certain individuals or groups into the problem that has to be solved.

Recent years have seen an alternative vocabulary develop around the idea of the 'neighbour'. This has its own baggage; after all, many disputes are between neighbours who cannot escape from each other but intrude on each other's lives in what are experienced as unmanageable ways. The closeness of neighbours can be supportive; but that same closeness can create bitter, unresolvable tensions. When neighbours are also 'others' to one another, for example members of different racialised groups with differing cultural practices, this can add to the mix. Simply calling others 'neighbours' does not in itself solve any problems.

Despite these important realities, however, there is something useful about reconceptualising the problem of dealing with difference as an issue of neighbours rather than others. The notion of 'others' implies a binary distinction with 'us' or 'self'. The other is always at a certain distance, always tending to slip into being perceived as somehow *alien*. Even in the positive frame that is sometimes used of offering 'hospitality' to the other, there is a distinction being made between the one who is a kind of landowner, who can decide whether or not to offer this hospitality, and the other, who is at best a guest. Hospitality is of course a good thing, emphasised as a virtue in many religious traditions, but it has a connotation of reaching out to an other who is by definition a stranger in need of help. That this need should be responded to positively is part of the ethical injunction described above, but it is still an unequal relationship in which one person or group is subject and the other object, with the former having the power to decide the fate of the latter.

Neighbours have to find ways to live side by side. This can go terribly wrong, as we see in civil wars and acts of internecine violence, when neighbours turn on one another and sometimes betray lifetimes of what had seemed to be relatively friendly day-to-day connections. The question of how to go on living together after this has happened is a key one for discussions of reconciliation and reparation, in the aftermath of the wars in ex-Yugoslavia, for example, or the partition of India and Pakistan, or in post-apartheid South Africa, or in the post-dictatorship period in Latin America. Neighbours who attacked one another now must be together again – a task that is demonstrably extremely hard. The South African writer Pumla Gobodo-Madikizela has written powerfully on this point, focusing on the responsibility of whole societies for crimes against humanity, including 'those whose votes and other kinds of active or silent support contributed to the flourishing of oppressive regimes.'[15] In response, she comments,

> This component of crimes against humanity, the one that resides at the systemic, institutional and social levels rather than at an individual level, leads me to suggest that in the aftermath of historical trauma, restoring human bonds requires a new vocabulary of re-humanization. This new mode of being human, what I have referred to as 'reparative humanism,' opens towards a horizon of an ethics of care for the sake of a transformed society.[16]

'Reparative humanism' here arises from the work of the South African Truth and Reconciliation Commission (TRC) and in particular from the notion of 'ubuntu' advanced especially strongly by its leader, Archbishop Desmond Tutu. 'The concept of ubuntu,' writes Gobodo-Madikizela, 'is an ethic based on the understanding that one's subjectivity is inextricably intertwined with that of others in one's community.'[17] Ubuntu is deeply embedded in an approach to social relations that emphasises the significance of community and the construction of an ethical human subject through intersubjective relations with others involving mutual recognition. This is consistent with the view I am presenting of the centrality of ethical relations towards others as a condition for becoming real. But as we shall see later, in a further discussion of the TRC, there is a real question of how possible this reconciliatory ambition can be in a context in which unforgiveable, murderous events have taken place.

None of these difficulties should be neglected; they are part of the reality of neighbours, of the challenges that arise from living in close proximity to one another, especially in conditions of historical injustice or oppression. Nevertheless, what adopting the vocabulary of neighbours achieves is to remind us that the binary 'self versus other' can obscure the fact of joint vulnerability, that the pressure on us is to find ways of living together where it is not the case that one group is 'entitled' and the other is a 'supplicant', but that each has equal rights and responsibilities. The closeness of neighbours creates real problems because of the inescapability of contact; but it also illustrates the inextricable connections between our different lives, how we simply must 'cohabit' (as some describe it) in the world rather than lay claim to bits of it as purely our own.[18] If we need to live together because we have no choice in the matter, because others are not in distant lands but right next to us – as they always are – then the small and large rubbings-up against each other that do so much to shape us have to be recognised as the result of the needful connections we have, requiring of us support and care.

I am suggesting in this chapter that the hatred we so commonly feel has to be recognised rather than denied, in order for it to be placed in a context in which something constructive can be done with and about it. The idea of a Death Drive makes the denial of hatred harder to maintain and pushes us to ask what we can do with it rather than pretend that all would be well if the world were only a better place – plainly true, but not very helpful.

Our shared vulnerability has much to do with this. All of us get hurt by others and are tempted to retaliate and protect ourselves by exercising our own hurtfulness, our own potential for violence. This happens both to individuals and to social groups and is abetted by the practice of 'othering', in which the lives of others are made less grievable, less valuable. The attempt to destroy them through hatred then feels less morally culpable. How we set about dealing with this matters deeply for the possibilities of living peacefully and in real contact with other people. Likewise, neighbours are forced to live together, with all the difficulties this poses, based on having equal rights to be present in the same spaces. This can be a political issue with important practical consequences, as we see for instance in the inextricable but immensely fraught relations between Israelis and Palestinians; it is also a matter of ethics, of treating people as equally valuable, as having lives that are grievable and of real worth.

Finding ourselves in a place which is also occupied by others means allowing for the fact of shared vulnerability and with it our shared responsibility for creating the conditions for survival. Being 'real' here means acknowledging this responsibility and taking the risk of mutuality, the entwining of our lives with those of our supposed 'others', and doing this without hate.

4

Defending Ourselves against Reality

Reality can at times be unbearable. In the midst of war or famine or a natural disaster (though most of the latter are caused by human activity, for example climate change, or civil war that destroys the infrastructure of a society, or corruption, or authoritarian violence) it can be very hard to process what is happening. Partly this is because so many of these events are emergencies: all we can think about is how to get through them on a day-to-day or hour-by-hour basis. Sometimes it is the horrific force of an event that overwhelms our capacity to reflect on it and make sense of it. Often, especially when there has been obscene violence, it is because what is triggered is either bewildered desperation or an automatic reaction of reciprocal violence. A reaction, that is, of rage.

There are also other kinds of unbearable events. Facing terrible losses can be hard to manage and sometimes gives rise to the melancholic 'I never loved so never lost' response. Abuse, perhaps especially in childhood, can also become impossible to think about. Psychoanalysts have long proposed that an important defence for children subjected to ongoing abuse can be to 'dissociate', cutting themselves off psychologically from the experience they are going through, either repressing the memory of it completely or shifting it around so that it is experienced only from the 'outside'. The child then becomes a kind of detached observer of what is happening to them. More commonly, perhaps, the child comes to feel somehow responsible for what is being done to them, a twist which is even more psychologically damaging and can be amplified still further if they are blamed by other adults, as sometimes occurs.

One classic account of this, by the early psychoanalyst Sándor Ferenczi, first published in German in 1933, describes how sexually abused children deal with their traumatising experience by a process he calls 'identification with the aggressor'.[1] Ferenczi emphasises the anxiety that a child will feel when confronted with the sexual violence of the adult, how they become 'physically and morally helpless', and comments,

> *The same anxiety, however, if it reaches a certain maximum, compels them to subordinate themselves like automata to the will of the aggressor, to divine each one of his desires and to gratify these; completely oblivious of themselves they identify themselves with the aggressor.*[2]

In this complicated way, the child gains a semblance of control over an unmanageable, confusing and frightening situation. The adult abuser's aggression is 'taken in' by the child so that it is experienced as coming from within, or in Ferenczi's words, the aggressor 'disappears as part of the external reality, and becomes intra- instead of extra-psychic'. Because the traumatising event has now become part of the child's inner reality, the child has a chance of fantasising some control over it by wishing it away. But this is by no means a solution: it leads to feelings of guilt, one of the harmful effects of sexual abuse that can also perpetuate it by making it less likely that a child will disclose what has been happening; and it also creates great confusion in the child between reality and fantasy. Ferenczi comments:

> When the child recovers from such an attack, he feels enormously confused, in fact, split – innocent and culpable at the same time – and his confidence in the testimony of his own senses is broken. Moreover, the harsh behaviour of the adult partner tormented and made angry by his remorse renders the child still more conscious of his own guilt and still more ashamed.[3]

These are some of the terrible effects of abuse on children, leaving them unable to 'work through' what they have experienced. There is every reason to think that the same might be true for adults undergoing severe abuse, like torture.

We are in various different territories here. In one of them, what is at stake is our ability to face relatively normal, or at least expectable, events in our lives – loss of people we love through death or separation, failures of one kind or another, maybe shame or guilt at things we have done. These can look relatively mild from the outside, but they may *feel* like extreme events and can be hard to deal with. Much psychoanalytic literature is concerned with this kind of thing, for instance when it understands (with Freud) the sources of neurosis as repression of sexual impulses that for one reason or another are deemed unacceptable, either because of social or religious constraints or due to their idiosyncratic meaning for a particular person.

Finding it hard to come to terms with aspects of ourselves that we do not like is a common source of resistance to recognising reality, which can be expressed through various psychological 'defences'. Someone might, for instance, 'forget' having done something they are ashamed of in an act of repression that relegates the memory to the unconscious, suggesting that it could be recovered under certain circumstances (in therapy, for instance) or might continue to have some effect even though it operates outside conscious awareness. Another person might simply deny that anything happened, or belittle it. In his book *The Interpretation of Dreams*, Freud presents a famous analysis of his 'Dream of Irma's Injection', which offers a nice illustration of how defences might work.[4] The dream itself was crucial for the development of psychoanalysis. Freud described it as the moment at which he realised that dreams are caused by unconscious wishes, and he even fantasised (in a letter to his friend Wilhelm Fliess in 1900) that in time the world would recognise this, so that 'some day a marble tablet will be placed on the house, inscribed with these words: 'In

This House, on July 24th, 1895 the Secret of Dreams was Revealed to Dr. Sigm. Freud.'[5] He added that 'at the moment there seems little prospect of it.' As it happens, there is now a plaque with this content on the site of Bellevue House, where Freud had the dream.

Freud gives as background to the dream his worry that his treatment of his patient Irma for anxiety and somatic symptoms was not being quite successful, and his annoyance at his friend Otto for pointing this out. The dream itself, as recalled and reported by Freud, is rich and in some ways hilarious. Here it is, shortened slightly:

A large hall – numerous guests, whom we were receiving. – Among them was Irma. I at once took her on one side, as though to answer her letter and to reproach her for not having accepted my 'solution' yet. I said to her: 'If you still get pains, it's really only your fault.' She replied: 'If you only knew what pains I've got now in my throat and stomach and abdomen – it's choking me.' – I was alarmed and looked at her. She looked pale and puffy. I thought to myself that after all I must be missing some organic trouble. I took her to the window and looked down her throat, and she showed signs of recalcitrance, like women with artificial dentures. I thought to myself that there was really no need for her to do that. – She then opened her mouth properly and on the right I found a big white patch; at another place I saw extensive whitish grey scabs upon some remarkable curly structures which were evidently modelled on the turbinal bones of the nose. – I at once called in Dr. M., and he repeated the examination and confirmed it ... We were directly aware, too, of the origin of the infection. Not long before, when she was feeling unwell, my friend Otto had given her an injection of a preparation of ... trimethylamin (and I saw before me the formula for this printed in heavy type) ... Injections of that sort ought not to be made so thoughtlessly ... And probably the syringe had not been clean.[6]

It is worth reading Freud's analysis of this dream, as it shows his method of taking a dream apart and associating to it as freely as possible. What becomes apparent is how much of the dream is self-exculpating, aiming to free him from the accusation that he has mistreated his patient. The wish it expresses is therefore that any continuing issues with Irma should be her fault, or that of other physicians. He writes:

> The whole plea for the dream was nothing else – reminded one vividly of the defence put forward by the man who was charged by one of his neighbours with having given him back a borrowed kettle in a damaged condition. The defendant asserted first, that he had given it back undamaged; secondly, that the kettle had a hole in it when he borrowed it; and thirdly, that he had never borrowed a kettle from his neighbour at all.[7]

The lack of consistent logic here is part of the point: if one defence doesn't work, perhaps another will. But at its root is the fact that the kettle was damaged somehow; similarly, facing up to the 'damaged kettle' within each of us – the damaged part of ourselves – can require a great deal of psychological energy and an orientation to the truth that not all of us can manage, and certainly not all the time.

If there is something normal about the defences we use to stop ourselves thinking about things we find unpleasant, the more extreme examples that I started with require something much more rigorous. There are even those who argue that it might be better *not* to recognise certain deeply disturbing events, especially if we cannot do anything about them. Just as there is debate about whether denying serious illness can be better for some people than fully acknowledging it, even enhancing the possibility of recovery, so it might be that finding ways to forget awful things can make it easier to get on with life. It is difficult to know how best to respond to this. While acknowledging that it could be true, it goes against the broader insistence that facing up to reality is important, whereas avoiding it produces precisely the sense of unreality that can lead to a psychologically and ethically impoverished life. Is forgetting a good thing?

Perhaps it would be useful to categorise the various ways of defending ourselves against reality as attempts at 'not noticing' or, more broadly, 'forgetting'. This is not always an easy thing to do. People may try hard not to notice what is going on around them when they are made anxious by it, for example because of the level of danger involved if they should get caught up in it. This is one source of the 'bystander' phenomenon, in which people take no action to intervene when an obvious injustice is being done in their presence. Will the gang attacking its victim turn on me? If the authorities have allowed this to happen, maybe there's more to it than meets the eye and I should trust that it's in a good cause? Am I sure that I am interpreting this scene correctly? Will I get any support from other onlookers if I act? And possibly, I am secretly (or not so secretly) pleased to see this happening – as was clearly the case for many Germans when observing Nazi attacks on Jews in the years leading up to the Holocaust.

Not noticing can be a sign of inner confusion, but it can also be highly motivated for these reasons and others; or it can be that the failure to take action is rationalised after the event, for example as a way of protecting our own community or family or because, in the end, it seems to us that the events we have witnessed and taken no action to stop might have been legitimate after all. What transpires from this is that 'bystanding' is not a passive stance, even if the behaviour it describes is indeed passive. Not noticing something involves psychic *work* – avoiding, justifying, denying, forgetting – and this is true at a social level too, where the events might be obscured, lied about, hidden or justified in political terms. This kind of work intentionally falsifies experience, changing it to a kind of lie in which our failure to respond to events is rationalised by a narrative of self-justification. We watch others suffer and absolve ourselves from responsibility; this is yet another way of not being real, creating a smokescreen behind which the lurking awareness of others' needs is killed off. Afterwards, after something has happened, we may also try to put it behind us. Not just because of the intense pain caused by a memory of suffering or loss, but perhaps due to shame at our own actions, regret for what we ourselves have done or not done, or for how this may call into question precious versions that we hold of ourselves.

Wishing away the past is a common ambition and one that many people pursue quite systematically. Yet, both the unnoticed present and the forgotten past have ways of intruding on us, returning like unsettled ghosts to haunt us even when we are not quite sure what it is that is doing the haunting. This pattern is one of the major discoveries of psychoanalysis: forgetting or 'repressing' memories does not delete them but only subdues them, forcing a silence where a speaking voice should be, thinning out our experience of ourselves. Motivated forgetting of this kind is not usually conscious, but rather a manoeuvre that the mind makes to protect us from the impact of realising the truth of our discomfort. It is a mechanism geared towards husbanding psychic resources that otherwise would be under strain from the full realisation of a damaging event, and as such it is understandable. Forgetting clearly has important functions, and its possible value should not be underestimated. It can protect us from some of the impact of potentially traumatising experiences and help us manage on a day-to-day basis when too much immersion in horror could destroy us. But the price paid for this forgetting can be great. Forgetting of this kind means that there are aspects of our experience and things that we really 'know' that cannot be acknowledged, no-go areas in our minds; and when this is the case, our mental landscapes are narrowed, so we see less of what surrounds us.

This can be an escalating phenomenon, again as psychoanalysis has often shown. We start with an area of experience that is not acknowledged; then there is a related area that points to the first hidden space, so that must be censored too, and then another and another. A person who has suffered sexual assault might understandably want to forget the terrible event and might adopt mostly unconscious strategies for doing so. This could help stabilise the person so that they can move on with their lives. However, it could also happen that any sexual feelings may then threaten to remind them of the assault, so these have to be reduced or censored too. Now a situation develops in which a large and important area of experience is being interfered with, even denied; and this can escalate further as any suggestion of intimacy becomes intolerable. This of course does not mean that the original forgetting was irrational and somehow 'wrong', but it points to the problem in this kind of understandable obliteration of reality – that it creeps outwards to create a shadow world in which people become alienated from themselves. There are ethical as well as psychological well-being arguments here. On the former, the question is whether it is *right* to forget what has happened, or whether we have a responsibility to remember so that truth is not maligned and lies do not infect us. On the latter, there is the more 'technical' question of whether there is too much of a price to pay when denial and forgetting take hold of the psyche. Perhaps we need to face our horrors in order to be fully alive.

This psychological account can be matched with the forgetting that occurs on a societal scale. This is not to say that they are the same thing – it would be naïve to assume that whole societies function in the same way as the minds of individuals. Nevertheless, there are connections. In part this is because each of us draws on the cultural materials at our disposal to make sense of the world, the 'discourses', as they are sometimes called, that encourage us to think in some ways and not so easily in others. In political theory, such discourses are often called 'ideologies', socially structured ways of experiencing and thinking about the world – for example, that gender is fixed or that some 'races' are superior to others. It can also be useful to draw on psychological ideas metaphorically, to suggest parallels with the way societies function. The example of motivated forgetting is a good one in this regard, given how much of culture is devoted to processes of remembering, reliving or rewriting the past. It has sometimes been argued that forgetting the past is necessary for the resolution of intractable conflicts.[8] This can be the case when ancient battles or hurts are constantly recycled in order to serve current political ends, such as nationalist war-mongering or what is termed 'revanchism', the demand for the 'return' of territories that might once have belonged, or are now imagined to have belonged, to the nation. It seems to be the case that some such conflicts can only be resolved when the past is forgotten, or at least set aside so that it is no longer allowed to keep a hold over the present and the future. The relatively successful attempt at a peace process in Northern Ireland is an important example: violent 'troubles' between the different communities dominated the scene there for decades from the 1960s, until at the end of the century an agreement around power-sharing created a precarious, narrowly sustainable peace. Yet every time the old battles between these communities, some of them reaching back centuries, are celebrated it causes more strain; these hoary triumphs and resentments need to be put to rest if people are to live in peace. Perhaps the same might be said of other impossible situations, such as that between Israel and the Palestinians: there is simply too much living history and reversion to ancient history, which is poisoning the ground. Forgetting some of this, confining it to history rather than keeping it alive in memory, might help in the crucial task of finding a path towards reconciliation between warring peoples.

But forgetting can be politically motivated in a more negative way. Turkey, for instance, has long refused to recognise the Armenian massacre of 1915, in which at least 650,000 and possibly more than a million Armenian Christians were killed by the Ottoman authorities. This genocide, and the prolonged refusal of the state to fully acknowledge it, continues as a running sore in Turkey. Sometimes forgetting involves a rewriting of history, as with the widespread emergence of a self-description in Germany after the Second World War that they were 'double victims', first of the Nazis and then of the Soviet Union, rather than perpetrators of the horror of the Holocaust. It can also be a way for a society to free itself of responsibility for wrongdoing, serving both political ends (no reparations are necessary) and the wish to build a positive national identity.

In British schools and in the story British people tell about themselves, the role the country played in abolishing slavery is emphasised, while the position of Britain as a proponent of the slave trade, and the way much of the country's wealth was built on the proceeds of slavery, is much less fully acknowledged. The forgetting of history here is clearly motivated to build up a story of progressive humanitarianism and of Britain as a beacon of enlightenment, and this continues to inform its self-understanding even in the face of the current 'hostile environment' towards migrants and refugees. Yet failure to note the underside of this, in this case its participation in the slave trade but more broadly its prolonged engagement in violent colonialism, distorts the picture that Britons have of themselves in a way that reduces the complexity of its history to a kind of banal nationalism ('Britannia rules the waves'). Truly understanding the society of which we are part requires open acknowledgement of its destructive elements as well as of its achievements – and of how these two things are often deeply connected.

Not only is forgetting the past liable to create distortions in how we relate to ourselves as individuals and societies, it can also mean that the ways in which the past continues to live on in the present are ignored and hence that old wounds, festering as they are, then repeatedly open up. Without resolution of important historical injustices their effects cannot be understood, recognition and acknowledgement cannot be offered, restitution cannot be made. As many writers have stressed, under such circumstances of non-recognition, the past is not past; the 'continuing disaster' recurs.[9] As we can see in the treatment of Black citizens in the United States, slavery there cannot be forgotten – precisely because the attempts to forget it, to write it off as a past event no longer relevant to today's society, involves denying the reality that the effects of slavery persist, creating conditions of deep and oppressive inequality. Justice is required before forgetting can occur; and justice requires remembering. Indeed, as the historian of Jewish culture Yosef Hayim Yerushalmi once wrote, perhaps the 'antonym' of forgetting is not 'remembering', but 'justice'.[10] The wish to forget the past is understandable and can even be seen as progressive under some circumstances, but it is too risky. It leaves hanging too many issues that need to be addressed, issues which have a habit of coming back to haunt us. A full life, whether for an individual person or a society, requires remembering what has happened so that recognition can be obtained, reparation made where necessary, and justice done.

Much of the discussion about witnessing and acknowledging the past has revolved around the question of trauma. Indeed, it has been convincingly argued that we live in a 'trauma culture' in which the concept of trauma has been extended to include a wide range of troubling experiences.[11] It might also be said that the *claim* to have been traumatised is characteristic of much contemporary communication, as if it were a necessary condition for being given the authority to speak about something. Nations root themselves in tales of national trauma out of which they have arisen, and which give them legitimacy. These events, such as genocides or the ravages of colonialism, were genuinely traumatic to those who lived through them, and subsequently they become markers of the difficult birth of the nation, attaining sometimes mythical status as they bind a society together. These traumatic origins may be real, but they are often simplified and magnified for political purposes, especially to justify the state's own violence against others.

At a personal level, trauma denotes overwhelming negative experiences that are so powerful as to leave the individual constantly plagued by them. Sometimes these experiences are so bad that people cannot get on with their lives unless they expend a great deal of psychological effort on excluding the memory of these events from consciousness. A common way of understanding this is that trauma consists of the inability to actively symbolise the event concerned. It therefore stays in the mind, unconsciously, as something that has not been fully processed but instead retains the attributes of the original: frightening, concrete, and felt as if it is happening now rather than as something located in the past.

Thought of this way, traumatic memories operate rather like ghosts. Ghosts are unquiet souls which have not been dealt with properly, but which keep returning to insist that something be done about them, yet causing such terror when they reappear as to make it hard to respond in a way that will lay them to rest. In the case of trauma, a person has been subjected to an experience that is so painful, physically, psychologically or both, that the necessary act of articulating it in some way, for example by speaking about it, is itself intolerable. This is because articulating it would bring the event to awareness too strongly, threatening to swamp the mind. Faced with such events, people might 'split' their consciousness so that they do not experience them fully; or, having experienced them, they might repress knowledge of what happened so as not to have to face it again.

The problem is, however, that this act of denying symbolisation to the traumatising experience means it is never, in this psychoanalytic account, 'worked through'. It can never be put in its place, made sense of and – in so far as this is possible – come to terms with. In the broadest sense, the experience cannot be owned by the person who has suffered it. Instead it continues to dominate that person, controlling their life. Using another metaphor, we might think of the traumatising event as a kind of concrete 'thing' that is swallowed whole without being digested; it therefore persists in its original form inside the person, causing severe pain whenever it is stirred up by new 'food' (that is, other experiences or thoughts or emotions). 'Digestion' here means being able to think about the event in an emotionally connected way so that it can begin to be integrated into the person's memory rather than constantly returning and causing unbearable pain.

There is much in this way of understanding trauma that is helpful, but it also misses some important points about why it might be that the original traumatising experience becomes inarticulable. Before getting to this, however, it is worth noting the history of the notion of trauma. While it is undoubtedly the case that people have always gone through terrible events that have marked their whole lives, the concept of 'trauma' is a relatively new one. The idea itself only really arose in the last couple of centuries and has changed significantly in that time. Originally, in the mid-nineteenth century, it referred primarily to severe physical injuries; then it was extended to the psychological impact of such injuries, and then, especially as a consequence of the wars of the twentieth century, to other events that have psychological effects. The development of the railway system, and the accidents that came with it, were vital to the early emergence of the notion of trauma. In the words of Didier Fassin and Richard Rechtman, historians of trauma,

> Railroad accidents remained center stage for some time, principally because they caused a major public stir. The novelty of the train as a means of transport, the anxiety of the first users, and a few spectacular accidents in the early days of the railways

sufficed to make it one of the great dangers threatening the population as a result of advances in science and technology.[12]

The radical newness of the railways was in many ways shocking, due to the speed and the sudden regulation and compression of time that trains produced (standardisation of the clock across different places only happened as a consequence of the need for reliable timetables). Railway accidents caused unexpectedly significant damage to people, leading to many insurance claims, and raising the question of how these events could have such profound effects on people's functioning when their physical impact was often unobservable. The controversial idea of 'railway spine' was invented to deal with this, but it did not silence the debates over whether people were really injured or were pretending or fantasising for the sake of insurance payouts.

Quickly, however, especially during the First World War, the concept of trauma became attached to 'war neurosis' or 'shell shock', the phenomenon that soldiers who were not necessarily physically injured (though they might have been) could be so deeply affected that they developed a severe, debilitating anxiety that prevented them from fighting. At this time, despite the term 'shell shock' implying that close encounters with fighting had damaged the soldiers' nervous systems, the common understanding was that there was something already wrong with these soldiers. They were constitutionally, morally or nervously weak, vulnerable to situations that others would be able to cope with. Considerable opprobrium was faced by these soldiers, who were regarded more as malingerers than as sufferers. Psychoanalysis operated here as one of the sources of a more sympathetic approach. Freud, for example, in testimony in a famous court case in 1920 against Professor Julius Wagner von Jauregg, director of the Vienna Neuropsychiatric Clinic and a proponent of electrical treatment for war neurosis, 'clearly stated his opposition to electrical methods, which he saw as useless and unethical', even though he defended the honourable intentions of the professor.[13] For Freud, the problem was that psychiatrists were neglecting the role of the unconscious by assuming that the soldiers concerned had control over their actions and were to one degree or another malingerers. By revealing that people could be provoked into disturbance by extreme events such as were experienced in wartime, psychoanalysis advocated for what we might now term a more 'therapeutic' approach – one that in the UK was famously instantiated in the Craiglockhart Hospital, run by the extraordinary W. H. R. Rivers, and including among its inmates the major literary figures Siegfried Sassoon and Wilfred Owen, a setting brought to life in a sequence of powerful novels by Pat Barker.[14] This was still a minority approach to shell shock, as Fassin and Rechtman point out, but it nevertheless showed a possible route away from a punitive approach to trauma and towards a more sophisticated understanding of what violence might do to the mind.

Much the same was true during the Second World War, when there were some important interventions, including experiments with group therapy, aimed at tackling the underlying sources of war neuroses and at mobilising a sense of community among suffering soldiers. Yet the attitude of suspicion towards trauma claims continued into the post-war years, for instance in the approach taken in the Federal Republic of Germany to applications for reparations by Jews who had suffered in Nazi concentration camps. As the historian Dagmar Herzog has documented, many of the psychiatrists and psychoanalysts who assessed these claims in the 1950s rejected them on the grounds that the claimants must have already been disturbed before they went into the camps, and/or their nervous disorders were motivated by the 'secondary gain' of financial awards.[15] It was only in the 1960s that a significant change came about, largely as a result of growing awareness of the extent of post-Holocaust suffering and of pressure in the US from Vietnam veterans. Soldiers returned home from Vietnam as national heroes, yet many were deeply troubled by their experiences, showing all the symptoms of what eventually came to be called 'post-traumatic stress disorder' – a term that only entered the official diagnostic manuals in 1980. These veterans, having bravely served their country, could not so easily be cast as malingerers or blamed for their own suffering. Instead, it was gradually understood that they were themselves victims (even if they had perpetrated war crimes) of a set of conditions that could only be called 'traumatic'. Since then, fuelled also by the belated recognition of the impacts of sexual violence on women (the feminist movement and rape crisis centres were vitally important in this) and of physical and sexual abuse on children, the centrality of trauma in many people's lives has become more widely recognised, and a shift has occurred towards an appreciation of the suffering of these people as being due to their circumstances rather than to any inner weakness.

It is worth noting some paradoxical implications of this move towards a more sympathetic, person-centred understanding of trauma. Until the latter part of the twentieth century, 'trauma' referred to an inner state and the psychiatric question might be, 'why does this person suffer when others don't?', implying that there might be a defect of some kind in the sufferer, perhaps neurological or due to developmental factors. Since then, having a traumatised response to certain overpowering events has come to be seen as 'normal': anyone who went through the concentration camps, or has been raped or subjected to intense violence, will be expected to show effects. The focus then shifts from why certain people are vulnerable to what it is in the nature of the *event* that can be expected to have traumatising consequences for most or all people. Indeed, as has been evident in the context of court cases of rape, it is sometimes held that a *failure* to display symptoms of trauma is an indication that the experience could not have been as bad as claimed. As an aside, it is revealing that the performance of rape victims in court has often been used as part of the evidence for the veracity of their claims. Being too incoherent and distressed means their testimony cannot be trusted; being too poised and rational suggests that they cannot have undergone experiences which would usually be expected to be traumatic. The narrowness of this tightrope is obvious. It is also curious to see how the shift in the understanding of trauma can have certain effects on moral judgements. If, for instance, soldiers are traumatised by actions they have taken, for instance having flashbacks and an overpowering sense of guilt for their involvement in a massacre, does this make them victims or perpetrators? Should they be entitled to compensation in the way that the victims of their abuses might be? Moving the focus of trauma theory away from the individual and towards the event has definite benefits, but it also obscures some important issues related to how we might deal with matters of responsibility and culpability in certain extreme, but unfortunately not rare, situations.

Let us go back now to the question of how we relate to trauma and what it means for the issue of feeling real. The historical account sketched above demonstrates just how much the narratives made available to us influence how we understand traumatised people: either as weaklings who cannot cope with stress or as victims of appalling circumstances that should never have been allowed to occur. Having an acceptable narrative, one that is recognised socially and therefore warrants a hearing, is precious and can mark the difference between the conditions that allow working-through to occur and those that prohibit such comings-to-terms with what has happened. If the culture cannot 'listen' but instead blocks out these experiences, hearing them as evidence only of neuroticism or manipulativeness, it is very unlikely that the sufferer will be encouraged to share their troubles and feel free to develop ways of dealing with them. They are more likely to lapse into silence, reinforcing the view that trauma cannot be spoken of. To my mind, this is an important lesson to draw from the history of trauma. The account of trauma as characterised by an inability on the part of the sufferer to speak of their experience can itself be a way of silencing people. If you can articulate it in even a remotely coherent way, this suggests, then you are not properly traumatised. The theory of the silence of the traumatised victim might be a way in which society excuses itself from the responsibility to give such victims their voice. In relation to Holocaust testimony, for example, Thomas Trezise writes in his book *Witnessing Witnessing*: 'The routinely repeated claim that the traumatic experience of the Holocaust is unrepresentable or unspeakable appears to stand in for a refusal to listen.'[16]

Taking this a bit more slowly, the issue is whether the difficulty around trauma is one of speaking or of listening. The dominant idea is that 'being traumatised' is a response to unbearable painful events that overwhelm normal psychic processes and require extreme forms of psychological defence to preserve the ego from destruction. These defences are important for the preservation of sanity, but they have a serious cost as well, cutting the person off from the reality of their experience and sometimes literally removing memories or 'encapsulating' them in an area of the mind that cannot be accessed. This potentially has two negative effects. One is to make the person feel less real. Highly significant events in someone's life have been scrubbed out of their memory, and much psychological energy must be devoted to maintaining the split that keeps these events 'unknown'. The other negative effect is that, because the memory is not integrated into the person's active psychological being, it remains unprocessed. This means that when it does break through, which may happen when the person is under great stress or when something happens to remind them of their past, the memory surfaces as a kind of 're-enactment'. It feels as if it is still happening; it has not been properly absorbed into the bank of memories, which requires a certain amount of facing up to the remembered events and making sense of them, but instead it is held in a primary, 'uncoded' form. The result is that when the (non-)memory reappears, it is with the full force of the original event. Evidence of this can be found in the characteristic phenomena of post-traumatic stress disorder: a feeling of being back in the traumatising situation, flashbacks and nightmares, uncontrollable anxiety and overwhelming sensations of dread.

One way in which this has sometimes been thought about is through the metaphor of 'encryption'. Although the notion has become familiar in the context of online security, well before that the psychoanalysts Nicolas Abraham and Maria Torok developed a similar idea from their work with Holocaust survivors.[17] Their account is sophisticated and relates as much to how trauma is passed on intergenerationally as it does to the traumatised reactions of individuals. For them, traumatic memories are like secrets that are hidden away in a safe place – a 'crypt' – where they lie dormant yet send out hints of their existence. We can imagine this as a situation in which we know that there is a hiding place containing something of importance but cannot get access to it; in that sense, the crypt simultaneously attracts us (because of the belief that something vital is stored there) and repels us (because the object is securely locked up in its encasement).

The parallel with encrypted messages is even stronger. The fact that a message is encrypted indicates that there is something significant there, inciting attempts to decode it, but it also repels those attempts. For Abraham and Torok, and others who have drawn on this idea, this is one way of thinking about the silence that follows atrocities which can continue to have effects even after generations have passed. The immediate descendants of Nazis and other Germans of that time, for instance, heard very little talk about what their parents had done. They were aware that this silence indicated the presence of something deeply troubling that cried out for revelation, but which demanded that it should be kept secret. As a result, few asked their parents about what had happened during the Nazi period. It was not until the advent of a third and fourth generation that such reckonings with history became common.[18] In a painfully parallel way, it is held that many Holocaust survivors refused to, or could not, talk about their experiences, leaving their children to puzzle over a silence that could sometimes be felt as a palpable cloud over their own lives. Many second-generation narratives have testified to the effect of this, including the frequency with which these children actually understood what had happened to their parents, in general terms if not in detail, without being able to speak of such knowledge. For example, in her powerful memoir called *After Such Knowledge*, Eva Hoffman describes the way in which the mostly unspoken memories of her parents meant that she often felt herself to be 'wrestling with shadows,' which, she writes 'can be more frightening, or more confusing, than struggling with solid realities'.[19] For some, too, there has been an effect now termed 'postmemory', in which the younger generation have 'memories' of events that they have not experienced, but their *parents* had.[20] Dreams of persecution, of Nazi violence, of being hidden or lost or orphaned – these seem to be frequent accompaniments to the lives of the second generation, even or perhaps especially when their parents have been silent.

All this would seem to confirm the theory that trauma works its effects by becoming unspeakable. The traumatising event festers inside, occasionally breaking into consciousness to renew itself but essentially controlling the sufferer by its radical unavailability to symbolisation and hence to working-through – to a process of coming to terms with the past. Yet we must ask some questions about this. Does this account place the responsibility for silence on the sufferer who cannot communicate their ordeal, becoming a smokescreen to excuse the society that cannot find a space to hear of such suffering? The 'trauma produces silence' model assumes a generally benign social context that the deeply troubled sufferer cannot take advantage of. If only they could speak openly of what they have been through, then the rest of us might be able to help. There may be some truth in this, but the big question is whether the surrounding context is genuinely benign, how willing it is to provide a listening ear with sufficient integrity to allow real speech to take place. For example, the belief that Holocaust survivors refused to, or could not, speak of their experiences was widely held, yet it has gradually become clear that it is mainly false. Many such survivors in fact spoke through testimonies in Polish and Yiddish in the late 1940s and early 1950s. The problem was not that there was silence, but that there was scant response to this speaking and, as a result, the survivors' voices dried up. Even one of the most celebrated and influential of Holocaust memoirs, Primo Levi's *If This Is a Man*, was not widely noticed when first published by a small Italian firm in 1947, when it sold only 1,500 copies; it did not gain traction until the end of the 1950s. That is to say, the text was there, but few read it.[21] The main difficulty of communicating trauma was not that it could not be articulated, but that any articulation was avoided or denied. Ironically enough, this mirrors an account Levi gives of a recurring nightmare he had in the concentration camp: that he would survive to tell his story, but no one would listen to it, a nightmare that he claims many other inmates shared.[22]

One might say similar things about responses to child abuse, notably children's disclosures of being sexually abused by adults. There had been very little registration of the prevalence of sexual abuse until it burst on the therapeutic and political scene in the late 1970s and 1980s, brought to light mainly by the feminist movement and especially by the work of rape crisis and women's therapy centres in uncovering historical and contemporary sexual violence. It rapidly became clear that this was not because no one had reported it, but because the voices of children and women were systematically stifled by the lack of response to their calls. This social deafness was compounded by a misreading of psychoanalytical ideas but was chiefly produced by a misogynistic culture apt to assume that women and children (and women treated as children) had nothing of value to say. The flood of disclosures that subsequently arrived revealed not only the prevalence of child sexual abuse but the many attempts that children and women had made to be heard, only to be met with silence or active rejection.

As Sándor Ferenczi pointed out back in the 1930s (demonstrating that the 'secret' of child sexual abuse has been in plain sight for the best part of a century), sexual abuse of children is much more common than was generally thought to be the case.[23] Children who try to tell an adult about their suffering and are rebuffed, because they are not believed or because the adult is protecting another adult or their own relationship with that other adult, quickly learn that they possess dangerous knowledge that must not be disclosed. This can convert itself into a secret held even against the self, in the sense described above of how trauma operates: something troubling exists that cannot be spoken about. What this means is that it is not necessarily the original event (in this case, the abuse) that causes the long-lasting silence, but the failure of the attempt to speak about it and be heard when faced with the indifference of those around. What Ferenczi calls the 'timid attempts' of children in this situation to transmit information about what was done to them requires adults to increase the volume on their receivers; instead, however, they too frequently fail to hear anything and treat the message as 'nonsensical' or as an outright lie. That is indeed an effective way to silence trauma.

Why is it that people cannot listen to the stories that sufferers of trauma try to tell them? Sometimes this refusal is clearly motivated by conscious or semi-conscious intentions, to protect oneself or someone else from accusation, as in the case of the abuser or someone dependent on the abuser. But leaving aside this possibility and also that of simple callousness, there are a range of more understandable, and in some cases potentially forgivable, defensive responses on the part of a listener. That these are understandable and forgivable, however, does not make them any less complicit in perpetuating a situation in which trauma is silenced and suffering goes on. One way of conceptualising these defensive, effectively rejecting responses is to consider them as a kind of 'Scylla and Charybdis', the two sea monsters of Greek legend placed either side of a narrow channel of water down which ships had to navigate. On the one side, let us call it 'Scylla', there is the temptation towards repudiation of the trauma narrative because it is too disturbing, perhaps even bringing up listeners' own traumatic memories that have not been dealt with, or frightening them or making them feel uncomfortably responsible for the speaker's troubles. The consequence of this can be a kind of backing away in which the trauma narrative is ignored or even actively rebutted as a lie or as something that cannot be listened to ('This is too much for me, sorry'). On the other side, 'Charybdis' is the danger of over-enthusiastic adoption of the trauma narrative as the listener's own, a kind of 'traumatic identification' in which listeners take on the trauma as if it is the same as experiences they themselves have had, or imagine themselves so strongly into the position of the sufferer that they end up sharing the traumatised state of mind. This has occurred a few times in very public ways, for example in Benjamin Wilkomirski's book *Fragments*, published during a period of heightened memorialisation of the Holocaust towards the end of the 1990s. This book purported to be a childhood Holocaust memoir but turned out to be a fabrication, the twist being that Wilkomirski seems to have believed it himself.[24] More commonly, this kind of response involves the listener adopting a stance that runs, 'I understand you because I have gone through the same thing myself.' This is not to deny that having had similar experiences can sometimes help understanding, nor to claim that people do not often gain support from this kind of solidarity. But what I am referring to here is the temptation to usurp someone else's narrative, translating it into our own life story, leaving the original speaker bereft of what is truly theirs. 'I know what you mean, hear what happened to me ...' can be a way of avoiding what we are being told and assuming that everyone's experience is the same, when clearly it is not. At base, we can never be sure about what a specific experience means to someone until we have fully heard them out, and even then there may remain an area of uncertainty that lies between the authentic attempt to imagine their experience and the actuality of what that feels like 'from inside'. But if we collapse into trauma ourselves, how can we be a resilient, meaningfully responsive witness to the suffering of others?

The challenge of imagining things from another's perspective is a general one, but in the case of trauma there is the additional difficulty of the enormous emotional load that a sufferer might be trying to communicate. It is not surprising that people defend themselves against hearing fully what they are being told: sometimes the knowledge we are being asked to take on board is truly unbearable. Yet that clearly is the task; otherwise, the silence of trauma is perpetuated not because sufferers cannot speak – indeed, they tend to speak a lot about their suffering unless they are silenced. It is rather that the communication of these experiences is blocked, listeners turn away, society neatly parcels up its response into specialist areas such as psychotherapy, and trauma sufferers are discouraged from telling others what their lives are really like. Unbearable it may sometimes be, but for the sake of truthfulness and in an attempt to re-inscribe into the world people who have undergone traumatising experiences, we have to find ways to bear it.

One problem in responding constructively to trauma narratives is that the magnitude of many tales leaves a listener feeling helpless, aware of how little they can offer. Some second-generation descendants have commented on this, documenting the difficulties of growing up as an 'ordinary' person with, say, regular teenage anxieties, while living with an awareness of the terrible ordeals that their parents went through and the correspondingly heroic scale of their history. Eva Hoffman describes this powerfully with the refrain 'Not the Holocaust': '"It's not the Holocaust," I would think in my adolescence as I met with some small but hurtful problem – an awkward social encounter, a summer job interview, a friend's rejection, a rebuke from a teacher.'[25] Yet these children had to find ways to get on with their lives, to have comparatively trivial problems that nevertheless felt real and loomed large for them, navigating the ordinary complexities of growing up. They had to relate to their parents not as survivors but as parents, even when the parents were having difficulties of their own, and they had to balance the demand to be sensitive to those parental difficulties against their own needs, desires and ambitions. No one thinks this is easy, but thousands of descendants have somehow managed it.

For the witness to someone else's trauma narrative, the task is more specific and limited, even if some of the demands it makes are parallel to those just mentioned. It is to navigate those waters between Scylla and Charybdis so that a destination can be reached in which something is offered to the trauma sufferer that neither rebuffs them nor escalates the trauma, but instead recognises what they have gone through, and are going through, in a way that communicates real listening and acceptance. Donald Winnicott's idea of the 'use of an object' is again helpful here.[26] The 'object', which for present purposes is the person doing the listening, must be resilient enough not to be destroyed by the narrative being directed at them, which could be inflected with hate, fury and resentment as well as tragedy, and might sometimes be felt as a personal accusation even if it is not intended that way. 'Not being destroyed' here simply means enduring the situation, staying in it with the trauma sufferer without turning away, neither trivialising the experience nor being panicked by it. The listener also must be responsive enough to be attuned to the speaker, demonstrating respect for the specificity of their account – 'it is not my story and I cannot ever fully inhabit it' – but doing whatever can be done to understand it. This all sounds ambitiously ideal, given the intensity of many of these witnessing encounters, and people are often left feeling helpless (that is, unable to help) and inadequate to the task. Yet it happens; people do feel supported by the solidarity of others and by the sense that something has been acknowledged even if it can never be rectified. It is like the therapist who manages to say to a very troubled patient that their pain will never fully go away, but that they, the therapist, will stay with them however hard the situation might become. Ambitious, yes, but possible too.

Perhaps the key point is about moderation and a kind of sympathetic realism. Some writers on trauma have made it seem as though the only way to understand such experiences is through a kind of nonverbal intuition in which listeners react to the underlying emotion of what is being said and mirror it themselves. This would be akin to the 'postmemory' situation, in which someone feels they are in the same predicament as the person who has actually suffered, dreaming their dreams and going through what they have gone through. This is surely empathetic, but also potentially self- and other-destructive. The trauma is being passed on rather than eased. I think something much more ordinary is desirable, which is to recognise that the traumatic experience cannot be magicked away, but still to offer a less-than-perfect ear to the other person, communicating a wish to understand and be helpful rather than a heroic ambition to make everything all right. Aiming to solve all the problems of the world will always lead to failure; sharing the burden a little might be a more responsible way of going about things. This is why it is important to move away from the notion that trauma reflects inarticulable, unbearable knowledge and instead to notice how trauma sufferers usually try repeatedly to express themselves, however haltingly and uncertainly. Similarly for the listener, the knowledge they gain of the other's experience may be hard to take but it is not 'unbearable'; it is, rather, genuinely *difficult* knowledge but (some might think, unfortunately) within the sphere of human possibility. Appreciating that there are limitations on our capacity to fully connect with another yet that the attempt is worthwhile is a non-idealising approach to responding to the distress of others; and some understanding *is* possible, with the use of our imagination.

We defend ourselves against suffering. The defences we use are important, they have a function in keeping us afloat in what can be choppy seas, and they are at times absolutely necessary for managing the difficulties we have. At the more extreme end, as with real trauma, we might even need them to help us stay alive. But they come at a cost, which is often paid in the form of a reduction in the sense of reality as we turn away from our experience or that of other people, silencing it through denial or other forms of non-responsiveness. This happens at the level of the individual, but it also happens socially in the way communities and societies can delegitimise certain forms of experience, making it very hard to recognise their reality. Key to combatting this denial of reality while also acknowledging the challenge of facing traumatic memories without reproducing a cycle of secrecy, is a process of recognition – person to person, but also social. Many of the defences we deploy, especially those that lead us to silence traumatised voices, are fuelled by an overriding sense that we are being exposed to unbearable knowledge and are helpless to respond to it adequately, without falling apart ourselves. Shifting the perspective slightly might help: this knowledge is genuinely *difficult* and requires a kind of robustness that may be hard to sustain, but it need not be *unbearable* if our sights are set on recognising our own and others' hardships rather than wishing them away. What is genuinely unbearable is the sense of an irrecoverable tragedy; yet finding small ways to reach out, even under those horrific circumstances, can help build a sense of being real in ourselves and in those who try to tell us of their lives.

5

Ghosts and Ancestors

The past, if not properly mourned, can come back to haunt us. Let me start with one example. In October 2018, Jair Bolsonaro, a far-right politician, was elected president of Brazil. The election campaign had been violent and characterised by widespread protests, street movements, and claims of corruption all round. It took place in the aftermath of what was dubbed a 'legislative coup' through which the then president, Dilma Rousseff, who belonged to the leftist Workers' Party, was impeached and removed from office. In the presidential election, Bolsonaro was regarded as a candidate of the militaristic right, and he certainly fitted that role, celebrating Brazil's civil-military dictatorship of the 1960s and 1970s and cannily playing on a public desire for a stable society. A specific instance captures both the shamelessness and brutality of Bolsonaro's candidacy. During the impeachment process, when parliamentarians had to cast their vote, Bolsonaro dedicated his to 'the memory of Colonel Carlos Alberto Brilhante Ustra, the dread of Dilma Rousseff'.[1] Ustra had been chief of Brazil's secret service in São Paulo and as such was responsible for torture, murder and disappearances; indeed, he was the only member of the military to be subsequently convicted of murder. As Bolsonaro knew full well, Dilma Rousseff had herself been the victim of torture at that time.

How could someone who so openly advocated torture and cruelty, who glorified a destructive regime of this kind, be elected as president of a major country? Obviously, there are many answers to this question, relating to economic decline, corruption, populist nationalism, American Trumpism and so on. But there is an additional factor, less extensively commented upon, that may play a part.

Here is a brief extract from an interview with a psychoanalyst who participated in the Truth Commission of Brazil, set up by President Rousseff before she was impeached. The psychoanalyst, invited by the president to join the commission, focused her work on the impact of the 1964–85 dictatorship on the indigenous people of the Amazon. In an interview in 2016, carried out as part of a research project on psychoanalysis during the dictatorship, we asked this psychoanalyst about her experience and in particular what overall effect she thought the Truth Commission had had.[2] Her response (in the original English) was definite:

> I think it was near zero, I was very disappointed. Brazil was the last [Truth Commission] from the countries in Latin America and everybody, the young people who had not lived in it and the old people, the ones who were not victims, had forgotten the dictatorship … In my personal research, sometimes I talked to someone at the bus station or on the streets by curiosity, [saying] I was from the Truth Commission. [For] most people I spoke to in the streets the dictatorship was better than now, there was not a mess, things were in order and they were right to arrest those communists.

Our psychoanalyst notes how 'most' ordinary citizens ('someone at the bus station') remembered or imagined the dictatorship as a better time, seeing it as more orderly and free of disruptive communists. This is after she has introduced herself as a member of the Truth Commission, so the reaction is undoubtedly meant to antagonise and impress. There is of course nothing systematic about this: the psychoanalyst is clear that she was engaging in 'personal research', but she is also a practised observer and political thinker well known in Brazil, and so we might give some weight to her testimony. It fits into something else, in any case: the question of what it takes to mourn a period of violence in such a way that it does not recur.

In Brazil, the dictatorship did not come to a dramatic close as it did in some other Latin American countries. It rather faded away, and its end was preceded in 1979 by the Brazilian military president, João Baptista Figueiredo, passing a law that granted a general and unrestricted amnesty to all perpetrators of political crimes, whether they were members or defenders of the civil-military regime or opponents of it. The consequence of this is that no one has been called to account for the violence of that period, even when Truth Commissions have provided evidence. It has also meant that many alleged perpetrators have been able to take refuge in denials. Our psychoanalyst described the scene:

> They only said 'nothing to declare, nothing to declare', you can do nothing. We had the power to force them to come but not to force them to tell the truth, we are not torturers, we made the question, 'Nothing to declare, it's false, no it wasn't me. Nothing to declare.'

Is it too far-fetched to suggest that the restoration of right-wing rule in Brazil and the nostalgia for the period of the dictatorship are linked to the failure of acknowledgement, mourning and reparation for past oppression? The perpetuation of injustice and refusal to come to terms with past horrors – which for many Brazilians is what they were – is precisely the set of conditions that militates against laying ghosts to rest. These ghosts come back to haunt, and one response is to deny them again, to try to exorcise them by violence. Perhaps we have in Brazil (and elsewhere, but those are other stories) exactly this scenario: our connection to a brutal past leaves us plagued by ghosts that demand recognition and justice; but this is a painful process, requiring openness and the courage to acknowledge the damage that has been done and who bears responsibility for it. Where the social order is insufficiently resilient to achieve this, the ghosts are banished again and in their place appears another kind of repetitive phenomenon, the return of the 'repressive authority' that blocks a coming-to-terms with the unquiet remains of the ancestors. This is indicated psychoanalytically under the heading of the return of the repressed and the death drive and is perhaps the real danger of intergenerational haunting: that we might try to rid ourselves of ghosts through violence.

Being haunted is usually a troubling experience, one which people seek to end by expelling or releasing the ghost that is disturbing them. Sometimes it is portrayed comically, especially in children's tales, which may say something important about how we might move towards a deeper understanding of ghosts. For children, it seems, they can be scary, but in a familiar way. The fright comes from the way ghosts are enigmatic, uncontrollable, inexplicable and unpredictable, not to say threatening. But children are probably used to that; they know that they do not fully understand the world and have to be cautious about it but also must trust that it is reasonably benign. The *attraction* of ghosts is partly that they dramatise this experience in a way that both brings it into focus and normalises it. In addition, there is something we might call 'metaphysical' about ghosts in relation to childhood. Not only does the existence of ghosts promise that death is an extension of life, mitigating awareness of the finality of death, so there is less to be frightened of, but there is also a kind of comfort that children feel in how the ghost can represent the *aliveness* of everything around them. The material world ceases to be blank and alien and instead becomes personified, inhabited by spirits that may be unquiet but are fundamentally recognisable. There is something in the air, even if it cannot be seen clearly, and that something is at root friendly, even if it might also give us the shivers.

If ghosts can be comic for children, this might be a way of dealing with the anxiety produced by encountering things outside their previous experience. Turning ghosts into figures of fun, even pretending (not) to be scared of them, transforms for a child the potential hostility of a dangerous world that cannot be fully understood or mastered into something that feels friendly and familiar. It is only my brother in a white sheet, only a dressed-up neighbour on Halloween. Or maybe, for children who have suffered significant losses, it is a dead parent come back to comfort and watch over them. The world is strange enough, what goes on within it mostly incomprehensible and sometimes deeply saddening. It can make us fearful. The best strategy is to mock it or convert it into a manageable tale of ghosts as fellow lost beings who need as much help as we do. Befriending a ghost not only allows children to move across different worlds, the living and the dead, but it also represents a kind of solidarity of the displaced and marginalised, those who have not yet found, or have lost, their place in the world.

Ghosts are, of course, unnerving, for children as well as for adults. Yet the acceptance by children of the possibility of a benevolent type of haunting is an indication that sympathy with ghosts is just as much a part of the natural response to them as is being frightened. Fright happens when we are unprepared for something, suddenly come up against it, cannot understand it and feel threatened by it. All this is part of what Freud called the 'uncanny' and can certainly set our teeth on edge.[3] But if the presence of ghosts is familiar (so we are prepared for them) and forms part of our general understanding of the world as alive in all its aspects (so we understand ghosts to be living beings), and if the ghosts are not threatening but instead are either lost, requiring help, or supportive, offering guidance, then we need not be overcome with fright when ghosts appear but might instead welcome them into our lives. Mastering fears by playing with the idea of ghosts is common in childhood, and indeed in adulthood if we include watching scary films or reading occult stories, but so is the sense that at least some ghosts are to be welcomed, perhaps especially in situations where otherwise we might feel abandoned and alone.

Not all ghosts are comforting, though, as my Brazilian example shows. It is likely that as children develop into adults they lose the knack of embracing curiosity and wonder and increase their wariness about the world, disabused by experience from the old conviction that all is fine and there is always someone there to look after them (though continued belief in God might well have this function). But let's think for a moment about the relationship between ghosts as lost, returning figures and the question of how we might come to feel that our minds have depth – that is, how we might sustain a sense of being real. One proposal that Freud made was that our 'ego' or 'I' is made up in large part of what he called lost objects – specifically, 'an object which was lost has been set up again inside the ego'.[4] Broadly, what he meant by this was that as we learn to differentiate between ourselves and others, and therefore experience the painful effects of not being able to control our loved ones – our precious 'objects' – we manage the situation by psychologically taking them into us and identifying with the treasured parts of them. This is a normal part of development, but it also hints at something that grief can do. In the face of actual loss, for example through death or abandonment, the object is somehow preserved through this process of internalisation, becoming a building-block of the ego, so that the real loss is tempered by memory and by the sense of having assimilated important aspects of the loved one. The object consequently becomes an influence on the ego; our psychic life is, to a considerable extent, constructed out of those we have loved and lost. This is nicely expressed by Freud in the important article *Mourning and Melancholia* that he wrote during the First World War, in part to explain the sense of guilt that often affects people who are bereaved: 'The shadow of the object fell upon the ego.'[5]

We can use this idea to explore a broader set of questions about how we gain a sense of what it is to be human, and how we build ourselves up so that we live the fullest possible lives. For Freud, the answer is that we incorporate the attributes of those we love and of necessity have lost, whether this is simply by the routine separations that constitute the process of development or by more severe means, including death. Internalising these attributes involves integrating them with our own experiences, wishes and desires to create a sense of continuity between ourselves and others, and between past, present and future. The people who matter to us live on inside us when they are not there (for instance, imagine children who can feel the presence of their mother even when she has gone to work) and when they are finally lost to us. In this important sense, we carry certain ghosts within and this 'haunting' is an essential part of being human. Without it, we are thinned out by being disconnected from our pasts, we forget our intimacies and are drained dry whenever someone leaves.

Friendly ghosts are therefore central to a feeling of belonging, of having a place in human society. Denying these ghosts a home within us means cutting ourselves off from one of the most important sources of nurture for our own being. It means forgetting the past, in ways that I have discussed earlier – denying that we have ever loved and lost, pretending that nothing matters much and that we can manage without support, blocking the essential relationality of human life. Silencing the ghosts of our loved ones may be a way of avoiding sadness, but the cost is that we are less connected with others and our personalities have much less content.

Welcoming these ghosts is consequently important. The feeling of being with someone who is absent or departed is a way of facing reality even if it is also a kind of fantasy. The person is not actually there, but we remember them and can feel their presence as if they were. This is not of course a kind of psychotic belief that the ghost is real but rather an inclusive subjective state, in which what comes back to us in the form of memories and sensations through which we recover a person's 'presence' is a source of strength and of increased intensity of feeling. In which, that is, loss is accepted as a route to deepening our experience, and the valued attributes of those we have lost are allowed to live on.

If ghosts appear, it is usually because they are trying to communicate something. Otherwise, what is the point of them coming back? If we listen to these ghosts, whether they are disturbing or simply sad, what messages do they bring? In fiction, these are sometimes very specific – where the murder took place, say, or where and from whom to seek help, what task has been left undone and now needs to be fulfilled. The ghost of Hamlet's father is the classic Shakespearean example, directing Hamlet and the audience to the heart of what is 'rotten in the state of Denmark' and fuelling Hamlet's arguably paranoid thirst for revenge. Sometimes ghosts are imagined as bringing a warning to the living, telling them who to watch out for and what dangerous situations to avoid. The successful romantic film *Ghost*, from 1990, plays on this idea with the lead character protected by her dead husband. Believing in the concreteness of these messages does require an openness to belief in the occult that strays too far from reason to be very convincing. *Ghost* is no more than a romantic comedy; but *Hamlet* is one of the greatest of all plays partly because of the ambiguity about the status of the ghost – whether it is real or a projection from Hamlet's mind. If we consider the issue more broadly, it is worth taking seriously the sense of something that needs to be put right before the ghost can find rest.

In much recent writing on this topic, loosely termed 'hauntology', the things that need to be put right are societal. The sources of the troubles that haunt people are unresolved and often unacknowledged tensions in the social world, perhaps a situation in which the promise that society makes to its members – basically to protect them and offer them sustenance – has been betrayed. Much has been written, for instance, and in many cases very powerfully, about the legacy of slavery in the United States. In one of the most significant novels of the twentieth century, Toni Morrison's *Beloved*, this legacy is presented as a ghost story, dealing both with the immediate aftermath of slavery and the resonance of this aftermath for contemporary American society.[6] How has the supposed freedom produced by the abolition of slavery, Morrison's book asks, hidden the actual continuation of oppression and discrimination, resulting in the perpetuation of anti-Black racism and its immense weight for more than a further century? The ghost that keeps returning in the novel is of the baby killed by her mother to protect her against being re-enslaved (a genuine historical occurrence); but it is also, palpably, the ghost of slavery itself, still haunting the American body politic in inescapable ways.

Beloved is, obviously, a novel in which being haunted by an actual ghost can be imagined as a real event. We are at liberty to take this literally or symbolically, or both. If we think about it *psychosocially*, however, mixing psychological and sociological perspectives, we can perhaps see that it brings to light how unspoken and suppressed societal iniquities can continue to make themselves felt, to *insist* on themselves, until they begin to be recognised. The Black Lives Matter movement, for instance, can be understood in part as an explosive resistance to anti-Black racism that has certainly not come from nowhere – the civil rights and Black Power movements of the 1960s and 1970s are just two examples of its precursors – but which represents the resurgence of a spectre that has haunted American society (and, of course, other societies too) precisely because the injustices it names have not been put right. Other postcolonial demands for reparative justice of one kind or another, sometimes material and usually involving formal apologies and acknowledgement of the continuing profits derived from historical wrongdoings, can also be seen in this way, even if they are not always quite as clearly ghostly in their appearance. And I have already said something in the previous chapter about how haunted the post-Holocaust world is, how the second-generation descendants of both survivors and perpetrators have often had to feel their way blindly towards the experiences they know have affected them but which they have not had 'permission' to really put in their place.

This example of the descendants of perpetrators is especially revealing due to the different levels on which it operates. On the social and national level, we know that the denial of responsibility by post-war Germany and the covering-over of the reinstatment of Nazi functionaries in its legal, civil service, political, cultural, educational and health systems – the rapidity, that is, with which the slapdash process of 'de-Nazification' was abandoned – only began to be reckoned with in the 1970s.[7] Even then, it was controversial within Germany to acknowledge the Nazi terror and the responsibility of the whole society for allowing it to thrive. Chancellor Willy Brandt's famous *Warschauer Kniefall*, his gesture in 1970 of kneeling at the memorial to the Warsaw Ghetto uprising, was deeply unpopular among a large section of the West German public who, neglecting to notice the murderous events it was recognising, saw it as bringing their country into disrepute. Yet if rampant denial was characteristic of the generation that had lived through the Second World War, the second and perhaps especially the third generation of post-war Germans gave ample and sometimes violent evidence of having been haunted by the unspoken histories of their predecessors. These descendants were driven to ask questions about the silence in which the immediate past was shrouded and often ended up challenging their parents or grandparents. The effects of all this continue today. On the one hand, Germany, like many European countries, is plagued by backward-looking extreme right-wing nationalists still in thrall to an imagined past of greatness; on the other, Germany has done more than many countries – perhaps most notably Austria, which is the closest comparison – to acknowledge its culpability through memorialisations and (eventually) material reparations. Both responses are haunted by a stain that will never go away, and that passes down the generations so that even people who have no conceivable link with this past must find ways of responding to it. Germany's unqualified commitment to supporting Israel, and the difficulty this creates when criticism of Israeli actions is needed, is another example of the hold that the past can have over present politics.

Ghosts speak about the injustices that have been perpetrated and that have not been resolved by societies that refuse to face up to their past, and in that refusal fail to recognise present iniquities. As the example of post-war Germany illustrates, this is not just an intellectual encounter with the ghosts of the past. For the children and grandchildren of Nazi Germany, it has often been a deeply personal, emotional experience to come up against the silence of their parents or grandparents and to realise just what they may have done, whether as active Nazis or as members of what has come to be called a 'bystander society'. This has been studied carefully in some important scholarly works, such as Mary Fulbrook's *Bystander Society*, mentioned earlier; it has also been explored by writers reflecting on their own discoveries of the histories of their German ancestors and subsequent struggles to come to terms with them.[8] For example, Jennifer Teege, a black, Hebrew-speaking German who in her thirties found out by accident that her grandfather was Amon Goeth, the commandant of Płaszów concentration camp (portrayed graphically in Steven Spielberg's 1993 film *Schindler's List*), and that her beloved grandmother had been his mistress, was pitched by this discovery into a deep psychological crisis.[9] The psychoanalyst and historian Roger Frie launched into a historical investigation of denial in post-war Germany after uncovering his grandfather's Nazi connections.[10] There have also been several documentary films about the tension between denial and acknowledgement of the actions of Nazi parents, notably Philippe Sands's 2012 film *My Nazi Legacy*, which explored the differing responses of the sons of Hans Frank, who as governor general of Poland was directly responsible for the destruction of the Jews there, and Otto von Wächter, governor of Galicia and Frank's deputy.[11] Frank's son Niklas, a well-known German journalist, is renowned for his condemnation of his father, a standpoint that came to very public notice with the publication in 1987 of his book *Der Vater: Eine Abrechnung* ('The father: A settling of accounts' – translated into English in 1991 as *In the Shadow of the Reich*).[12] Von Wächter's son Horst, on the other hand, is shown in the film as wriggling out of this: he is troubled (that much is clear), he sees what was done, but his own father, he believes, was fundamentally a good man who had no real choice. He argues that we have to understand how resistance to the Nazi decrees was not easy, even for a Nazi. Despite considerable pressure from Niklas Frank and Philippe Sands himself, Horst von Wächter maintains this position throughout the film; he is shown receiving with pleasure the admiration for his father expressed by some Ukrainian neo-Nazis.

For the people on the 'other' side, the survivors of atrocities ranging from the Holocaust to South African apartheid to genocides in different places around the world, the ghostly apparitions are of a different nature. Nevertheless, some elements of their general structure are shared. Something has not been done to make good the damage, to ascribe responsibility to where it belongs and to achieve recognition of what people have gone through. In the case of survivors, the struggle to be heard has in many contexts been immensely challenging. Their haunting is connected to the genuine silence that followed this experience of being *silenced*: having spoken to deaf ears, the survivors often withdrew. For this reason, and also as a protective strategy, they often did not unburden themselves within their families, leaving a vacuum that their children were aware of but did not know how to fill. Alternatively, some survivors projected into the next generation a demand for *them* to repair the damage that had been done, perhaps to make up for their own difficult lives, or even at times as an 'answer to Hitler', a statement about survival. Intense investment in their children, over-protectiveness, anxiety, expectations of high achievement: these and similar demands, both consciously and unconsciously transmitted, are reported by many of the second generation. Eva Hoffman writes, from her own experience:

> The parents so often hoped for rescue. They invested so much in these children, and imbued them with so much yearning. To replace – revive – the dead ones; to undo the losses; to repair the humiliations wrought by the abusers; to provide the redress of unconditional love and protection against deadly danger.[13]

For those next generations, sometimes driven to distraction by their parents' behaviour and by what they suspect but do not know, the haunting is often profound. These ghosts are saying, 'repair the world for us', an injunction that may be unachievable, especially when the recipient has all their own normal human uncertainties and vulnerabilities, now magnified by those they have received from their parents.

Ghosts of these kinds, the haunting remains of past suffering, need to be recognised for what they are: living remnants that keep injustices alive until something is done about them. In this respect, they can also be thought about in relation to the concepts of 'melancholia' and 'trauma' discussed in previous chapters. In both these states, what is being described is a set of experiences that remain 'unprocessed', unavailable to the kind of thinking integrated with emotion that is necessary for coming to terms with indigestible events. In trauma, the big difficulty is of finding ways to convert the here-and-now experience of being overwhelmed by the event into a different experience of that event as *past*, the subject of distressing memories no doubt, but *memories* nevertheless. The hard task placed on later witnesses to find ways of listening to trauma narratives that recognise their reality and intensity but also manage to stay with the sufferer is based on the idea that such witnessing can be a path to allowing the trauma to be looked at or symbolised, to make some kind of sense. In this way, a certain 'difficult knowledge' can substitute, for both speaker and listener, for what was previously felt to be unbearable.

With ghosts too what is noticeable is the sense of a voice not heard, of something speaking and trying to find a listener so that things might change. There is an event, perhaps a continuing series of events; it is known about yet also not known, because this knowledge is painful either in itself or for how it implicates us or others in culpability. The ghostly reminder, never quite in focus and often at the edge of what is perceptible, calls out to the haunted person or society, demanding a hearing. If this listener can be found, then just as with trauma and melancholia, the possibility arises of some lessening of suffering, a kind of reaching back into the past that then alters the present. In myths and stories, ghosts represent the cries of lost souls who have often suffered violence. Psychologically, this is quite a precise statement: we are haunted by unfinished business related to righting injustices; and finding ways to respond to this might mean not that the ghosts are destroyed, because that would wipe out history, but that they find their appropriate place in the order of things.

A famous psychoanalytic formula suggests that the task of therapy is to 'turn ghosts into ancestors'.[14] In many ways, this captures both the task of dealing with trauma and the sense that people might have of being 'possessed' by events from their own past or from the history of their families or their culture. People come for help because they are distressed by something in their lives. This might be a specific problem such as an eating or sexual difficulty, or a more amorphous but no less troubling set of issues around relationships, or (even more existentially) a sense of purposelessness or emptiness. The therapeutic arc begins with these experiences and moves downwards, exploring psychological 'depth', or (speaking in terms of time periods) backwards. The aim is to create an understanding, hopefully shared between therapist and patient, that these difficulties relate to wishes, desires, losses, hurts and memories that are in important ways unresolved, and because of that they remain 'alive' in the mind. In psychoanalysis, these are usually assumed to be 'unconscious' phenomena, meaning that they are not easily available to reflect upon. The purpose of therapy is to find a way to bring them into consciousness so that they can be articulated, discussed, made sense of, and in some fashion helped to find a place in the client's sense of themselves. The idea is that in this way, the underlying issue is given voice and integrated into the narrative of a person's life, losing its sense of strangeness and becoming more available to change.

The parallel between this (idealised) account of therapy and the relief of haunting is strong, especially if the trouble that is brought to therapy has its roots in some past experiences that have left the patient traumatised. The ghost that haunts is something that began in the external world but has become lodged 'inside' the person and is seeking to make its presence felt without being explicit enough for it to be clear what needs to be done to relieve its suffering. The therapeutic task is for the voice of the ghost to be set free so that its message can be heard and the patient can respond to it. Put in another vocabulary, we can see the ghost as some kind of 'split-off' part of the patient that acts as if it were a separate being, whereas in fact it is an aspect of the patient's own psychic life. It is split off because the events that it wishes to speak of are too troubling, disturbing the patient's equilibrium and requiring the application of strong defences to keep it at bay. While these events – as memories, fantasies and anxieties – remain disconnected from the patient's consciousness, they are confined to a kind of half-life in which they fight for expression but can only achieve it indirectly, by speaking as a separate being from the patient (a ghost) or by forcing what are called 'enactments' in which the patient does things without fully knowing why.

Possession by a ghost can take many forms – that of a 'dybbuk', for example, in which a dead soul inhabits the body of a living person, or that of poltergeists that bang on the furniture. These can be understood as emanations from the suffering person, parts of their mind that have been denied integration into the self and instead are pushed 'outside', to be encountered as if they come from somewhere or someone else. A ghost appearing as a visual apparition is, in this account, a *projection*, meaning it really belongs to the mind of the person concerned but is experienced as if it comes from elsewhere – rather like the phenomenon of hearing voices that many people report (not just those labelled 'schizophrenic').

People who believe in the reality of ghosts will not necessarily accept this psychological account but might still agree that the act of reconciling sufferers with their ghosts involves recognition being granted to the ghostly demands so that a more benign relationship can be forged with the troubled history that they represent. This is where the notion of 'turning ghosts into ancestors' can link the two approaches, the occult and the psychological. In relation to trauma, the task is to make memories that can be acknowledged and tolerated, rather than to experience past events as recurring in the present, usually uncontrollably. Facing these events again in a safe context, for example through therapy, is a way of entering into a kind of dialogue with them so that they are made more tangible but also less frightening, precisely because they are allowed out into the light. The idea, shared across many psychological approaches, is that exposure to the feared 'object' in conditions that allow the patient to feel relatively safe and supported will reduce the anxiety the object causes and allow the patient to integrate it into the array of objects and events in the world that can be lived with. In this process, the living ghost that keeps returning – for example, the flashbacks that bring glimpses of an original trauma – takes its place in the line of memory, as something that can be thought about and, precisely because of this, is much more under the sufferer's control.

All this makes a lot of sense, but it might also be missing something important about both traumatic suffering and ghostly recurrence. It seems reasonable to assume that if a troubling memory or impulse is not recognised and confronted, it will continue to trouble; it is like the cry of a lost and hurt person who has not been heard. The crying continues until something is done or the one to whom it belongs has given up hope or has died. Facing, acknowledging and reconciling ourselves with this crying person, finding a space for them in our life, eases the suffering, quietens the cry, makes a relationship with the loss and hurt possible. Moving on, the cry can be recalled in memory as something that happened and was meaningful but is now past. Without the act of recognition, however, it will more likely come back to plague listeners – the 'witnesses' – as a continuing reminder of the suffering and of our culpability in not lessening it. And if the sufferer is the same person as the witness, if the 'cry' comes from inside us and is not acknowledged, the situation is the same: it continues, pressing against us as an endless sore. Finding a way to hear the cry and tolerate it sufficiently to act by dealing with its source makes it possible to relieve the trouble and set the (mind of the) sufferer at rest, especially so if it is one's own mind. An example might again be people who have lived for many years with the knowledge of having been abused but whose attempts to confide in others have been rebuffed, so that this knowledge becomes a source of shame, and the abuse itself lives on inside them as something that cannot be thought about. This might then have the consequence that it cannot be put into the past.

'It happened, but now it's over' is the state of mind that therapy aims for in those who have been abused or suffered other traumatising experiences. Gaining this perspective emotionally as well as intellectually, so that it is *felt* to be true rather than just being a moralising formula, will not be easy. It can be achieved, however, if the therapeutic frame is robust enough to allow such people to feel that everything that needs to be said has indeed been aired and that someone – the therapist in this context – has been able to listen and thoughtfully respond, without being rejecting or descending into madness themselves. The 'ghost' that has kept on haunting the survivor of abuse can now be laid to rest, recollected as the representative of something real ('I suffered because of what was done to me') but no longer plaguing the survivor with its continuing after-life.

While this is a powerful and useful account of how to deal with ghosts, what is missing is recognition of the value of these ghosts in keeping alive something that *needs* to be preserved. In the version presented above, haunting is treated as a *problem* that must be dealt with, a voice crying out that demands being responded to and appeased. But if, as I have been emphasising, ghosts draw our attention to suppressed knowledge that we need to access – knowledge, for example, of damage that has been done, of oppressive acts and unjust situations – then it could be argued that laying these ghosts should not be our first priority. Indeed, this is why I have not been adopting the language of exorcism, in which a ghost is removed by an act of symbolic violence. Driving a dybbuk out of a person or a poltergeist out of a house, as dramatised in many stories, without fully understanding what the ghost is trying to say or what it represents, preserves rather than addresses the injustice that has blocked its peaceful demise. Likewise, simply helping someone to dismiss their recurrent anxieties by rationalising them away or by behaviourally exposing them to the situations that alarm them until they feel better able to cope with them, may well relieve some suffering and so should not be rejected outright as a treatment strategy. But the question of what it was that produced these anxieties in the first place, and what sustains them, might still need addressing. This is not just because without doing so the symptoms could recur (a longstanding point of contention between behavioural or cognitive-behavioural therapists and psychodynamic ones) but also simply because these events might have meaning in themselves, whether or not they continue to trouble the patient. Perhaps someone who has been traumatised by abuse has become frightened or ashamed to go to social events; it may be that a treatment programme focusing on supporting them in social situations helps significantly, improving the quality of their life. This is clearly worthwhile, and I would not criticise it as a way forward for someone in that situation. But it still leaves the original abuse untouched as an issue.

Some might argue that this is fine, and perhaps there are circumstances in which it is justifiable, for instance when a person's well-being could be actively impaired by reviving painful memories. A 'therapeutic' avoidance of the traumatic event could be upheld on those grounds. However, ethically, in terms of what *should* be confronted, brought into awareness and understood in relation to psychological and social issues of truthfulness and justice, neglect of the abuse is an unsound way of proceeding. Of course, it might be argued that dealing with the symptoms first could fortify the sufferer to look at the original trauma, that it is only once the socially phobic person, say, has overcome their anxiety about being with others that they find the ego-strength to examine their past. This too seems a legitimate argument, so long as the motivation of both the therapist and the patient to do this does not dissipate with the reduction of the symptom, and so long as this does not mask a fear of what might be called 'facing the truth'. A room into which gas is leaking could be made habitable by opening the window, but if the leak is not dealt with, then once the window is closed again there will be continuing poisoning of the atmosphere. And if this is the case for individuals, who deserve respect in, and help for, their suffering, it is just as true at the social level, where the persistent efforts of ghosts to keep alive the voices of those who have been dispossessed by history might need recognition and support. In short, what if we turn some of this on its head and ask, how can we keep ghosts alive?

The continuing existence of ghosts is purposeful; they have something important to say. The things that haunt us are not so much memories, which are basically conscious, but intimations of events and experiences subjected to some kind of repression, meaning that they are held outside awareness. They are a kind of 'unknown known': we somehow know of these things without being able to access that knowledge, so that it comes through as forced upon us, usually in partial and mysterious ways. The sense of being inhabited by someone else, the glimpse of a traumatic memory that gives us the shivers, the uncanny nature of a house that should be a home but feels alien: these 'occult' experiences are indications that the knowledge we hide is really present, that we partly 'know' this 'unknown' but, because we do not give it its due, it keeps having to find ways to communicate its existence.

Thought about this way, the primary aim in relating to a ghost would not be to rid oneself of it, or at least not by expulsion. The aim should be to allow the hidden knowledge that the ghost represents to come more fully into consciousness, so that there is less need for the ghost to continue pressing its claims. Put more directly: if the source of haunting is an injustice, then that injustice demands recognition and action to put things right. It is only under those terms that the ghost can depart. Until that happens, we need our ghosts to remind us of the work that remains to be done.

An instructive example is the recent discussions and agitations around colonialism. The legitimation of what has come to be called 'extractivist colonialism' – the expropriation of wealth from colonised societies to enrich the colonisers, a practice that underwrote much of the development of Europe over a 400-year history – was couched in terms of the superiority of the Europeans over the supposedly 'primitive' or 'savage' societies that they conquered militarily and economically. The actual history, cultural sophistication and moral standing of those societies was denied as they succumbed to the military technology of the colonisers (and, of course, to their diseases). The rationalisations for this, when it became necessary to have any – that is, when simply asserting the right of the more powerful to govern the less powerful became insufficient – included Social Darwinism (development is based on the 'survival of the fittest'), religious imperialism (Christianity as the sole truth), and racist paternalism (the 'savage' races are inferior, too childlike to successfully govern themselves and needing the benefits of 'civilisation' even if imposed on them by force). The whitening of the world follows from this, with devastating effects on what have recently come to be called 'majority cultures'.

It is striking how both colonising and colonised societies still struggle with this history in what is notionally a 'postcolonial' world. For the colonisers, the often unmet challenge has been not only to come to terms with the loss of power and wealth that effectively had been gained by theft, but also to acknowledge the damage wrought by the colonial project on colonised societies. The failure to fully manage this has led to a kind of national nostalgia in which the present, often dire, state of things is compared to an idealised 'memory' of past greatness, coupled with a racialised intolerance of migrants, including those from former colonies, who are seen as somehow degrading this fantasised national purity. The regressiveness of this postcolonial melancholia has resulted in attitudes that are often self-destructive as well as morally reprehensible. For the previously colonised, the struggle has been to enable their new states to emerge from out of the long history of depredation, destabilisation and extractivism that characterised the colonial era, with its destruction of indigenous societies and systematic debasement of traditional religious, cultural and governmental practices. In many places this is linked to the devastating impact of slavery over several generations. For these reasons, the shadow of colonialism continues to fall on the emerging selfhood of these relatively newly decolonised societies.

In South Africa, where colonialism morphed into a deeply racist republic, this shadow was even darker in the post-apartheid period. This is because of the overwhelming force with which the white minority sustained its dominant position right into the end of the twentieth century, entrenching this in land ownership, the military and the law. Thanks initially to an extraordinary, charismatic leadership that has not been renewed, post-apartheid South Africa managed to avoid the civil war that seemed programmed into it as a kind of delayed fuse; and yet the problems apartheid bequeathed are profound, manifest in continuing violence, extremes of still-racialised disparity in wealth, and corruption. The remarkable creativity of the South African people and their capacity to renew themselves has been sorely tested, but was helped by the Truth and Reconciliation Commission (TRC) headed by Bishop Desmond Tutu in the 1990s. This process was undoubtedly flawed – too strong on Christian forgiveness and insufficiently committed to recognition, acknowledgement and redress for the suffering under apartheid. The disappointment this produced was huge. People's hopes for reparations and the punishment of perpetrators were left partially or wholly unmet. Nevertheless, it constituted an important symbolic and practical attempt to face the violence of the past, and has served as a model for Truth Commissions in many other countries.

Over the years, the TRC's various weaknesses have become increasingly apparent. But still it resonates as a necessary step in exorcising the ghosts of the past; or rather, in allowing the subjugated and silenced voices of those ghosts to be heard. The hearings in the TRC involved testimonies by witnesses of various kinds: those who had suffered directly, those who had lost loved ones to state-sponsored and state-inflicted violence, and those who were themselves perpetrators of that violence. Whatever the inadequacies of the process, the effect of these testimonies was electric. At times it aggravated wounds, as the full horror of the apartheid years was exposed; but it may not be fanciful to suggest that the process of revelation, while it did not bring closure, enabled South Africans to begin moving away from the 'retributive' cycles of violence that have occurred in many other places and towards a more 'restorative justice' model. In this, the focus is on allowing the voices of suffering to be heard so as to develop a society in which people who have to continue living together become capable of doing so. As I have mentioned, the success or failure of the TRC, or the relative balance of these things, is the subject of controversy, but the model is nevertheless an important one. Without recognition of what happened and acknowledgement of where responsibility for it lies, it is hard to see how there can be avoidance of repetitive cycles in which enactments of further violence take the place of reconciliatory thoughtfulness. To work through the legacy of a tragic past, that past with all its losses has first to be brought into open view.

A second example comes from the history of antisemitism. Anti-Jewish hatred has taken many forms. For most of its history, it has been best coded as 'anti-Judaism', an antagonism to the Jewish religion based on Christian, and to a lesser extent Islamic, beliefs. From the middle of the nineteenth century, this was first complemented and then largely displaced by 'racial' antisemitism, which treated Jews as a distinct racial group and opposed them as such. One effect of this was that religious conversion could no longer reliably protect Jews from persecution, something that became grossly evident in the Nazi period. Religion then as now had little to do with the increasingly violent oppression of Jews; it was rather their status as a separate (and often 'separated', in the sense of socially marginalised) people that was the focus of discriminatory and, in the case of the Nazis, genocidal practice. Subsequent to the Holocaust and the formation of the State of Israel, the situation has become more complicated, with antisemitism at times being integrated into anti-Zionism so that the latter escalates into forms that veer well beyond criticism of Israeli policy and action. This lives side by side with a recrudescence of old-style antisemitism, drawing on conspiracy theories in which claims of a Jewish plot towards world domination are recycled and linked with additional fantasies, such as that Jews are working to flood the West with migrants who will overwhelm the 'indigenous' white population – the so-called white replacement theory.

One thing that is noticeable here is a remarkable forgetting of history, in which the Nazi Holocaust is denied or displaced so that its echoes can no longer be heard. What was once, briefly, a widely shared recognition that antisemitism could poison societies as well as have murderous effects on Jews, rapidly lost its force. Today, antisemitism has become once more a tool in the arsenal of demagogues and of authoritarian factions seeking populist advancement, as well as of more 'traditional' racists.

The manner in which 'classic' religious anti-Judaism created the conditions for modern antisemitism to thrive has also been forgotten, yet it is arguable that without it there would have been less appetite for singling out Jews for special 'racial' opprobrium. These are acts of motivated forgetting and denial. Where the theme of haunting becomes especially relevant is regarding the belated acknowledgement of the impact of the Holocaust, and in what can be claimed as a failure of mourning in the European countries where the Holocaust mostly unfolded. The former point has been discussed already: how the silenced voices of Holocaust survivors created conditions such as 'postmemory', in which their descendants found themselves battling with their parents' unspoken memories and anxieties, their irredeemable losses that were sometimes passed down as a powerful melancholic atmosphere in which inexpressible grief recurs. For the children and grandchildren of perpetrators, as we have seen, the situation was different but parallel. The unspoken guilt of the parents, the hidden secret of complicity and conformity, the construction of a 'crypt' in which lies an unsharable but central secret – these failures of memory and communication have created in many descendants an unease, a sense of responsibility, sometimes activating further denial and at other times provoking a quest to make reparation. In both these cases, revelation of the secrets held by the older generation has been crucial to release their children and grandchildren – the later generations of their societies – from the haunting vestiges of those terrible times. It is in acts of remembering that the silence can be broken and forms of working-through can become possible. Remembering in this sense is not the route to forgetting – to exorcism of the ghosts – nor necessarily to forgiveness, especially when what happened is unforgiveable. It is, however, the only possible route towards accepting the truth of what the ghosts say: 'This really happened, and something needs to be done about it, or it will happen again.'

The idea that Europe itself still suffers from the unmourned, or insufficiently mourned, loss of its Jews is a more complicated one that has been discussed in some work on post-communist societies and, less explicitly, in projects for European unity.[15] Jews were part of the European world for a thousand years or more; they were also major drivers of modernist culture, perhaps most notably in the German-speaking heartlands of the old Austro-Hungarian Empire and in post–First World War Europe. In music, literature and the arts and also in science, not to speak of psychoanalysis, the 'marginalised insider' status of Jewish intellectuals provided a powerful impetus towards creativity. In industry, trade and banking, the newly emancipated Jews were important forces for innovation; and the more general integration of Jews into German society, including through high levels of intermarriage, was a spur to development. This was all destroyed in the Nazi period, as was the intense and more religious Jewish culture of Eastern Europe. Post-war, along with all the issues around reconstruction and the urge to develop self-preserving narratives in places where atrocities had been routinely facilitated or perpetrated – not just Germany, of course, but Austria, France, Hungary, Poland, Ukraine, Lithuania, Latvia and so on – the loss of these immensely creative communities and intersections should have been mourned. On the whole, however, it was not. Instead, in the Eastern bloc the specific suffering of Jews was largely denied; in the West, the self-congratulatory narrative of resistance and eventual victory was promoted over any reckoning with complicity and loss.

The exigencies of the Cold War took priority over punishment of Nazis, while surviving Jews became a kind of embarrassing historical relic. It is much too big a stretch to suggest that this failure to recognise and mourn the loss of the Jews is the sole source of modern antisemitism, and even more of a stretch to make it responsible for Europe's problems. Nevertheless, the denial of loss has had its effects, enfeebling the European community politically (for example, in its attitude towards migrants and its susceptibility to right-wing nationalist populism) and culturally. What does it mean for a country to have lost its Jewish citizens through genocide, to have been a site for the Holocaust? Arguably, this question has never been fully addressed, a failure that paves the way for a prolonged sense of unresolved guilt that also contributes to the resurgence of antisemitism.

What is clear is that the failure to hear the voices of ghostly suffering not only leads to continued haunting, but also has destructive effects on the well-being of societies as wholes. Coming to terms with the past, whether as individuals or as communities, requires first appreciating what lies in that past. This is why we need to value the ghosts that appear to us: they give voice to the inexpressible and hidden, alerting us to their presence; in the words of the philosopher Walter Benjamin, they allow the oppressed to 'flash up' so that we can see and hear them.[16]

It is here that there is a link with the idea of 'being real'. Failure to acknowledge the injustices of the past entails an exhausting, relentless process of self-deception, denial and self-justification in which wilful ignorance triumphs over truth-seeking. This can be an escalating phenomenon. Refusal to grieve and mourn can turn into more intense attempts to deny reality and eventually to violent repudiation of those others who remind us of what we have lost or demand compensation for what has been done to them. Listening to what haunts us, at personal and social levels, involves a process of deepening our commitment to truthfulness, however hard this might be and however attractive or even necessary the short-term gains of denial might seem. This truth might be difficult to fathom, even more difficult to face; there may be conflicting accounts and continuing uncertainties around memory and evidence. But being open to truth is an important path to take, whether for the individual or for a whole society that has suffered trauma. Otherwise, the energy that should go into developing ourselves or our society gets dissipated in a narcissistic attempt to keep the truth at bay. The important thing about ghosts, then, is not to banish them, but to hear what they are trying to say.

6

Psychopolitical Reality

As part of a study of boys in London schools, carried out in the late 1990s, my colleagues and I interviewed a thirteen-year-old white boy who we called John.[1] Here is a short section of the interview.

> John: Yeah. But it's racism I really hate. [Interviewer: Do you, yeah?] Yeah, I hate racism. Think it's just out of order. It's wrong.
> Interviewer: Do you ever come across racism?
> John: Not as much as I thought in this world would be. No. Not at all. Um. But there are quite racial things, like say if we go to a shop and it's run by Asians and um they can't speak very good English and um so people go in there and they get, and they get cussed because of their race and then they said stuff like 'You shouldn't be over here. You should go back to your own country.' And stuff like this.
> Interviewer: Who says that?
> John: Some boys round my area. I didn't like it. I didn't wanna say that, but I mean round my area if you go into a shop, they want something and they can't afford it and then they say 'Put it back. You can't afford it.' And then they start cussing them because of what their race are. I've never really taken part in that. [Interviewer: Yeah] Yeah. I've just always stepped away from racism. I hate racism. It's not, it's not a good thing to do really.
> Interviewer: Right. Are these boys that, that you go around with then, or, these boys who, who cuss them this way. Do you go around with these boys?

John: Yeah, I go around with them but I mean I don't really take part in anything they really do. Because they're, some of them are real troublemakers, but I try to step away from that, and I try to keep clean and um just keep away from racism. And they use, they cuss a lot of people. They could cuss people in the street, and stuff like that. And they could get themselves into trouble. Say um they start cussing a boy that's from a different country and um the boy from the different country could come up to them, start pushing them about and then they could be themselves in serious trouble. Because they can get beaten up really badly by these, this Asian kid.

Interviewer: Do you, do you say anything to these boys at all, these friends or do you just …

John: Well if they go too far I just say, 'Oh just leave it now 'cause I think they get the message.' Yeah, and if they, they just stop at their own account, I just leave it. But I mean if they just carry on and carry on, and everybody else has stopped and there's one kid just carrying on and I say 'Oh just come on. Leave it.' And I just tear them, tear them apart for cussing.

John wants to position himself as antagonistic to racism, but his description of his actions contradicts this: he goes around with boys involved in racist abuse, and he tries to limit it to avoid trouble, rather than actively opposing it. What is not clear is why he is at such pains to present himself as so fervently anti-racist in the first place ('it's racism I really hate'). It sounds like a straight negation, in which the opposite of what is asserted is the truth. The dynamics of the interview almost certainly come into play here, in that John has formed quite a good rapport with the (male) interviewer and might be eager to hold on to this, particularly as he has previously said that his connections with other adult males are starved of emotional content. It would be surprising if John did not assume that the interviewer would have a non- or anti-racist position, given the professed values of most adults working in schools and the then-current general norm against prejudice. Yet the confusion of this narrative, which demonstrates racism while asserting anti-racism, suggests that something more might be going on than simply presenting a conforming, non-racist face to the interviewer while participating in the racialised masculinity of his immediate environment. In other parts of the interview, John presents himself as a violent person caught up in a rough and dangerous male culture, with numerous examples of fights, some involving weapons, and participation in racial abuse. He is not interested in academic work and hints that he finds it difficult to understand complex ideas. His description of his relationship with other boys is in terms of hardness and aggression; 'reputation' is important, and tenderness between boys is automatically connected with homosexuality. Given the strength of his homophobia ('I mean that's just grown on me and I just can't stand gay people'), this is a particular worry for him.

The constant need to demonstrate hardness is frequently reiterated, but there is also a recognition of the price he pays for this: 'So people try to help me and then I just push them aside and then they don't come back. So I feel sorry for them and I feel sorry for myself.' Movingly, he tells the interviewer of feeling 'upset and angry' towards his father, who has left the home: 'But then now, he's, he's like stopped ringing and he's, he's got his other family now. I think he's just, I don't think he just wants to see me anymore.' Perhaps we might speculate (cautiously, as John is not a patient and cannot respond to this suggestion) that his denied but visible racism is a socially congruent way to express these 'upset and angry' feelings. With the interviewer, it is not acceptable, and this matters to John because there is a hint of a reparative element in their relationship. But with his peers, it manifestly is: racism has become the language whereby they express their affinity with one another, and perhaps also their bravado in the face of inner and outer conflict. John's racism, then, channels his feelings away from his own loss and sadness into a socially prescribed form of hatred – 'hate' being the dominant term in his emotional lexicon, and racism being a structural component of much social life.

If we are to live full lives, we must resist social processes that distort our experience of reality. These social processes are especially implicated in patterns of historical and contemporary oppression, yet they are often obscured by practices of denial or of other-blaming ('the migrants/Muslims/Jews/Europeans are responsible for our troubles'). They are politically motivated in the broad sense, serving the interests of dominant groups, and they have profound social and psychological effects. They perpetuate injustice in the here-and-now and from one generation to another; they encourage antagonism between different groups; they foster discrimination and prejudice; and they block progressive change. By generating material and social suffering, they also have significant mental health impacts in the well-established links between levels of inequality and general unhappiness, or the more specific connections between poverty and depression, anxiety and other forms of psychological distress. They also, ironically, provoke resistance. This resistance is both a symptom of social conflict, produced by what Freud called 'unease' or 'discontent' with civilisation, and a potentially creative, but also risky, response to it, bringing to light discriminatory practices and abuses of power and fighting back against these through protest, attempts at legal change, and occasionally through force.

Traditional Marxist theories understood the way in which social conditions are hidden as 'ideology' – the sets of beliefs and practices that *naturalise* them, making it seem as if they are inescapable aspects of reality. Ideology presents the world as 'given' to us as we find it, and there is nothing we can do about it other than to exploit it and, if possible, ameliorate its worst attributes. This idea is nicely caught in the slogan that it is 'easier to imagine the end of the world than the end of capitalism,' which has come to be attached to Mark Fisher's idea of 'capitalist realism'. Fisher, in a widely-read book, comments:

> That slogan captures precisely what I mean by 'capitalist realism': the widespread sense that not only is capitalism the only viable political and economic system, but also that it is now impossible even to *imagine* a coherent alternative to it.[2]

The concept of capitalist realism is perhaps best understood as a variant on the classic understanding of ideology. Capitalist realism operates in the interests of the dominant class, deliberately obscuring the constructed nature of capitalism and instead presenting it as necessary and without alternatives. What is at work is a systematic practice of truth-representation that is especially aimed towards the reduction of social processes to individual psychology. In the dominant liberal and neoliberal versions of this, each person is held responsible for their fate without anything more than a vague gesturing towards the contribution of the social world to what that fate might be. This was famously represented in then Prime Minister Margaret Thatcher's assertion to a British women's magazine, when in answer to her own question, 'Who is society?' she said: 'There is no such thing! There are individual men and women and there are families and no government can do anything except through people and people look to themselves first.'[3] Interestingly, a later 'clarification' of Thatcher's point, expanding and accentuating it, was published in the *Sunday Times* a few months after the original interview. This explained:

> All too often the ills of this country are passed off as those of society. Similarly, when action is required, society is called upon to act. But society as such does not exist except as a concept. Society is made up of people. It is people who have duties and beliefs and resolve. It is people who get things done. [The prime

minister] prefers to think in terms of the acts of individuals and families as the real sinews of society rather than of society as an abstract concept. Her approach to society reflects her fundamental belief in personal responsibility and choice. To leave things to 'society' is to run away from the real decisions, practical responsibility and effective action.[4]

The idea that society is merely abstract and that the responsibility for our fate rests on our choices as individuals, suggests that the structures of the social world are fictions used by people as excuses for failure. It presents the perpetuation of inequalities in income, health, education and housing, which are largely a consequence (and a descriptor) of social class, as a function of 'meritocracy' – the belief that people can be, and are, stratified by their inherent ability and life choices. This is an ideological move that hides the real operations of class-based society, which are geared towards the preservation of wealth by those that already have it. We live 'as if' it is obviously the case that people get what they deserve. Put more fully, society structures us according to a set of ideological premises that point us in the direction of believing and feeling that the world is organised in the only way it possibly could be. This is why ideology and 'common sense' are tightly tied together: claims are 'obvious' because their supposed veracity is already preordained.

Similarly, social assumptions around gender, sexuality and 'race' are all presented as if they were universal truths; quite commonly, people also *experience* them that way. This has fuelled some intense and sometimes troublingly emotional, even hate-filled, debates, especially in recent times around trans* (some people taking deep offense at the idea that one could be other than 'obviously' a man or a woman) but equally over race and sexuality. The history of homophobia stretches back, after all, to biblical times. Yet variations in gender identity and experience, in sexuality and in cultural and ethnic identifications, make it apparent that these 'truths' are at most only partial, and that the ways in which the world is made are much more flexible, and more complicated, than the dominant ideology would suggest.

This raises another issue: is there a 'true' way of experiencing the social world, or are we always subjected to ideology of one form or another? Classical Marxism seems to promote the former idea, claiming that objective knowledge of how society is organised according to class formations and their conflicts, is obscured by the ideology promulgated by the ruling classes. Ideological struggle is therefore a product of class struggle, and ideology will be displaced once revolution occurs. More recent Marxist thought, associated especially with Antonio Gramsci and Louis Althusser, has developed this argument differently. In Althusser's case, this change was in direct conversation with psychoanalysis and produced a nuanced understanding of ideology as always present in one form or another.[5] For Althusser, we never live life in direct contact with the 'truth' but find ways of engaging with reality that are always mediated by fantasy, wishes and imagination. What differentiates capitalist ideology from more progressive, socialist ideology is the latter's appreciation of the role of social structures in constructing the world as we experience it, and its commitment to emancipation and egalitarianism. Ideology is therefore itself a site of struggle, with progressive ideology aimed at producing better conditions for living, at creating life worlds that are more open to complexity, more tolerant of difference and more committed to social justice. In a sense, ideology becomes a site in which people fight to create ways of being that construct the social world in a more ethical way. Who is to say what is more ethical? That too is a contested matter, but here we might argue that it connects with the ethics of being real, of doing our best to unpack the social assumptions and conditions that surround us in order to grasp more fully the meaning of our lives. Just as we use psychological defences to stave off reality when it is too uncomfortable to face it directly, so social defences operate to protect society itself from too much reality, from being challenged by the damage it does. An ethical stance here is one in which this damage is recognised in order for it to be confronted and prevented or, if that does not happen, repaired.

This chapter focuses on how oppressive social structures come to seem like the only reality that is possible and on how this state of affairs might be challenged. It therefore concerns itself with the experience of 'psychopolitical reality', drawing on psychoanalytic insights to explore how gender, race, class and the like take hold to make resistance and renewal more difficult. It is worth noting that psychoanalysis itself has always been embroiled in political and cultural 'wars', in relation to conservative and more radical tendencies in its own thought and practice. Yet it also offers ways of thinking about what can broadly be called 'political experience' by giving us tools to consider how forms of oppression are perpetuated. The injunction to face reality reaches beyond the language of values and ideals and instead defines an emotion-laden attitude that involves searching out and naming whatever actually exists, however destructive, painful, guilt-inducing or shameful that may be, however much it impugns the good name of the individual or the society (or, for that matter, the institutions of psychoanalysis itself), and however much that might then place on us a responsibility for difficult actions. 'Truth' here is not a thing, but an activity, a way of approaching life that is inherently political.

The intersection of psychoanalysis and politics does not reduce to questions of whether to take up the political issues clients raise, or what weight to give the external world in clinical contact, or whether psychoanalysts and psychotherapists have special kinds of social responsibilities. These are important questions (at the time of writing, there is a lively debate going on within the British Psychoanalytical Society about whether and how to pronounce on major human rights abuses), but alongside, or rather in excess, of them lie more challenging questions still: how to gaze unblinkingly at what exists and how to respond to it analytically by examining its contours and its underlying drive, its desire and its hidden recesses, its violence. The analyst's capacity not to look away can be translated into the political injunction to refuse ideological distortions, to look clearly at the world and not be afraid to speak about what can be seen, particularly in relation to justice and injustice, truth and its suppression, which can perhaps be understood as social parallels to the dynamic processes with which analysts are familiar.

My use of psychoanalysis to help articulate what we could call the 'psychosocial' dimension of politics needs a little expansion. It is not obvious that psychoanalysis – intrinsically individualistic in the sense of focusing on therapy for individuals and on their personal concerns – might be a place to look for help with understanding social phenomena. In fact, the whole gamut of political positions is visible in the history of psychoanalytic institutions and practices, from the conservatism evident in some of their approaches to femininity and homosexuality through to social welfarism and on to radical, socialist or Marxist activism, and more recently to what might perhaps be unexpected engagements with queer and postcolonial critiques.

The conservative elements in psychoanalysis have roots in a variety of sources, including Freud's personal attitudes; the strong, yet relatively unacknowledged implication of much early psychoanalytic thinking in colonial assumptions and racialisations, in which the 'savage' mind of the indigenous African or Australian was contrasted with the more 'civilised' mind of the European; the medicalisation of psychoanalysis in the course of its development, driven by the search for professional respectability and fear of 'quackery'; the way psychoanalysis settled down, especially post–Second World War, into a middle-class profession never fully integrated into public health provision; and psychoanalysis's tendency to reduce complex social experiences to 'internal' psychological events. On this last point, despite paying homage to Freud's great, late social texts in which he strove to develop a theory of what he called 'civilisation', including critiques of religion and war, psychoanalysis has largely focused on the struggles of individuals to survive their tumultuous inner world and often difficult early circumstances. This is not unwarranted, given its therapeutic focus, and has produced a rich array of concepts relating to what might be required of a caring society that allows people to develop their internal resources and capacity to manage themselves, but it has had relatively little to offer in direct relation to political thought.

Nevertheless, there is also a strong radical tradition within psychoanalysis, quite often developed by social theorists rather than clinical psychoanalysts themselves. Freud's personal commitment to social democratic politics was demonstrated in the speech he gave to the 1918 International Psychoanalytic Congress in Budapest, in which he stated very clearly that everyone, no matter how poor, should be entitled to receive good mental health care, specifically psychoanalysis. The speech ended on a note that was stirring and effective:

> Compared to the vast amount of neurotic misery which there is in the world, and perhaps need not be, the quantity we can do away with is almost negligible ... On the other hand, it is possible to foresee that at some time or other the conscience of society will awake and remind it that the poor man should have just as much right to assistance for his mind as he now has to the life-saving help offered by surgery; and that the neuroses threaten public health no less than tuberculosis, and can be left as little as the latter to the impotent care of individual members of the community. When this happens, institutions or out-patient clinics will be started, to which analytically-trained physicians will be appointed, so that men who would otherwise give way to drink, women who have nearly succumbed under

their burden of privations, children for whom there is no choice but between running wild or neurosis, may be made capable, by analysis, of resistance and of efficient work. Such treatments will be free.[6]

Note how clearly Freud lays out the relationship between material privation ('the poor man') and neurotic suffering, and also how contingent this is: there is a 'vast amount of neurotic misery ... in the world' which 'perhaps need not be'. That is, misery is unnecessary; or rather – because Freud did not believe that people were capable of prolonged happiness – the *quantity* of misery was not determined by the propensities of the human psyche.

Freud's 1918 speech fell on fertile ground, in that many of the analysts who heard it were social democrats, sick of the suffering of war and of the corrupt politics that had fomented it. It was seminal in rousing them to action, with the result that 'free' psychoanalytic clinics were formed in Berlin, Vienna, Budapest and London, aiming to offer high-quality psychoanalytic treatment gratis to all who needed it. The history, traced by Elizabeth Danto, of such clinics in the 1920s and 1930s shows them to have been a very practical example of how European psychoanalysis tried to maintain a social-egalitarian perspective, despite all the pressures placed upon it.[7] Freud himself seems to have treated many patients for free during the 1920s (charging exorbitant prices to his American patients to cross-subsidise this), and other analysts, out of purely altruistic motives, committed themselves to financial contributions and voluntary work to sustain the clinics.

The promise and limitations of this psychoanalytic radicalism, which was embodied particularly creatively in the Berlin Psychoanalytic Institute until the onset of Nazism and the collapse of German psychoanalysis, gave way after the Second World War to more conservative practices, especially in the US and Britain. This was in part as a response to the deathly effects of the explosion of irrationalism that engulfed Europe mid-century, which made many psychoanalysts hesitate to side too strongly with unconscious wishes. It was also because many analysts were refugees, trying to adapt and make their way in new countries that were in some respects suspicious of them. Nevertheless, it is striking how little work has been carried out on social class from a psychoanalytic perspective, perhaps reflecting the dominance of the liberal ideology mentioned earlier, in which the causes of suffering are attributed to individual choices; furthermore, psychoanalysts have worked mainly in private practices, and their fee-paying patients have of necessity come from relatively affluent backgrounds. That said, not only have there been practical initiatives towards more socially aware psychoanalysis, for example in the resurgence of free clinic projects in several countries, especially in Latin America,[8] but there have also been some penetrating psychoanalytic analyses of the effects of social class.[9] These emphasise how questions of shame have often been pivotal, for analysts and patients alike, and have also offered explorations, and a growing awareness, of how class oppression, poverty and discrimination intersect with race and gender to produce strong effects on mental health.

From the 1960s onwards there has been a return to various politically active strands in psychoanalytic thought, notably in the profound challenge to psychoanalysis arising from feminism (discussed more fully below). On the other hand, at times, especially in Latin America, there has been collusion between psychoanalytic institutions and oppressive social regimes. In Brazil, for example, in the period of the dictatorship that stretched from 1964 to 1985, psychoanalysis was characterised by 'neutrality', understood as not taking sides on any issue, alongside a focus on the family that was easily appropriated by reactionary rulers. The upshot was that the official psychoanalytic societies collaborated with the regime and even flourished, obtaining financial support and remaining silent on the question of human rights abuses and social violence. This does not mean, of course, that no Brazilian psychoanalysts ever took brave stands on these issues; there were certainly such individuals, as there also were in Argentina and elsewhere at that time.[10] Nevertheless, psychoanalysis as a professional discipline was not a source of resistance to authoritarianism, as we might have expected and hoped it would be.[11]

The history of psychoanalysis in relation to politics is therefore a complex one, and its tendency to 'regress' to more conservative stances has been in tension with its capacity to offer incisive critiques of what Freud early on called, using ironic quote marks, 'civilised' (for his purposes, sexual) morality. Psychoanalysis is especially well attuned to questions of how what lies *outside* the person as features of the social setting, such as classism, racism and sexism, come to be experienced *inside* and often 'enjoyed' by people. Why is 'lower' social class sometimes a stimulus for feelings of disgust? The American psychoanalyst Lynne Layton suggests as follows: 'The emotions that underlie the internalization of class relations … entail a great deal of anxiety about being contaminated by poverty, of getting too close to need.'[12] This might be reflected in psychoanalysis itself: dealing as it does with the sordid, the disreputable, the uncertain, the passionate and the supposedly perverse, it has to work hard to maintain its credentials as a legitimate bourgeois profession. This is accompanied by a fear of falling into the 'necessity' of working-class life – a term that seems to have numerous associations with other words pertaining to psychoanalysis, such as 'primitive' or 'unanalysable'. *Necessity* means connection with the fundamental elements of capitalist exchange, in which we work because we must, because money is needed to keep us alive – and not because we care, or love, or seek to 'recognise' the other, as might be assumed of the so-called helping professions. Could it be that part of the psychoanalytic occlusion of class in favour of other elements of identity politics is due to the way class issues throw up this discomfort so clearly? More generally, part of the perpetuation of class distinction may be due to a psychic tendency to deprecate poverty, to turn away from the realisation that all of us are needy and vulnerable and that we are implicated in the neediness of others.

While psychoanalysis has left the dynamics of social class relatively neglected, perhaps mirroring how class itself is tied up with the politics of neglect, it has had quite a lot to say about identity politics. Why are some people such enthusiastic racists; why is it so hard to escape the feeling that gender is absolute and that there is something wrong with those who express their gender differently; what is so enticing about homophobia and what so threatening about homosexuality that it is legislated against so punitively in so many places? These and other questions concern the relationship between people's emotions and the realities they face. They are also questions about how social structures enter the soul, making us what we are. Psychoanalysis offers tools for understanding these processes, which I hope briefly to use in examining two important areas for psychopolitics: firstly, gender and sex; secondly, 'race' and racism.

The multiple ways in which we experience our sex and gender make this a confusing area to examine. All we know for sure is that there is a great deal of uncertainty, and a lot of heated disagreement. If it is possible to distinguish between sex and gender, which some people dispute and others strongly assert, then it might be along the lines of anatomy versus psychosocial identity. Sex then refers to the bodily and chromosomal differences between males and females, which themselves have variations but are still recognisably distinct most of the time. Gender, however, refers to the ways in which these biological differences are expressed behaviourally (often termed 'gender role') and to felt, subjective states of being ('gender identity'). This gender–sex distinction has served useful purposes in making it possible to discuss how fluid gender roles and gender identities might be, even given a clear binary of sex; how, for example, there is no necessary determination of the way a man might behave just because he is anatomically a man. There are many kinds of masculinities, intersecting with class, race and ethnicity; and these are expressed in different ways in different contexts. Aggressive physical masculinity, aligned with traditional 'macho' social expectations, is not the same as supposedly 'soft', scholarly masculinity, yet both are recognisably gendered. If anything, traditional 'femininity' has been even more deconstructed in the last century or so, revealing just how much it depended on, and was used to reinforce, the rigorous maintenance of a gender-stratified society. There is no one way to 'do man' or 'do woman', just lots of overlapping ways of being.

However, the differentiation between sex and gender does not always go unchallenged. Trans* is an obvious issue here, especially for people who do not see themselves as genderfluid, but rather as fixed in the wrong body by their anatomical sex. Their gender identity is experienced as at variance with their sex, which in one way demonstrates how sex and gender are not the same; on the other hand, this difference is also experienced as deeply troubling, even existentially impossible, and the task of reconciling sex and gender can become a matter of life and death. We might also note that at a social level, sex is usually taken to be determining of gender, with boys and girls separated from each other through familial expectations, religious and cultural practices, educational and sporting opportunities, employment and life chances. In many countries, these factors have changed in the last few decades, demonstrating their malleability; but there are plenty of places around the world where the effects of sex remain constricting rather than empowering.

In addition, a third term, *sexuality*, comes into the mix, referring both to the experience and the expression of sexual feelings. Sexuality also is not determined by sex, as we can see with both homosexuality and bisexuality. Psychoanalysts are not the only people to know that sexual desire and sexual experience are highly complex, that for example a person might engage in heterosexual sex while being homosexual in their fantasy life (or vice versa), and that expressions of sexual impulse and feeling are heavily influenced by social as well as psychological factors, as everything from religion to pornography demonstrates.

The regulation of sexuality is clearly a social issue. The legalisation of homosexuality in the UK was a social and political decision based in part on the principle that the state should not intervene where no harm was being done, but also in recognition of the reality of sexuality as a mode of self-expression, the blocking of which is unethical in a liberal, secular society. However, the regulation of sexuality is also a profoundly personal concern, shaped by what people find tolerable or exciting, what makes them feel alive or guilty, what fulfils desire and what constrains it. The 'internal' defences against sexuality can be even more stringent than the external ones; yet they are linked in that these psychological inhibitions are at least partially derived from the social messages that define some forms of sexual expression as 'normal' and pathologise other forms. In a society in which homosexuality is widely accepted, the inhibition of homosexual desires is likely to be less powerful than in a setting in which they are actively derogated and prohibited. In the latter situation, homosexual desire does not wither away but may be attached much more strongly to personal anxieties and an unsettling mix of frustration and persecutory distress. Staying 'real' in such situations, being aligned with the desire that one is feeling, is potentially a difficult struggle.

Concentrating on gender for a moment, let us consider how and why it might be that there is such a strong commitment to maintaining gender distinctions, in some societies so strong that the roles men and women can take up are severely delimited by cultural and religious norms. If we can agree that there are many ways to 'do' gender, then what is it that impedes these possibilities, that seems so desperate to maintain a model of masculinity as 'hard', instrumental, active and aggressive and of femininity as the opposite – 'soft', emotional, vulnerable and passive? These are stereotypes, of course, and there is immense variation in how men and women live their lives within and between cultures. Nevertheless, the tendencies remain pervasive, even in liberal societies; and there is plenty of evidence that they are deeply engrained ('men should be like this, women like that'). At the same time they are often resisted, as people find that they do not do justice to the reality of their life experiences or indeed their ambitions for who they would like to become. More technically, the continued sway of certain discourses about ideal masculinities and femininities needs explanation, especially as these discourses are demonstrably out of step with the actual experience people have of themselves. They present a kind of impossible ideal (which does not mean that the ideal they present is a desirable one) and in so doing obscure the paths we might take to a more flexible, inclusive understanding of gender and indeed more realistic ways of living our gendered lives.

A great deal has been written about women's lives. Feminism has not only illuminated the ways in which women have been, and continue to be, oppressed, marginalised, discriminated against and often abused; it has also provided many tools for resistance which have made a positive material impact, even if much remains to be done. The intersectionality of gender and race, for instance, or more precisely sexism and racism, has never been fully engaged with, and debates continue about which should take priority, the struggle against racism or that against sexism and misogyny.

My own view is that both are necessary and that they should not be differentiated tactically, but not everyone agrees. In relation, however, to feminine gender identities and roles, there can be little doubt that there have been massive shifts in the past half century in many countries, leading to a major expansion in what it is possible for women to aspire to and enact without having their gender 'appropriateness' questioned. This does not mean that all the old problems have disappeared. They include how to manage mothering and childcare in a gender-stratified society in which maternal labour is denigrated or at least goes unrecognised; how to avoid being objectified by a sexualised male gaze; how to navigate vulnerability in a world in which sexual violence is prevalent, especially but not only under conditions of war. Yet we could argue that these problems are problems *for* women, but not *of* women; that is, they are much more to do with the way *men* behave. The same could be said about how some women may have 'internalised' patriarchy so that it is hard for them to see a way out of it, and there are certainly many women who feel more secure and comfortable with conventional arrangements that might, from the outside, seem overly restrictive of their life choices. Again, however, it is not the women that are the 'problem' here, even if their resistance to change is an issue to consider; it is rather that the social context (patriarchy) is such as to make it hard to imagine and live out alternatives. We could perhaps call this 'patriarchal realism'.

The perpetuation of what has been called 'hegemonic masculinity' is another issue. Despite shifts in the acceptability of expressions of alternative, or 'subjugated', masculinities, some dominant forms of masculinity still display a great deal of staying power. These promote a set of attributes such as hardness, propensity for violence, resistance to emotional vulnerability, and competitiveness that was once prescriptive of ideal masculinity and that retains its hold in the imagination and in much of popular culture. Masculinity, like femininity, is an intersectional phenomenon, as boys and men of different cultural groups may find themselves more or less close to this dominant vision. Working-class male competitiveness is not the same as economically privileged masculinity, where the drive for power is apt to be expressed by academic or material competitiveness – though physical prowess is still likely to be highly valued. It is also notable that many boys and men, perhaps even the majority, do not see themselves as living up to this hegemonic ideal.[13] Finding a way to live with this 'insufficiency' impels them to do the psychological and social work of establishing that they remain 'real men', even if they are not quite made in the mould of Superman.

In more extreme cases, where there is vulnerability of various kinds, it may prove too difficult to bring together the demand to be a certain kind of masculine person with the reality not just of what is possible (not everyone can be a sports star) but also of what feels right. Gender determinism might then lead to significant psychological distress. That is to say, the challenge of being real in these circumstances is to be able to free the self from the pervasive message that there is only one way to properly enact masculinity, and instead to find more openness towards masculine being, with all its complex variations. And perhaps this requires destabilising the masculine–feminine binary if we are to live out the reality of our desires.

Why should masculinity be 'hard' and tough? Psychoanalysis, especially in forms influenced by feminist thinking, has moved a long way from Freud's original view that masculinity is always active and femininity passive. It has also problematised the notion that gender can be defined by the sexual 'object' taken by the person – that there is an innate sexual orientation towards the opposite sex and that psychic structure follows from this. Even Freud was not wholly convinced, as shown by his idea that the famous 'positive' Oedipus complex, whereby the boy desires his mother and the girl her father, is balanced by what he called the 'negative' Oedipus complex, which is characterised by love for the parent of the *same* sex, and jealousy of the parent of the opposite sex. The complete arrangement of the actual Oedipus complex as found in any individual involves a mix of both positive and negative complexes, laying down a rich tapestry of possibilities for homosexual as well as heterosexual love. In their account of the Oedipus complex in their psychoanalytic dictionary, *The Language of Psychoanalysis*, Jean Laplanche and Jean-Bertrand Pontalis comment:

> The description of the complex in its complete form allows Freud to elucidate ambivalence towards the father (in the case of the little boy) in terms of the play of heterosexual and homosexual components, instead of making it simply the result of a situation of rivalry.[14]

This is a very useful counterweight to the tendency to reduce developmental stories to a simple 'loves mummy hates daddy' scenario, and it also normalises homosexual love in a way characteristic of much of Freud's thought, if not always of that of his followers.

The debate over whether identification with parents is more nuanced than classical psychoanalysis allowed, and more relevant to development than sexual desire, remains quite active and varies between different 'schools' of psychoanalysis. What it highlights, whatever the final outcome of this debate (if ever there is one), is the need to think more flexibly about both masculinity and femininity, to not become confused by stereotypes but instead to look closely at what men and women, boys and girls, actually do and who it is that they feel themselves to be connected with. Issues around dependency and autonomy feature quite largely here, but so does the more straightforward (but still very complicated) question of the role of love and care in relation to gender identification. For example, the American feminist psychoanalyst Jessica Benjamin rejects the apparently clear Oedipal account of classical psychoanalysis, which splits gender roles between a desirable mother and a regulating father, to emphasise the potential of fathers to be nurturing and loving towards their children. Benjamin's focus is on the father's ability to be a loving figure to the young child, to balance the repressive, prohibiting Oedipal father. Boys and girls both identify with this loving father, just as they do with the powerful and loving mother. 'Disidentification', the process whereby boys are held to move away from their mothers, is not a major issue; rather, children make multiple identifications with figures who matter to them. The effect of these multiple identifications, Benjamin claims, is to produce in the child a greater range of possible gender positions, particularly enhancing 'complementarity' rather than the kind of exclusivity which results in the triumph of one gender position over another. She writes:

> In linking identificatory love to the rapprochement [i.e. nurturing, pre-Oedipal] father, I was emphasizing that the father figure is used not merely to beat back the mother, to defensively idealize someone other than mother, but also to extend love to a second.[15]

Benjamin is what is known as an 'intersubjectivist' theorist, emphasising the importance of relationships rather than (but not excluding) sexuality. Her ideas link with those of psychoanalysts working from an 'object relational' perspective, often drawing on the writings of Donald Winnicott and others in the 'British School' of psychoanalysis, in which what matters most in development is not so much the direction of desire as the nature of identifications, of who we feel ourselves to be connected to and what we take from those around us. This has some drawbacks, tending to de-emphasise sexuality, the proving-ground of psychoanalysis's distinctiveness. However, it offers a suggestive account of masculine development not as the assertion of inborn activity, but as a set of defensive manoeuvres against vulnerability.

For feminist object relations theorists such as Luise Eichenbaum and Susie Orbach, children begin life deeply attached to the mother on whom they depend and to whom they feel linked.[16] The girl continues in this vein of identification, gradually enlarging her engagements with the world but always immersed in a kind of intimacy that develops her capacity for emotional connection. This can cause difficulties, especially around separation, but it means the girl is helped to have an awareness of emotional depth and empathic concern. The boy, however, as he becomes increasingly aware of the social demands around masculinity and his difference from his mother, must find ways of *disidentifying* from her, of cutting himself off so that he can become independent and a player in the world. The boy has to harden his defences so as to restrict his closeness with his mother and to feel less vulnerable. Given the usual structure of a sexually differentiated society, in which fathers are less available emotionally than mothers and in which the likely pattern of father–son relations is an outward-oriented, competitive one, identification with the father and with the masculine role in society is more precarious than the girl's identification with femininity. The result is that the boy is more intent on bolstering his fragile selfhood, and hence also more prickly and liable to resort to violence rather than allow himself to be overwhelmed by too much feeling. From one generation to the next, these patterns are replicated, underpinned by a society that is itself structured around the manly rejection of emotion. Yet at the bottom of it is a kind of masculine rage, in which the actual vulnerability of the psyche, our dependent need for connection with others, is desperately felt yet never fully acknowledged.

This account is no doubt simplistic and contains dubious assumptions about how the psychic life of the boy child is necessarily constrained by the patterns of childcare approved of in society, about how gender roles around parenting are distributed, about the relationship between mothering and fathering, and about the fixity of social conditions from one generation to the next. In fact, notwithstanding considerable continuity in attitudes and gender roles over time, including in violence against women, there has also been very significant change. In many societies, gender roles have become increasingly equalised, with patterns of employment and social behaviour shifting, and with the educational prospects of girls and women and their level of achievement dramatically improving. In some other societies, especially where religious fundamentalism rules, there has been a shift towards *greater* gender segregation. These developments, some welcome and some not, at least demonstrate that gender roles are malleable and that when there are changes in social conditions, they too can and do change. None of the psychoanalytic speculations should therefore be taken too literally. Nevertheless, the relational model promoted in much contemporary psychoanalysis allows us to think about how the patterns of sociality impact upon the psychic life of individuals.

In relation to gender differentiation, norms that are deeply embedded in society travel by way of the practices of social groups and of families to lodge 'inside' each of us as patterns of expectation and understanding, and also as emotionally charged principles through which we experience the world. If the surrounding culture is built around divisions made on gendered lines, meaning that the assignation as male or female carries with it directives on how to live, then these divisions will find their way into our psychological spaces, so that we come to accept their universality. As I keep emphasising, this is not a once-and-for-all situation that cannot be resisted; not all men are macho, not all women are vulnerable, and people can change over their lifetimes. Jessica Benjamin has proposed that a more realistic attitude towards gender would require moving away from a binary in which 'masculinity' is contrasted with 'femininity' towards what she calls the 'polymorphism of the psyche'.[17] This involves acknowledging and welcoming the multiplicity of different identifications that children make and the many ways in which we can express our gender. Freeing ourselves up in this way is, as ever, a step we might need to take to become more real. But the problem is always there: social conditions lay down what is desirable and make out that it is also what is necessary ('There Is No Alternative'), which means that finding more fulfilling and meaningful ways to live requires active resistance.

It is arguable, though perhaps quite a large claim, that 'race' has become the primary way in which the political landscape is divided up, more even than social class, with which it intersects. What has come to be called 'race' operates on numerous levels. It differentiates between groups, through the lenses of 'ethnicity' and 'culture' but also as a supposed biological marker of difference. Such distinctions produce sometimes quite radical disparities in social opportunities, with discrimination in health, employment, education and housing as well as, in many cases, direct subjection to racist attacks. Race is treated as something that really exists and can be accurately named, so that the terms 'Jews' or 'Asians' or 'Orientals' or 'African-Caribbeans' are understood to denote pre-given, naturally identifiable categories of people. Yet while there obviously are important cultural and historical differences between different groups, and while these terms will often be valued identity markers for members of those groups, they are also *racialised*. Race is not a pre-given but is constructed out of the historical and cultural differences between people, becoming attached to variations in biological markers (skin colour being a major one) and therefore a procedure whereby lines of demarcation are drawn and hierarchies created. Racialisation is a process of reducing the many differences between people into one purported biological difference, termed 'race', and reading into this difference a significance that goes far beyond describing variations in cultural practices – variations which in any case are often malleable and small. At the social level, in which discrimination is present in the social and political system, race materialises as a pattern of stratification based on categorisation processes that have their own histories (among others, European colonialism, slavery or Church-based anti-Judaism) and that continues to serve the political and economic interests of powerful groups.

Understanding that 'race' is a term that does specific kinds of *work* is important. It helps us see how the complex plurality of social and cultural differences becomes reduced to one primary difference, which is proposed as somehow fundamental and immutable. This classificatory process, like the procedure for forcing gender into a binary division between masculine and feminine, is a way of simplifying the manifold differences between groups, but also of refusing an encounter with them so that a structure of dominance can be maintained. This is because race-talk is not just about celebrating difference; it is an ideological mechanism for establishing hierarchy. The 'white races', as they were referred to by Freud and his contemporaries, are placed at the top of an imaginary tower in which blackness is usually at the base. Other groups – Muslims and Jews especially – are seen as disruptive outliers, sometimes adding exotic spice to whiteness, at other times threatening it through their alliance with the racialised underclass. Jews in America, for instance, on the whole have higher status than African Americans and other minoritised groups yet are easily re-racialised so that their status of 'provisional whiteness' is removed. The chant of the 2017 Unite the Right rally in Charlottesville, 'The Jews will not replace us,' is evidence of this, here casting the Jews as the hidden hand behind the fantasised 'flood' of black and Hispanic migrants that are imagined to be displacing white Americans. This notion of the civilised world being undermined by a Jewish conspiracy is an age-old antisemitic trope, prevalent in Christian Europe since medieval times and now transmuted from religious bigotry into modern racist thought. A parallel trajectory can be traced, to some extent, with anti-Muslim or Islamophobic racism, which also has a history mired in religious antagonism and persecution that remains visible in its contemporary racialised and politicised forms.

Racism is clearly a social phenomenon, serving social and political ends. Historically, it has been used to justify colonialism – colonised 'natives' being too 'primitive' to manage themselves without the help of 'advanced' Europeans, who under cover of this ideology proceeded to rob the colonised of their material wealth and wreck their customs and cultural heritage. It also offered a legitimation of slavery, with 'undeveloped' black Africans being seen as 'naturally' serving their white masters. And it continues to operate, sometimes in the foreground (as in police anti-Black violence in America) and sometimes in the background (as in the global trade in domestic semi-slavery) to serve economic and political ends today. The upsurge in Europe of antisemitism and the demonising of migrants are two examples of how racialised groups are made to bear the brunt of popular dissatisfaction with governments and hence to shift attention away from the actual sources of inequality and hardship in their societies. Racism is mobilised by right-wing populists apparently without any compunction, with victim groups often being blamed for it (for example, migrants are held to cause racism by their very presence), a displacement that is visible in much media coverage of the migrant 'crisis' in European countries and the UK. The carceral culture of many countries in the West, in which black people are imprisoned in highly disproportionate numbers, is another instance of the everyday workings of racism. All these contemporary expressions of racism have deep historical roots that help entrench them as they take their modern forms.

How does racism maintain its hold and continue to present itself as rooted in reality? After all, there is considerable resistance to racism and also plenty of public rhetoric against it from mainstream politicians and others in positions of power and influence. Nevertheless, it grinds on, with racist activity and racist ideology just below the surface, ready to bounce again into the limelight as soon as conditions allow. We have seen this both with the resurgence of antisemitism in Europe and America since the financial crash of 2008 and in the overt manifestations of anti-Black racism in Trump-led America.

While the sources of this are clearly structural and social, there is also something about racism that appeals to people, winding them up into states of fear and excitement as well as the 'enjoyment' that I discussed in the chapter on hate. Racism is a space of pronounced psychosocial suturing, where the social and the personal are stitched together. Racism operates powerfully in society and is also experienced and maintained by individuals, serving psychological functions which support and are supported by their social conditions. Put simply, there is a lot of *emotional* investment in racism (including for the racist who fervently denies being racist), and combatting it effectively requires us to understand this just as much as we might need to understand the economic and political conditions that make racism thrive. It can even seem that the intensity with which racist ideas are embraced exceeds what is required to sustain it on a social level. It is certainly clear that under some conditions, such as the Nazi regime in Germany, racism becomes a norm that is almost irresistible, one that can offer people a way of understanding their situation, along with opportunities for identification with others in their group (the 'Volk' or nation, in Nazi times; the 'white race' in ours) that can be deeply satisfying and seemingly life-enhancing. What might be going on here? What is it about racism that excites people so, that moves them to cling to the most irrational ideas and explanations for their troubles, and that can so easily motivate them towards verbal or physical violence?

This is where it is useful to draw on psychoanalysis for its understanding of the emotional hold that racism exerts. Historically, many psychoanalytic accounts of fascism and authoritarianism in general and racism in particular, have focused on how the bourgeois family is designed to reproduce ideology through sexual repression. This was the case for the famous inter-war psychoanalytic radical, Wilhelm Reich, who held the dubious distinction of being expelled in the 1930s both from the psychoanalytic movement (for being too 'political') and from the communist movement. Whatever his excesses, of which there were many, he offered some profound insights into the ways in which the structures of the authoritarian, patriarchal family might be reproduced within the individual as a kind of 'character armour,' defending the self against multiplicity and fluidity. That is, a certain kind of rigidity enters the mind, rendering us unable to face up to the complexity of the world. At certain times, when that complexity is threatening and especially when the governing politics is itself authoritarian, we might respond by submerging our personality in the mass. More generally, Reich was convinced that sexual repression was at the heart of political repression and that sexual revolution would be needed if ever a political revolution was to succeed. Reich's analysis was directed more at fascism than at racism, but this broad understanding of the authoritarian or fascist state of mind as one in which the confusing complexity of the world is managed 'internally' through repression, accompanied by the projection of unwanted feelings onto the derogated outgroups in society, is quite widely shared among those using psychoanalytic ideas in the psychopolitical field.[18]

Other thinkers have developed this basic paradigm to explain how the internalisation of social norms creates inner racist states. Theodor Adorno and his colleagues, in a classic post–Second World War investigation of prejudice, traced the source of racist psychology to a family scenario in which an authoritarian father and the absence of affection produces a sado-masochistic personality structure unable to deal with the complexity of the world.[19] Any feelings and ideas that are confusing and disturbing have to be got rid of through a process of projection in which they are expelled into the outside world as 'not me'. This creates a persecutory environment full of hated beings, confirming the person's vision of being ensnared in a dangerous situation in which the other must be wiped out for the self to survive. *Difference* always constitutes a threat. Adorno and his colleagues called this 'psychological totalitarianism', mimicking the political structure of totalitarianism in which nothing that diverges can be tolerated. This psychological rigidity entwines itself with the systemic racism present in society and adds energy to it, creating a situation in which racist ideas are enthusiastically embraced and reiterated as part of a process of psychic survival.

This idea can also be seen at work in the most influential of all writers on race to have used psychoanalysis (among other theories), the Martiniquan psychiatrist, political philosopher and activist, Frantz Fanon. Much of his book, *Black Skin, White Masks*, published in 1952 at the time of the major decolonial movements, is given over to an impassioned and brilliant exploration of the impact of racism on the psyche of black men (Fanon has much less to say about women).[20] However, he also pays attention to the white colonial imagination that fuels this racism, emphasising its sexually repressive character. For Fanon, whiteness, supported by an ideology of 'purity' and a disavowal of sexuality that comes with the demands of colonial claims to civilised superiority, *needs* the black 'other' as a repository of its own discontent if it is to survive. The white man projects his repressed sexuality onto the black man, constructing him in fantasy as a sexual paragon and an object for his homosexual desire. This creates a circuit of disturbance in which the white man finds the black man's sexuality returning as an envied aspect of his own disavowed sexual embodiment. The white's relationship to the black is then mediated by this sexuality: the black man, freighted with the projected elements of the white's sexuality, is imagined to be a constant threat to the potency of the white man and a stimulus to the desire of the white woman. Racist persecution of the black is therefore fuelled by sexual hatred, as is borne out by lynchings throughout history. There is a general idea at work in these early thinkers that has continued into more contemporary analyses of racism. This is that the racist imaginary is not constituted by 'mistaken beliefs' of the kind hypothesised in many psychological theories of prejudice, which suggest that the situation could be remedied by better education in cultural differences. It is rather that something weak or unbearable in the psyche of the racist is dealt with by splitting it off from the consciousness of the person concerned and then projecting it outward, where it finds a ready receptacle in the existence of an already demeaned outgroup. The choice of outgroup is, psychologically speaking, *contingent*, in the sense that it depends both on the nature of the projection and on the structure of prejudice in the society at large. Thus, sexual repression is lodged in the body of the Black, reduced to animality and physicality; and this is a ready-made stereotype especially in erstwhile slave societies. On the other hand, antisemitism, rife especially in places where Christian anti-Judaism predominated for centuries, is a great vehicle for feelings of dispossession, or corruption, or infection. It draws on images of Jews 'poisoning the wells', a familiar medieval allegation, as well as the still prevalent fantasy of a 'worldwide Jewish conspiracy' aiming at power.

The argument throughout is that because 'race' is a constructed notion with very little basis in reality, it serves as an excellent conduit for projections of troubling ideas and deep-rooted anxieties and desires. The force with which sexual fantasies in particular are projected onto the racialised other (the potent Black, the depraved Jew, the homosexual Asian) lends persuasion to this idea that it is the 'dark' underside of whiteness that is being expressed in this way. Racist thinking is paranoid not simply because of its content ('everyone is against us; we are in a battle for survival') but because of the emotional charge attached to the expulsion of intolerable fantasies into others. The 'election' of the racialised other as an object of hate is a way of closing down the thinking that would be necessary in order to deal properly with these unwanted fantasies, to integrate them into the person's mind and so make them survivable. Instead, these 'unthought' impulses are evacuated into the other. This is also why racists are fascinated by the object of their hatred and sometimes express their racism counterintuitively in admiration, for example of Jewish 'cleverness' or Black 'athleticism' or Indian 'family life'. These too are stereotypes with social and cultural sources, but they are treated as natural categories.

Recently, some psychoanalysts, especially in America, have turned their attention to trying to understand *whiteness* as a defensive structure linked indissolubly with racism. Some of this work is quite controversial and is arguably too binary in its own account of racialised difference ('whiteness' versus 'blackness' as an inescapable conflict), but the general theme aligns with the focus on how what is unbearable in the white psyche is projected into the black other. This is because whiteness only exists in opposition to something defined as blackness. The problem for whiteness then becomes at least twofold. On the one hand, much that is core to liveliness and hence to a sense of subjective being – but which is also troubling – is projected outwards towards the other. This creates a sense of emptiness that means the identity of the white subject can only be sustained through a form of character armour that blocks the encounter with this empty self. On the other hand, the non-white subject also becomes a threat, both because that other is so much more real than the white subject and because the way in which whiteness survives is by domination of the other. If black others come close, their very presence threatens whiteness not just with what it has discarded, but also with the guilty non-secret of its oppressiveness, the action it constantly takes to maintain itself by keeping the other subjugated. Even the failure to mourn lost aspects of white subjectivity becomes weaponised: it creates guilt, which is repudiated and projected outwards, leading to a situation in which the black other is seen as guilty for the trouble that whiteness causes. In this manner, the whole system becomes a kind of destructive feedback loop. Whiteness projects disturbance onto blackness, understood generically here to refer to all racialised and marginalised groups, the specific ones 'chosen' at any time to be the receptacle for projections determined by social as well as psychological factors. This means that the unwanted material that has been got rid of now resurfaces as imagined characteristics of the racialised other, who then becomes a threat to the white person. The source of danger is thus located outside, which makes it easier to deal with; but this also sustains a fantasy of persecution and a paranoid state of mind in which racism flourishes. In addition, the racialised other becomes an object of fascination for the white, who recognises something in it that has been lost from the self – a kind of liveliness, of feeling real. Guilt, hatred, eroticism and attraction all mix together to form something combustible that, especially under circumstances of generalised precarity (for instance, economic disaster), hardens into a racism that feeds on, and is fed by, the racism embedded in so much of the social world. Resistance is not futile, but it is hard work.

Racism, then, is deeply embedded in the psychic life of people who live in racialised societies. The choice of the racialised other as the repository of unwanted psychic projections is facilitated by the fact that such others have already been nominated as derogated and disempowered, yet also as dangerous threats. The racist dynamic is one in which feelings that belong 'inside' are rejected and relocated in the external other, who is then made responsible for them. However, the point about projection is that it reveals the *permeability* of personal boundaries: what is supposedly 'inside' does not stay there but leaks out and finds its place among networks of identification and relationality that are socially organised. These are also part of the 'self' and so have a strong emotional charge: racist ideation is intense precisely because it is *felt*. Yet internal disturbance should not be seen as the cause of racism. There are many ways to deal with anxiety and vulnerability; it is when the social context promotes rigidity and externalisation of blame and provides racialised categories into which people can be made to fit, that these inner passions come to be expressed in racist ways.

What we can see from the twin examples of gender violence and racism is that obscuring social reality is itself a way of blocking attainment of the state of 'being real'. Ideology is not a once-and-for-all pulling of the wool over our eyes, so that as soon as we see through it we have the truth. But even if we can never reach that truth, the way in which certain prevalent ideologies actively promote falsehood needs to be examined, understood and exposed. Remaining fixed on absolute categories of gender difference clearly reassures some people for whom notions like 'non-binary' or 'gender fluidity' create existential alarm. That is one major reason why so much heat is generated by this issue. However, rigid opposition to acceptance of the intensity, variability and complexity of gendered experience is a way of avoiding reality and of preventing access to more emancipated lifestyles for many people. There have been many changes in gender expression in the last few decades, along with much resistance to them; some of this resistance has been violent and a lot of it brutally intolerant. I think that we need to understand such reactions as part of the difficulty of facing the fact of how complicated our gendered, as well as our sexual, experience can be, and how poorly we seem able to cope with this complexity without being overwhelmed with an anxiety that is also reinforced by certain aspects of our social world. Similarly, racism is a prominent feature of many societies and takes specific forms in the West as a consequence of slavery, colonialism and historic antisemitism. Like the preservation of gender inequalities, it fulfils social and political functions in maintaining existing patterns of domination. And like gender identity and gendered hatred, it is an arena for the expression of personal passions that cannot be easily faced.

The social and the personal run together to make the psychosocial and the psychopolitical. Finding what is 'real' in these areas requires us to do our best to work out how they are constructed, not to take them as fixed and natural. When we succeed we are better placed to understand how often we use politics as a vehicle for our defensiveness, denying what is real in us. And we can also see more clearly what politics does to us, how regularly it plays on our vulnerabilities in the interests of social denial.

7
Endurance

What is it that makes it so hard to bear the burden of another's suffering? In Chapter 4, I mentioned the idea of 'sympathetic realism' as a counterbalance to the tendency to believe that we can solve all the problems another person might have, an expectation that is bound to be unfulfilled. Holding onto the heroic idea that we can make up for all suffering is a route to failure; it can leave us feeling depleted and guilty, distressed by the sense that we are helpless in the face of such trouble. There might also be a directly damaging effect of listening to trauma testimony, which may raise in the listener memories and associations to experiences they themselves have had. This can result in a kind of transmission of trauma, in which the suffering of one person is passed on to another without being resolved, and it is helpful to no one. Indeed, at its most damaging it can become a second trauma for the original sufferer, who is now 'responsible' for hurting someone who is trying to help. 'Traumatised witnessing' of such a kind, added to the sense of impotence that comes from seeking to do too much, is a way in which trauma spreads and means that the witness to it becomes less useful to the sufferer than they might have been, increasing distress all round.

What is the difference between 'unbearable' and 'difficult' knowledge? The former invites us to turn away from the experience, full knowledge of which would be impossible to tolerate. In psychoanalytic terms, it is an incitement to repression and denial aimed at protecting us against a kind of assault by a reality that, psychologically speaking, cannot be survived. *Difficult* knowledge, on the other hand, is recognisably hard to deal with but is in principle manageable. No one should deny its force, complexity and threat, yet the very notion of 'difficult' suggests something that is possible, however hard it is to accomplish. We can work to overcome difficulties, whereas things that are unbearable stay that way. But *work* it is nevertheless; nothing comes easily here.

Trying as a listener to be supportive and helpful to someone who is attempting to communicate the depth of their suffering is obviously desirable, but as most people know – ranging from parents dealing with their distraught children to psychotherapists probing the previously-hidden details of torture or abuse – it can rebound on the listener in numerous ways. As well as the danger of being 'triggered' ourselves by what we are hearing, the sufferer might find re-engagement with their trauma so horrific that they blame the listener for drawing it out of them. Difficult knowledge is difficult for all parties and can become the source of interpersonal conflict and mutual rejection. Sticking with the task of sympathetically realistic listening is a matter of endurance, with all the strain that this term implies.

Being 'real' means engaging with the fullness of reality, however hard it might at times be to bear. We have many ways of backing away from this, of hiding from ourselves what we and those around us are going through, especially when we feel that we cannot control events to make them tolerable. This is marked in a special way when we feel called on to respond to the suffering of others, to our 'suffering neighbours', for whatever reason – because, for instance, we feel implicated in their suffering as a consequence of our own actions when we have hurt them, or even when the link is much less direct, perhaps historical in form (the violence done in previous generations), or because of cultural, ethnic or religious connections. But, of course, we might also have a simpler, ethical reaction to the suffering of others, in which everyone is seen as a kind of neighbour. If we hold that view, all of us are implicated in the fate of other people. But how can we deal with such a universalist demand? At what point does facing the reality of difficult knowledge and our implication in the lives of others become absurdly idealistic? Or should this always be the ethical standpoint from which we see things? That is, are we always 'implicated subjects' and, if so, how do we deal with it?

The idea that we are implicated in the lives of others is straightforward enough when we think about family and friends and all those with whom we are intimately involved. We rub up against those people all the time. What happens to them is connected to what we do. With some relationships, for example parents with their children and intimate partners with each other, the implication is profound. Everything done by or that happens to one person in that context implies some kind of responsibility to and from others. Even events that have no direct connection to others, such as an accident that happens to one person when another is far away, ripples out to impact upon the other. Psychologically, we might feel responsible for, or guilty about, what happens to a child or loved one even when we have no control. 'If only I'd been there, this would not have happened,' or 'I will never forgive myself for allowing him to make that decision' – these are quite common laments when bad things happen to people we are close to, and the logical weakness they often display (you cannot be everywhere; the decision was his and he insisted upon it) does not make them any the easier to dismiss.

As the American scholar of Holocaust and literary studies, Michael Rothberg, has shown, the idea of implication can be extended to various situations, some more easily challenged than others.[1] A common one is in relation to the kind of intergenerational connection remarked on in Chapter 5: that we might *feel* responsible for the legacy of events that we are not literally responsible for, because they took place before we were even born. Slavery, colonialism and the Holocaust were the examples given there, but there is a more general point about how, because we identify with past generations (our parents and grandparents, or more broadly the earlier history of our communities or nation), we also have to acknowledge that the lingering effects of any of their actions might be part of our heritage. Similarly, we might feel implicated in geographically distant events that we have no control over yet take a stance towards. Being somehow 'called to account' for the violence in Israel–Palestine is an especially complicated and fraught example for many contemporary diasporic Jews. We might object to being automatically linked with Israel, whatever our views, and regard the assumption that Israel and Jews are interchangeable as antisemitic, reducing the nuanced nature of Jewish identity to a 'yes or no' attitude towards Zionism, itself reduced to certain stereotypes. On the other hand, most diasporic Jews feel some degree of connection with Israel and recognise that its claim to be a Jewish state means that there is pressure to position ourselves in relation to it, even if critically. Objecting to the antisemitic position that Jews are automatically responsible for whatever happens in Israel and Palestine, or that Israel is somehow a racist state of the Jews, does not mean that there are no intrinsic links between Jews and Israel. The emotional intensity of identification with, and disputes over, Israel within Jewish communities testifies to this and is part of the argument that even if diasporic Jews have no actual power over Israeli policy and no direct connection with what goes on there, we might still feel implicated.

Feeling implicated has resonance for an ethical approach to living with others, motivating people to act and urging them towards an attitude in which all lives are seen as 'grievable'.[2] If simply by being human we are responsible for the hurt done to others, or at least are required to respond to others' pleas for help, then we are always implicated in suffering; and if we have a demonstrable connection to these others, then this universal responsibility is fuelled still further. This is the basic philosophy of implication: that all human lives are connected simply by virtue of *being* human lives. Problems arise, however, from the material and psychological consequences of this universal injunction. Not only are there reasonable questions to ask about where responsibility ends, including how to prioritise when necessary, but there is also the resistance that sets in once implication is recognised.

Materially, this resistance is to the demand for reparation once responsibility is acknowledged. Psychologically, the resistance to implication itself is equally strong, indeed perhaps even more powerful. The resistance here usually takes the form of rejecting the idea of implication altogether. 'I have a good excuse' is the blanket slogan to describe this state of mind: 'The events occurred long ago, in a far-off place; my links with them are precarious; I objected to what was happening and never took part directly; we have paid our dues; it is time to stop complaining and get on with life.' (The echoes of Freud's 'damaged kettle' excuses might strike us here.) Resistance of this kind is part of a broader philosophy that places the individual at the centre of things rather than prioritising relationality and social connections. In this philosophy, I am only responsible for acts that I commit myself. But more relevantly, it is a way of protecting ourselves against the knowledge that we are called on to examine our implication in the suffering of others and react accordingly, moving out from the small circle of responsibility to our immediate family and friends to a much broader awareness of how we affect and are affected by others. In this model of ethical responsiveness, everyone becomes close to us, and this can be an uncomfortable feeling; we often prefer to be left alone.

A different example might be helpful here. Many of my PhD students have worked on projects that connect in some way to their personal lives. Usually, this choice of topic has been consciously based on an experience or situation that a student has had or found themselves in, which they wish to research in more detail both to bring it to wider awareness and to help them understand it personally. Sometimes, the link with their own experience has had additional components that can be called 'unconscious' in a psychoanalytic sense, when the motivation for it is partly hidden or when the wish to remedy the situation becomes visible only as the work goes on. One former student of mine was researching women who had been adopted in early life, looking specifically at their experience of reuniting with their birth fathers in adulthood.[3] The connection between this research topic and the student's own difficult process of seeking out her biological father was clear from the start, but the intensity of her investment in it and its richness, both positively and negatively, gradually became fused with the process of writing and understanding other women's experience. This certainly contradicted the approach to social science that decrees it should always be 'objective' and could trouble some people who think this should be the case. However, the student's open recognition of her implication in her work, including her strong sense of responsibility towards the women she interviewed, was both an acknowledgment of reality and a strong motivator of a powerfully empathetic and reflexive set of encounters. Her implication in the topic made her extraordinarily alert to the ethical requirement to allow these women to be heard and to treat them in a way that recognised the pain and longing that haunted their accounts of themselves, without this meaning that she abandoned the capacity to think for herself about what they told her.

Similarly, other students researching issues of migration in their national communities (Colombian or Turkish migrants to the UK, for instance), or rape or sexual violence or cancer survival, have known about and acknowledged their investment in their topic from the start, but have not necessarily been fully aware of their *implication* in it, in the sense of feeling responsible, until the work has been under way. To my mind, the sense of implication has always enhanced the research, even when – as has usually been the case – it has placed strong emotional demands on the researcher and indeed on myself as project supervisor. These situations are not, of course, examples of how someone might feel implicated in something they have 'done wrong', but rather of a sense of responsibility towards others that arises from an awareness of mutual interdependence and connection. My students understood their research as an act undertaken towards others, 'neighbours' in the sense of people having shared experiences, an act that would also reverberate in themselves. What this demanded of them was an openness to the hurt and suffering that might be involved, along with a capacity to remain stable even when things that were said triggered their own feelings and at times distress.

There is a general point that can be extracted from this. The emotional strain of staying with a person or topic that is troubling and personally resonant can be very demanding. It can make us feel that it is better not to open this proverbial can of worms, better to sidestep the direct encounter by deploying some of the defences mentioned earlier – turning away, dismissing the other's experience, too quickly embracing it without really listening to the specifics, choosing a safer topic to explore. This is not necessarily consciously intended; it just happens, as a way to protect ourselves from the challenge and disturbance of the other person or of the material under consideration. There is no moralising involved, as there can be no absolute requirement on anyone to face things that deeply upset them. Why not defend ourselves if it leads to a pleasanter and safer life? Stepping away from danger is often a sensible thing to do. Yet the problem is that it involves closing down parts of ourselves in order to preserve the whole. We choose, consciously or not, to turn away from trouble, but the effect of this is to reduce the range of experiences we can have and to constrain our own engagement with the world. This impoverishes our inner lives, which are narrowed and bulwarked against things that disturb us, and our connection with others.

The consequence is both psychological and ethical: we are less open with ourselves and can take less responsibility for others. Being implicated makes this dilemma all the stronger. Spaces of emotional rawness within each one of us can be opened up as we encounter neighbours who have similar troubles, or whose experiences resonate with our own; and this is magnified when we feel responsible in some way for their predicament. The idea that 'only one can live', as described by Jessica Benjamin, is relevant here: it can sometimes seem as though there is only room for one victim in a situation of competitive victimhood, the refrain being 'My suffering is worse, or more significant, than yours.'[4] In relation to implication, one danger is that there will be a response of 'whataboutery' ('What about other countries that have done wrong? What about what happened to me?') that seeks to clear us from responsibility – another defensive move that shuts out relationships of solidarity and support. The emotional pressure of feeling implicated can then compound the general difficulty of dealing with traumatic and other disturbing situations in which demands are being made of us. Once again, all the familiar manoeuvres we deploy to manage this by utilising techniques of distancing and denial can come into play. Yet we *are* implicated after all; if not directly (though this can be the case), then as witnesses who can be called on to take action, or as bystanders, who should be witnesses of this kind but are failing in that role. How, then, can we come to handle these difficult situations in ways that allow us to have fuller encounters with them, in the process finding the strength to be effective witnesses of our neighbours' troubles as well as our own?

Maybe we take on too much, trying to resolve problems when all we can manage is to stay with them in a process of watching, observing, listening and being-with. This does not, of course, mean that we should never take action; still, the belief that we should be able to deal successfully with all difficulties, our own or those of others, can turn into a damaging, either-or state of mind. Either a solution is found, or there is no point in doing anything: this is a common yet largely unproductive approach to struggle at all levels of social life.

At its most politically grand, it marks the difference between revolution and reform. Is a failed revolution, leading to heightened repression, preferable to a graduated process of progressive change, however frustrating it might be? There is plenty of scope for dispute about this, involving balancing the destructive elements of revolution against the way social reform can be used as a fig-leaf to mask continuing inequality and oppression. Enduring these conditions in the name of gradual development may itself be a way of defending against the need to take effective, risky action. But at the level of interpersonal relations, the question of endurance is somewhat different. It does not mean accepting things as they are, but rather staying with the difficulties of reality so that something new might happen. This is most apparent in the way people often go over and over an experience in order to gradually find a way to live with it and, if possible, transform it. In psychoanalysis, the working-through of a set of conflicts or traumatic memories needs to be contained within a structure that allows repetition, disturbance and failure without recrimination or adverse consequences, without the witness to the process turning away in despair or disgust, and without impatient reaching for brisk solutions or undue disappointment when such solutions fail to appear. In other words, it requires a capacity on the part of both the sufferer and the witness, or the patient and the analyst, to stay with the problem and let it unfold in its own manner and in its own time.

Let me work with another example here. There is a well-known and much discussed passage in Claude Lanzmann's powerful 1985 film, *Shoah*, a film largely made up of interviews with Holocaust survivors and perpetrators. Throughout, Lanzmann demonstrates determination to get the information he wants, including the use of hidden cameras when filming ex-Nazis but also demanding of survivors that they speak fully about their experiences. At times, this calls into question the ethics of the film, and it has certainly been an element in the debates that have revolved around it since it was first released. One especially contentious encounter is with Abraham Bomba, a barber in Treblinka tasked with shaving women's hair before the women entered the gas chambers. Bomba is first filmed on a balcony in Tel Aviv, and then in a barber's shop where, while cutting a man's hair, he describes what he had to do. At a certain point, he stops; this is when he has just said that it was impossible to feel anything in Treblinka, 'working there between bodies and dead people'. Some of the women whose hair he cut, he tells us, came from his hometown. He knew them. Another barber found himself faced with his own wife and sister. Bomba stops talking, the camera fixes on him, he wipes his face, shakes his head, and over several minutes there is this dialogue:

> *Lanzmann:* Go on then, you must go on. You have to.
> *Bomba:* Can't do it. It's too hard.
> *Lanzmann:* Please. We have to do it. You know it.
> *Bomba:* I won't be able to do it.
> *Lanzmann:* You have to do it. I know it's very hard. I know and I apologise.
> *Bomba:* Don't make me go on, please.
> *Lanzmann:* Please. We must go on.[5]

Eventually Bomba says something to himself and does 'go on' to describe his terrible experiences. This scene is important in numerous ways. But I want to pick up an ethical question here. By what right does Lanzmann make Bomba speak, and extending this, what is the real purpose of such testimony, and of our desire to hear it?

Before saying more, it is worth knowing that the scene was partially staged. Lanzmann had met Bomba and heard his story, and set up a fake barber shop, deciding it would be too much to ask Bomba to cut women's hair, but wanting the drama and immediacy of reconstruction nevertheless. Just before the moment when Bomba stops speaking, Lanzmann has sensed something will happen and has got his cameraman to reload, so there will be enough film to catch it. Lanzmann's account is revealing:

> The scene is famous ... he and I begin to talk, a conversation between two supplicants, he pleading with me to stop, me gently urging him to continue because I believe it is our common task, our shared duty. All this happens at precisely the moment when, had I not reloaded the camera when I did, there would have been no film left. And the loss would have been irreparable: I could never have asked Bomba to start crying again as one might if rehearsing a play. The camera kept turning; Abraham's tears were as precious to me as blood, the seal of truth, its very incarnation. Some people have suggested some sort of sadism on my part in this perilous scene, while on the contrary I consider it to be the epitome of reverence and supportiveness, which is not to tiptoe away in the face of suffering, but to obey the categorical imperative of the search for and transmission of truth.[6]

Is this exploitation, the use of someone's pain for dramatic effect to bring home a message? Do we have a right to demand of those who suffered that they tell us exactly what they went through, however terrible, however much they may have wanted not to speak of it? Some writers on memory and Holocaust suffering have challenged the ethics of Lanzmann's film generally, and this passage in particular. For example, the filmmaker and academic Agnieszka Piotrowska quotes many critics of Lanzmann's approach to his participants, including Dominick LaCapra, who regards Lanzmann as '"acting out through the film", ruthlessly exploiting the subjects of the film for his own purposes, verging on the sadistic'.[7] Other commentators, such as the literary theorist Shoshana Felman, have argued that the process Bomba went through during filming was likely to be helpful to him as a way of encouraging him, albeit brutally, to turn his unspeakable memory into something that could be articulated, recorded and thought about. In that way, it brought it into the domain of what is liveable, rather than left as an impossible memory.[8] This aligns with the vision of trauma as perpetuated by the failure to symbolise the traumatising event. Lanzmann's insistence that Bomba continue ('Go on then, you must go on. You have to') has the effect of releasing Bomba from the past that still grips him, and the enactment that Lanzmann sets up in the fake barbers' shop is a way of intensifying the cathartic process that eventually enables Bomba to speak. Witnessing, on Lanzmann's part and on that of the potential viewer of the film, is an active process of making something happen, of 'walking with' testifiers but still ensuring that they do not stray from the path of facing up to what they cannot usually bear. Felman has written about this section of the film,

> To have to *go on* now, to have to keep on bearing witness, is more than simply to be faced with the imperative to replicate the past and thus to replicate his own *survival*. Lanzmann paradoxically now urges Bomba to break out of the very deadness that enabled the survival. The narrator calls the witness to come back from the mere mode of surviving into that of living – and of living pain.[9]

Perhaps this is right, perhaps what happens in this section of the film is that Bomba comes back to life as the horrific experiences he has had are recognised by Lanzmann and, behind him, by the whole process of making the film. Yet Lanzmann makes no claim to be acting with a therapeutic aim. Indeed, the scene is clearly not done for Bomba's sake, but for the historical record that is so precious to Lanzmann. Can we do this to victims, say to them that whatever they feel, however distressed it might make them, they have a responsibility to speak out for the sake of history, for the archive, in aid of 'the search for and transmission of truth', as Lanzmann does? For Lanzmann, the process was one of 'gently urging him to continue because I believe it is our common task, our shared duty'. It must be said that the urging does not look particularly 'gentle', but the point is an important one: speaker, witness/filmmaker and audience must go through this as a 'shared duty' to historical accuracy, to the dead, and to life as well, to the fullness of knowledge of what happened and what people can and did do to one another. They must look it straight in the face, which is Lanzmann's term and exactly what his camera does: it looks straight at Bomba's face, barely allowing him to turn away, using the mirrors in the barber's shop to get access to it. Lanzmann says that it is this search for truth, which is achieved by dramatising, by setting up the barber's shop, that justifies what might otherwise appear to be his 'sadism'. Indeed, the reverence for truth is absolute and weighs much more heavily on the filmmaker than any concern for the therapeutic well-being of Bomba as survivor-witness. It is, says Lanzmann, embodied in the decision 'not to tiptoe away in the face of suffering, but to obey the categorical imperative of the search for and transmission of truth'.

Ultimately, Lanzmann is right in insisting on a responsibility to document suffering in as open and truthful a way as possible, and this often entails giving the exact record of what he here calls the 'face of suffering', individualising it so that it can have precise meaning. However, this has its paradoxes: if we value the individual story, in which every life matters and is grievable, then what is our responsibility towards the individual who tells it: are we really entitled to put Bomba the man through such pain just to get his story on film? If the difference between a relational ethics and a totalitarian ethics is that we think 'the person who saves one life has saved a whole world', as the Jewish saying goes – that is, that every life is precious, that you cannot say twenty are worth more than one – then what right have we to 'unethically' drag a story out of someone who cannot bear to tell it?[10]

More generally, we must challenge ourselves when we act as witnesses, when we hear some kind of testimony. What rescues this passage is not so much historical duty, though I can see the strength of that view; it is rather that Lanzmann says to Bomba, when he cannot go on, '*We* have to do it.' He saw it, he says, as 'our common task, our shared duty'. Maybe it is this act of solidarity that stops this being sadism, and instead binds everyone together, the testifiers and the witnesses to that testimony, those who can speak and those who must find dignified ways to listen. Endurance would then mean staying with a process of uncovering and engaging with whatever arises, whether it is, as in this example, horror and traumatic distress at the unimaginable barbarity of what Bomba has been through; or whether, in other circumstances, it might be disturbing or exciting dreams and wishes, confusions and hatreds. Endurance of this kind does not signify passivity. Clearly, Lanzmann is highly active in setting up the situation for the filming and in his insistence that Bomba continue with his narrative even when he explicitly states that he cannot. The same is true in the psychoanalytic situation, where the analyst's task is not only to listen sympathetically, but to question and at times to challenge a patient, especially by noting their attempts to avoid thinking about troubling things. 'You have to do it' or 'we have to do it' is rarely a phrase that an analyst would use, yet it is implicit in the conditions of the analytic setting: otherwise, why bother to come? Facing the 'truth', however hard it is to pin that down, as 'our shared duty', is precisely what endurance involves.

In the psychoanalytic situation, the 'reality' of the psychoanalyst is a significant issue that bears heavily on the technique of psychoanalytic psychotherapy. It also has a strong theoretical, even philosophical, edge. It is this edge that gives it wider significance for the question of how to be real.

Psychoanalysis is a crucible in which relational issues can be explored and then extrapolated to provide ideas about witnessing and relating in more 'everyday' settings. Of course, we should acknowledge that all relationships have their own peculiar constraints. We behave differently in the intimacy of our family, with close friends, with work colleagues, with strangers; these different interpersonal situations are governed by different rules and expectations, and to muddle them up (treating strangers as close friends, for instance, or the reverse) will create significant problems. The psychoanalytic setting is in that sense just another one with its own rules and expectations. But what distinguishes psychoanalysis from most relationships is that disruptions to the 'frame' of psychoanalysis – what in other contexts might be the muddling of situations in which, for example, a boss at work is treated like a hated parent – offer the greatest evidence for the analyst's work, the best material for thinking with the patient about what is going on for them 'behind the scenes'.

What psychoanalysts tend to term 'enactments' appear in analysis partly because of the intensity of patients' feelings. After all, most come for help with issues that trouble them, sometimes deeply. But enactments also reflect aspects of the relationship between analyst and patient that trigger in patients' minds connections with other relationships and situations in which important issues have arisen. These are located mainly in past relationships with important developmental figures, parents especially, but they might also reveal ways in which other, contemporary relations are being negotiated or are failing to be managed realistically and successfully. Precisely because the peculiar structure of psychoanalysis encourages a certain kind of frustration, it enhances the visibility of these enactments. The psychoanalytic encounter is usually constrained by firm boundaries of time and place, and perhaps most distinctively by non-reciprocity: the patient speaks, the analyst mostly listens; patients talk about themselves, analysts tend to give little away about their lives; patients may become highly animated, while analysts usually try their best to remain thoughtful and measured. As a result, the fantasies surrounding the analytic encounter are much *less* constrained than in many other situations, despite the overt restrictions of the setting. Indeed, insofar as these restrictions minimise patients' knowledge of their analysts, they are freer to imagine all sorts of things about them. According to analysts, patients are especially concerned about the thoughts and feelings that their analyst might have towards them; that is, because analysts give away relatively little, patients tend to fantasise more about what they are thinking.

This all means that the psychoanalytic situation is uniquely instructive in revealing the kinds of expectations, fantasies and anxieties that people bring to their relationships with others, their starting-points and underlying assumptions about what other people are like and especially about how they relate to the patient. If I rapidly assume that my analyst is bored by me when that analyst has said or done nothing to indicate this, it suggests that I carry with me a sense of being boring, or maybe misunderstood, which invites such a reaction from other people. Similarly, if everything my analyst says is felt by me as a criticism or as a seduction, even though the analyst is mostly silent and then speaks in a moderate, thoughtful way, it is likely that I am somehow primed to fantasise along those lines. My 'reality' is tied up with these fantasies, and one point of psychoanalysis is to allow them to come to the fore so that this reality can be explored.

This set of ideas about what might go on in psychoanalysis is usually theorised under the rubric of 'transference', loosely indicating how patients locate their analysts in terms of their own unconscious fantasies, behaving towards them as if they were reincarnations of their parents, or perhaps embodiments of aspects of their own selves (for example, a propensity to self-criticism) which they find hard to tolerate. But it is the other side of the relationship that interests me here: what can we learn from what goes on 'inside' the analyst faced with a disturbing patient?

The response of the analyst to the patient is commonly discussed under the heading of 'countertransference'. There are various ways of envisaging this. Sometimes it refers to the problems that analysts have in thinking clearly about their patients when troubled by events in their own lives, or when emotions and unconscious conflicts that they have not resolved for themselves are triggered by what the patient says or does. An analyst struggling to deal with a crisis in their marriage might find it hard to remain attuned to a patient who is talking about a similar thing; their own feelings might get in the way of identifying what the patient needs from them, especially if the patient has a different response to the situation from the analyst. Countertransference in this view is a kind of inhibition or blockage that analysts might need to overcome to be more 'realistic' in their relationship with patients. It is certainly the case that analysts, like anyone, can be distracted from their work by events in their personal lives; and some may have longstanding difficulties with certain kinds of patient (aggressive or seductive ones, for example), difficulties that relate to their own histories and have not been sufficiently resolved through their own analyses.

But perhaps it is useful to refer to this under a slightly different term than 'countertransference'. Calling it 'the analyst's transference' clarifies that what is being described is what the analyst brings to the session from their own background experience, rather than what is being evoked by the reality of a particular patient. That would reserve the term 'countertransference' for something different and more specific. In this narrower usage, countertransference refers to what is produced in the analyst *by a patient*, for sure in the sole context of the consulting room, and not as might be the case if analyst and patient encountered each other in other settings – but nevertheless as an honest response to what the patient brings. This treats countertransference as a kind of communication to the analyst *from the analyst about the patient*, where the message is encoded as a set of feelings and thoughts. To try to put this more clearly: countertransference might usefully be understood as the analyst's emotional response to the patient, made visible to the analyst through a process of reflection. This can be used to guide the analyst's understanding of the patient's unconscious life, expressed and communicated through the patient's transference – the way in which they 'use' the analyst as a matrix in which things can be worked out. Analysts thus need to have a capacity for feeling; they have to direct this towards the patient, be receptive to both spoken and unspoken parts of the patient's communications and be capable of reflecting on these feelings in order to make sense of them for themselves and, in one way or another, for the patient. No easy task, as one might imagine.

The state of mind that is called up by this has been well-described by the twentieth-century psychoanalyst Wilfred Bion as 'reverie'.[11] Bion compared this to a (somewhat idealised) mother's ability to receive from her young infant anything that that infant might put 'into' her: distress, excitement, fury, desire, need. The mother who can maintain a relatively even mental state in response to what might feel like a kind of relentless assault, especially if she is exhausted by broken nights into the bargain, can accept these mental 'projections' from her baby and hold onto them, making them safe for both parties. Translated into the situation of the psychoanalytic encounter, the analyst too must work towards being able to receive whatever the patient brings, taking it 'in' both as intellectual understanding and as emotional resonance, and finding a way to tolerate it so that it loses some of its sting, can be reflected upon and, where appropriate, fed back to the patient without too much damage to either party. The additional point here, central to Bion's theory but not quite conveyed by the term 'reverie', is the *active* way in which the material received from the patient is worked on. The analyst feels it, reflects on those feelings and relates them to the patient's unconscious life, and through this process transforms something felt but 'unthought' into something that can be symbolised, making it present and real.

The endurance of the analyst is central to this process; the analyst's capacity to stay 'alive' and thoughtful even under stressful psychological circumstances – when treated outrageously by a patient, say, or, perhaps more commonly, when having to listen to extremely disturbing, even potentially traumatic, material. This kind of resilience does not come easily and is usually supported by a variety of props, including the analyst's own past or ongoing analysis and supervision from another analyst who can help them make sense of what they are dealing with. The relevant term here is that of emotional 'containment' for analysts, sufficient to help them contain their patients; and for this to happen, examining the countertransference is crucial. 'What am I feeling here and how much of it is my business and how much is a reflection of my patient's feelings; and more particularly, what does it tell me about the nature and significance of those feelings?' Those are the kind of questions that might be asked by analysts of themselves and by their supervisors. The additional practical question is how these reflections can be used to support a way of being in the therapy that makes a patient feel safe enough to face difficulties they have previously shied away from. An analyst who responds to disturbance by becoming disturbed, or to trauma in a traumatised way, is not going to be much help to a patient, even if their response is in some respects a clear recognition of the patient's experience (if I am traumatised by what you tell me, it implies that I am acknowledging the reality of what you have gone through). The analyst's task is to be present in the relationship without being overwhelmed by it, to remain both in it and out of it, or on the border between inside and out, so that the relationship can be as intense as it needs to be, yet still available for careful reflection.

In the psychoanalytic movement, there has long been a debate about how 'real' analysts should be. Should they be active, telling patients about their feelings and revealing aspects of their lives that they think relevant? Interestingly, while the tendency of most modern analysts is to reveal relatively little about themselves (albeit in the knowledge that patients will pick up quite a lot and might also be able to find out a good deal from the internet and other sources), Freud and other early analysts were much less inhibited about imposing their own personalities on their work. Freud's consulting room indicated this: whereas most contemporary analytic offices are relatively bare, the better to encourage patients to fantasise about their analysts without being guided too heavily by visible personal belongings, Freud's was crowded with objects and pictures, lined with books. There was nothing neutral about it, as visitors to the Freud Museum in London can see; and Freud seems not to have been wary of telling his patients about himself or his theories or guiding them with advice.

Over the generations of analysts, a lot has changed, but strong differences persist on the question of the active involvement of the analyst. Are analysts relatively detached observers and commentators on what their patients bring to them, or does the work entail involvement in a relationship that becomes therapeutic because it allows a working through and gradual remedy of patients' disturbances? Today, analysts of the more 'relational' schools tend to see themselves as in a kind of supportively mutual relationship with their patients, which is necessary if there is to be sufficient trust and security for difficult issues to be broached. Other analysts severely disapprove of this stance. Differences in style and technique are clearly apparent here, but I am not sure they get to the heart of the matter. Whether an analyst is more or less active, more open or closed, more relaxed or formal, might not be the key issue. The important thing is to remain sane through processes of reflection and, where necessary, supervisory support, so that what is happening to the analyst *because of the patient* can be recognised and understood – allowing the analyst to endure the presence of that patient, and in turn to recognise and acknowledge what the patient is and has been going through. In this model, analysts do not hide from their feelings, but they also do not act on them, or at least not immediately. Instead, feelings are treated as real but not given the final say; they have to be felt, recognised and transmuted through thought.

Outside the analytic situation, this also holds true. In this chapter, I have been concerned with different ways of staying connected with the distress of other people without becoming traumatised oneself. This model of endurance is one that is watchful, cautious and slow, yet is by no means passive. It requires an active process of monitoring ourselves as well as the neighbour who is trusting us with their trauma; and just as that neighbour might become a little more real, a little freer, through being recognised and acknowledged, so the witness-listener becomes more real in the process of receiving, responding to and acknowledging the neighbour's testimony. In the end, of course, we are all from time to time in both roles: the one who speaks of trouble, the one who hears this and must find a way to respond. The same demands perhaps apply, even if they act in different ratios: how to create conditions in which speech can be free and hearing can be open and non-defensive; and how to respond to one another in ways that connect us, rather than perpetuating isolation. Returning to the real means making such connections without destroying ourselves in the process.

An aspect of the psychoanalytic situation that has paradoxical implications for these issues is that the setting, while highly privatised, also offers insight into the public conditions that might make endurance possible. The privatised nature of psychoanalysis almost goes without saying: it is a transaction between one person and another, usually (except in a relatively few socialised mental health settings) mediated by money, focusing on the 'inner world' of the patient and bracketing off wider social issues, even if their significance is recognised (and sometimes it is not). The advantage of this is that it allows for undistracted attention to be paid to the core issue that interests psychoanalysts – the state of the patient's unconscious life. The gravity of this should not be underestimated: especially when really distressing material is being explored, it can feel like life itself is at stake. Yet it is also clearly a practice that does not try to take account of much that operates at the social level. On the other hand, this highly refined situation demonstrates something very significant about what makes it possible to endure and respond to suffering. We can imagine this as a series of concentric circles, one inside the other. At its heart is the encounter between analyst and patient; outside this is the physical and temporal setting of the encounter – the regularity and safety of the analytic meetings and the place in which they occur. Outside this again is a set of professional requirements and systems that facilitate the analyst's work. These include personal therapy and supervision, professional support and ethical guidelines from institutions, and the material circumstances that make analysis possible, which ideally (but rarely) include the provision by society (the state) of good mental health services. The point here is that the capacity to endure is not solely a personal achievement, but one that relies on a set of facilitating social conditions.

We might say the same about the characteristics of social groups that create solidarity of the sort to allow suffering to be recognised and appeased or remedied. I have already discussed how societies can deny their implication in the damage done to their own citizens and to others, and the importance of moving towards a more ethical and truthful acknowledgement of responsibility. This is necessary in its own right, otherwise repetition of suffering, in which historical wrongs repeat into the present, becomes embedded. It is also essential for the creation of structures that support caring and the prospect of repairing damage in society.

Let me try to make this more concrete. In Kleinian psychoanalysis, there is a notion of *reparation*, the idea that a crucial component of mental health is the capacity to recognise the damage we do to ourselves and others and to find ways to make this good by acts of creative recompense. This refers to past events: damage has been done, and we need to own up to it and do something about it. But there is another component of reparation that is forward-looking: we know that we are likely to do harm, because the tensions and ambivalence in ourselves and in the world around us are such that damage will always occur. In that case, what is essential is to take this reality on board and plan for it, to develop within ourselves an ability to anticipate when and where things will go wrong and be present enough, psychologically speaking, to acknowledge and respond.

The same thing is true societally, and we have occasionally seen how it can work in practice. Perhaps the best example in relatively recent times is how, after the Second World War, a reforming Labour government was elected in the UK, clearly as a result of a widespread popular feeling that something new had to happen in the wake of the war's destruction and loss. This government introduced major changes to health, social care and education, inventing what became known as the Welfare State. I think it is reasonable to understand this huge sociopolitical event as a reparative one, in both the historically focused, responsive mode and in the future-oriented mode. In the former, it was a response to the deep damage of the war and could be framed as an act of contrition, a move to recognise the responsibility of political leadership to bind up people's wounds and ease the guilt for having caused them in the first place, however essential the battle to defeat Nazism might have been. In its future-oriented mode, the construction of the Welfare State arose from an awareness that no matter how hard we try, there will always be damage. People will fall ill; accidents will happen; inequalities and mismanagement and misdeeds will always push some people into need; repair of some kind will always be necessary. Creating a society in which these contingencies are planned for so that the reality of suffering can be witnessed rather than denied, and acted on constructively, is a form of what we can call 'proactive reparation'. We know that care will be needed and that it is society's responsibility to provide it, because so much suffering is caused by social forces themselves. This is not, of course, to say that the Welfare State was without defects, and it can also be argued that patching things up in this way can be a means of not attending to why there is so much suffering in the first place. Yet I think there is something genuinely 'care-full' in thinking this way, that a society's first priority is to create structures of care for its members, who are inevitably going to need them. And all this makes it even more painful to observe the current political attacks on care and welfare, as if they were signs only of the inadequacy or malingering of those who resort to them. A society that does not recognise the universal nature of need and of entitlement to care is one that backs away from accepting its fundamental responsibilities.

Social solidarity demands this level of political action. It is built out of an awareness of the pervasiveness of real inequality and the suffering it brings. When people bind together in groups to oppose these inequalities, they are acting in solidarity with one another and creating conditions to recognise and respond to suffering. Solidarity of this kind is also a mode of endurance, in which the presence and support of others enables us to face the pressures of dealing with entrenched social structures and often disturbing societal events. The difficulty of this is reflected in how frequently progressive social movements fail, falling apart because of their own intense dynamics and the opposition to them by vested interests. Nevertheless, the act of coming together to resist oppression and remedy suffering is a crucial one for keeping alive awareness of social reality and hence an important aspect of being real. At what we might call the 'macro-social' level, that of whole societies, the example of the Welfare State shows that it is possible for forms of social solidarity to develop that have at their base a reparative, ethical urge and that command huge popular support. After all, despite its enormous problems and failures born of chronic underfunding, the British National Health Service remains the UK's most cherished institution. We must hope, I suppose, that such social solidarity can be forged afresh without the stimulus of another world war. In other words, perhaps endurance can also be a proactive state: we know what we need, so must prepare for it, believing that the preparations are meaningful even if they are never going to be perfect in every way.

8

The Sense of Ending

Dealing with the end of a life, our own or someone else's, is probably the most profound experience we can have. Whether it is indeed our own or someone else's might not be that important; facing another's death, especially that of a loved one, is likely not only to provoke feelings of sadness and loss, but also to remind us of our own mortality. With every death, a little of ourselves dies too, and we get more in touch with the closeness of our death as we experience that of others. The circumstances obviously matter: whether the death is sudden or untimely, perhaps befalling a young person, the result of disease, accident, violence or war; or whether it is long, drawn out and painful so you wish the end would come, or slow and peaceful so that it feels reconciling and complete. Slipping away or violently truncated, brutally extended or gradually fading. These differences are important and frame experiences of accompaniment and grieving. Even at their best, they are not caught by the cliché of the 'good death' as no one knows what that is for any given individual, but they become part of the narrative that those 'left behind' might use to console themselves and make sense of their loss.

Sometimes death is denied, in stories of how someone has 'passed on' to a better life, for instance, or, less blatantly, how they have at last been freed from suffering 'here below'. The spiritual associations of these ideas give them heft even for those who are not especially religious, as if their grief or their own mortality encourages them to regress to infantile fantasies of everlasting life. When I overhear someone saying to a child that their grandparents are 'looking down on them from heaven', I cringe; but I also recognise the appeal of this, the wish to create an illusion of continuity and permanent presence. The popularity of ghost stories links with this, but there is more happening here, a form of whimsy and nostalgia, another mode of denial. We try to comfort ourselves and others through fantasies of afterlife and this impulse is easily understandable: why should the truth get in the way of feeling better? Yet if the idea of being real has any substance, this is precisely what the truth must do when what is at stake is a full encounter with the actuality of experience. By which I mean, simply, that a death is a death, and there is no turning back.

Freud was well aware of the ambivalent feelings we harbour towards death and the dead. He suggested that we are never fully reconciled to the idea that the dead will lie still, but somehow expect them to return. This can be a pleasant hope for some people, as when a dead parent is thought to be guiding them, but Freud also noted how disturbing it is, how 'the primitive fear of the dead is still so strong within us and always ready to come to the surface on any provocation'.[1] He also noted that it is not easy to fully accept the fact of our own mortality, that we find ways to avoid this knowledge, projecting it into the future and also taking refuge in various forms of narcissism. Most of us hope to leave a legacy, which includes the belief that our children will carry us onwards within them, indirectly extending our life. Yet Freud also invented the idea of a Death Drive that operates as part of what we might call human nature, which is to say, as an inborn tendency to self-abolition, an impulse to return to the 'inorganic', to rest. While later in his thinking Freud emphasised the destructiveness of the Death Drive and its link with aggression, in its earliest formulation in his 1920 book, *Beyond the Pleasure Principle*, the Death Drive is a tendency towards quiescence, a kind of 'nirvana principle', as Freud terms it; and is also the backdrop against which life is played out.[2] 'Freud writes:

For a long time, living substance was thus being constantly created afresh and easily dying, till decisive external influences altered in such a way as to oblige the still surviving substance to diverge ever more widely from its original course of life and to make ever more complicated détours before reaching its aim of death.[3]

It is these 'circuitous paths to death' that we mistakenly classify as the phenomena of life. Actually, they are exactly a detour, something that takes us away from the straight line from the disturbance caused by birth to the relief of extinction and rest, but nevertheless always brings us back to the same place. The Death Drive produces an unconscious wish to stop, to rest, against which all our liveliness is a defence.

Am I the only person who finds this idea, that we might long to return to sleep, attractive and repellent at the same time? Does it make sense to think that people might have an unconscious wish for death? That we busy ourselves with life, invest in our relationships, seek pleasure, fight off illness and abhor murder and suicide, yet all the time have something operating inside us that is secretly pursuing the opposite?

It sounds crazy. It is certainly counterintuitive. But as with much that is like that, it is perhaps wise not to write it off too quickly, but rather to try to understand what is being intimated by this idea. For one thing, we might argue that the very strong injunctions against murder and suicide in most religious and moral systems suggest that there is a tendency *towards* them that must be opposed. After all, it would surely not be necessary to invoke such powerful sanctions were it not that without them there might be unconstrained self- and other-killing. Wars certainly suggest this, and it is no accident that Freud's invention of the Death Drive came in the immediate aftermath of the First World War, where evidence of the destructiveness and deathliness of 'civilised' society was undeniable. Freud well understood that civilisation was organised on the basis of force, that it did not represent an abolition of violence but rather was the attempt by the state to monopolise such violence; this too was part of his evidence for the pervasiveness of the Death Drive. But more to the point, if death stalks us from inside ourselves, then the capacity to hold onto life is terrifyingly precarious and a great deal of psychic energy will need to go into this and into denying the reality of the death that hovers so closely over us all the time.

This is almost certainly overstated. It makes little sense to assume that deathliness is the primary human motive and that life is just a detour from it. Nevertheless, the complexity of our relationship with death is undeniable, and the tendency to hide from its reality very visible. We comfort others with assurances that they will recover from illness; sometimes we even hide the truth of their condition from them; and while we might do whatever we can to protect ourselves, it seems almost impossible to fully imagine our own demise. What will I be after my death? Even the idea of 'nothing', if we can embrace it, seems misleading, because this kind of 'nothing' is so often imagined as a *something*, for example absorption into the universe or 'back' into the earth, or into the winds, or scattered everywhere. This kind of nothing is not really nothing at all, but nothing made positive; a truly *negative* nothing, a full state of nonexistence, is very hard to come to terms with. Others survive in our memories, and we might even sense their continuing presence; we hope and unconsciously believe that the same will be true for us. This is another reason why ghosts are comforting as well as potentially disturbing: they confirm the fantasy that something of us – perhaps our essence – will remain alive.

The title of a book by the American philosopher Alphonso Lingis speaks to the question of what it means to face death. *The Community of Those Who Have Nothing in Common* is a precise but also double-edged commentary on what is involved in staying with someone who is dying, continuing to be a presence in their life even as they leave it, and even if they seem unaware of that presence.[4] At such moments, the living have *nothing in common* with them – they are on their own, and have to make whatever journey they are on all by themselves, crossing the threshold into nothingness while we stay on the side of life. At this point, the 'community' being referred to is the accompanying community, witnesses and watchers-over, who allow the death to happen in the most supportive circumstances we can manage. Yet we also have *nothing* in common in the sense that everyone, indeed all living creatures, will inhabit the 'nothing' that death brings and – especially if Freud is right, though this is not exactly a point that Lingis makes – we harbour that knowledge of 'nothing' inside us. *Nothing*, in this reading, is a possession or presence that we share with others; it is a *positive* entity built out of a pure negation: we all have in common this 'nothing', whether we welcome or fail to acknowledge it.

Lingis expresses this rather wonderfully, in evocative if complex language. Writing about the experience of being in the presence of someone who is dying, he describes how some kinds of communion do not rest on the exchange of meaning through the transmission of messages in verbal form, through a conversational exchange, as this is often impossible when someone is close to death. Rather, there are situations in which it is the 'mere' capacity to stay with the dying person that communicates solidarity and care and that also insists on how shared our experiences can be, as we are all rooted in what Lingis (following Emmanuel Levinas) calls the 'elemental'. This elemental is what we share with each other, the ground of our being; it acknowledges that the 'nothing' of death is precisely what links us, however different we might take ourselves to be from one another. Lingis writes that this kind of encounter depends not on reaching agreement between people who are similar but on drawing on the other's existence in all its *alien* form, so that we mark out the vista of a world that is not the same as our own yet which still links us together. At base, there is a human connection founded on the universality of death. Here is a characteristic passage from his book:

> We communicate to one another the light our eyes know, the ground that sustains our postures, and the air and the warmth with which we speak. We face one another as condensations of earth, light, air, and warmth, and orient one another in the elemental in a primary communication. We appeal to the others to help us be at home in the alien elements into which we stray: in the drifting and nameless light and warmth of infancy, in the nocturnal depths of the erotic, and in the domain of dying where rational discourse has no longer anything to say.[5]

It is worth noticing here that Lingis does not regard the pattern of connection around dying as unique, but rather as a particular iteration of the stance (which I have been calling 'endurance') that allows people to feel present with one another at various points in their lives. Lingis refers to these points in terms of what is 'alien' as well as 'elemental', by which he seems to mean those states and situations that are particularly difficult to communicate in words (though he has a good go at it). What connects 'the drifting and nameless light and warmth of infancy', 'the nocturnal depths of the erotic' and 'the domain of dying'? These are moments of immersion in something not easy to comprehend, perhaps also of great privacy, in which the presence of a concerned and sensitive witness can 'help us be at home'. It is the breathing, listening, sharing being-with that such a witness can offer that links people together, without the necessity for 'rational discourse'. We hear the noise of the other person, their breathing and murmuring, and respond with our own being, without seeking to make meaning out of it but merely to register it as a kind of nameless, yet human, cry.

This might all sound overly poetic and idealistic, and of course it is aspirational rather than a straightforward description of what happens between people when one of them is dying. We might like things to be like this; sometimes they are, and sometimes not. It also overlooks some of the differences that surround the distinct conditions of death, the scant opportunities for accompanying when a death is sudden, such as after a catastrophic bodily event or in a fatal accident, or when it is homicidal, whether in war or on the streets or in a hate-filled home. The *inequality* of death is striking and demands to be struggled against – how some people's lives are more 'grievable' than others, how death comes too soon, too regularly in some communities compared to more privileged ones. Indeed, sudden death can become a norm in situations of – usually human-induced – precarity, because of violence, subjection to oppression, callousness and neglect. Such circumstances can leave survivors shocked and bereft, not only of the deceased but of what we might call their own relationship to that person's death.

Murder does this, as do other situations in which people perish either suddenly and unjustifiably, or alone. During the Covid pandemic, when so many died in isolation, there was a quite widely acknowledged sense that people had been 'robbed' of the proper experience of death. This had various aspects. It referred in part to the lonely experience of the dying themselves, often on breathing-machines in hospital, their closest contact being with the technology and the masked and shielded medical staff who, however sympathetic and caring they might have been, were inevitably distanced by the exigencies of the pandemic. But it also referred to the experience of those to whom the dying person mattered, their friends and family, whose monitoring of the death could only be remote, mainly through medical reports, and whose ritualised grieving in funerals, wakes and shivas was abruptly cut short. Not being able to get to the bedside of a dying parent; separated from a spouse; unable to visit a close friend or other loved one – this was a form of robbery, in which people sometimes came to realise that they treat the sharing of death as a duty but also as a kind of *entitlement*. This loss of death, indeed, shows that accompanying another's dying has the power to be life-enhancing, not as a moment of triumph ('I at least survive' or even, hatefully, 'I have survived you') but as an important moment of grounding and connection.

Perhaps 'entitlement' is the wrong term here, and 'privilege' would be better. Still, the sense during the pandemic of being robbed of something that we might have expected to have been gifted to us was real and apparently widespread, leading people to feel that the grounding of shared experience had been left too shallow and in many cases that the loss of their loved one could not be made to feel quite real. We want to be there, to say goodbye for our own sake as well as for the dying person; we want to experience the completion of a life and know that we have accompanied it to the very border of being. Think how important it can feel to be present for the actual moment of death, partly out of a sense that this will support the dying person to the last, making the singularity of dying as far as possible a shared moment in which the person is not left alone. And think too about how often it seems to be the case that someone dies just after the witness has left the room, as if the dying person feels responsible for the well-being of the watchers and does not want to cause them distress.

There is a touching story about this from the Talmud, concerning a great rabbi (Rabbi Yehuda Ha-Nasi) who was gravely ill. Other rabbis came to pray for his recovery and stayed with him all the time. At first his maid joined in with the prayers but, realising that his suffering was too much and that he needed to be released from it, she also understood that this could not happen while he was surrounded by so many well-wishers. So she went onto the roof of the building, taking with her a jug which she then noisily smashed. The rabbis were startled and distracted from their prayers, and at that moment Rabbi Yehuda's soul was freed from his broken body and could escape, as it needed to, into death.[6] Watching over someone as they leave us is a hard task, but at some point the leaving is essential and the watching-over becomes a matter of allowing the way to open up.

There are some significant points arising from this. It is no secret that the act of attending to a dying person, hard as it may be, is often important for the witnesses, perhaps even more than for the dying person themselves. It is a duty and a responsibility, and many people treat it as such. It roots the dying person in a community at their moment of greatest loneliness, acknowledging their continuing significance and their right to be considered a person, even if their awareness of what is happening is poor. For the witnesses, it has the power to make the death real, because the connection with the person's passing is immediate; this is why the Covid restrictions were so damaging (which is not to say they were unnecessary, a separate debate) and why it is so hard to come to terms with a death where someone has disappeared, their body left unrecovered and their fate sometimes unknown. We often need a *place* to allow us to deal with such things. If we have not been present at the death, we need to be able to visit its site, or at the very least – often crucially – the place of burial or of the scattering of ashes. Without these physical connections, death is too abstract and loss too distant and unresolved. This is a recipe for melancholia.

More even than this, there is something we might imagine about the profound impact of accompanying a person in their dying process, testified to by countless relatives and others who have taken on this task, perhaps as a duty at first, and then experienced it as a privilege. This is not because the dying are always haloed by a new wisdom, or by the exceptional nature of their physical state, which might be hoped to be sublime but is more often marked by loss of dignity, pain and suffering and, at best, gradually increasing unconsciousness. It is rather that the act of presence demanded by the situation, the kind of being-with evoked by Lingis and, however idealised it might seem, enacted daily across the world, intensifies the witness's experience of life. Being in the presence of death, neither shying away from it nor disintegrating in the face of it, watchfully awaiting the end in solidarity with the dying person, is also a way to deepen our appreciation of the significance of human contact and consequently of the human itself. How might we steel ourselves to manage this? Perhaps a type of relaxation is required, in which, just as the dying person has eventually to set aside their demand on life, so the witness must at some point relinquish the desire to hold the person back, to keep up their struggle, to save them. This is not of course to suggest that nothing should be done to promote a sick person's recovery. It is merely to say that we need to work towards a recognition of when that stage has passed and what matters is to be in a kind of communion with the dying person as they go through their process, rather than trying beyond reasonable hope to prevent it. Relaxing our desire to make things better, possibly also our own fear of loss and death; not necessarily embracing it but tolerating it; these are necessary for letting someone go. They are also potentially enriching. Touched by the truthfulness of death, there is a chance that we might deepen our awareness of the reality of life.

'Rage, rage against the dying of the light', runs the refrain of Dylan Thomas's poem, 'Do not go gentle into that good night'.[7] If we need to accept the death of others, how might we approach our own? Should we rage or 'go gentle' – the rejected alternative Thomas gives? And what exactly might either of these options involve?

In the poem, 'raging' is on the side of life while going gently is to give up, to fail to assert ourselves against the 'good night' that calls us. It is worth noting, however, that the night of death is still marked as 'good'. This 'good' has the sense that death is seductive, much as in Freud's Death Drive. It calls to us as a space of rest ('goodnight') and an end to trouble, an enveloping darkness that will offer some comfort. It is precisely this mollifying, mortifying goodness that Thomas wants his father (the subject of the last stanza) to resist; he wants also to call his father back into a relationship with him, something intense and ambivalent. His entreaty to his father is to 'Curse, bless, me now with your fierce tears, I pray,' the ferocious commas after 'curse' and 'bless' forcing the reader, forcing his father, to place weight on each of the words. Maybe intentionally, the echo here is of the biblical patriarch Jacob, whose deathbed speech to his twelve sons is indeed a mixture of cursing and blessing and relentlessly dissecting their personalities. Such deathbed cursing, such ill temper, testifies to the power of speech that doubles as an indication of the intensity of a life fully lived.

It also has echoes of the literary critic Edward Said's identification of a 'late style' in some great creative figures, a late style that he strove to emulate as he approached, knowingly, his own death from cancer. Late style, according to Said, is the very opposite of the fantasy of a contented old age in which we aspire to die at peace with ourselves and the world, summing up our achievements, integrating them, making sense of life as a whole. Creative people, Said argues, often do the *reverse* of this. In their old age, when they are revered and looked to for wisdom and solace, they turn their backs on what they have done before, or at least challenge and subvert it; and they do so with irritation, intolerant of those who would wrap them up for a tidy death. Beethoven is Said's favoured example, but in his little book *Freud and the Non-European* he embraces Freud too:

> In Beethoven's case and in Freud's ... the intellectual trajectory conveyed by the late work is intransigence and a sort of irascible transgressiveness, as if the author was expected to settle down into harmonious composure, as befits a person at the end of his

life, but preferred instead to be difficult, and to bristle with all sorts of new ideas and provocations.[8]

Said is writing specifically about Freud's last completed work, *Moses and Monotheism*, which was published in 1939, the year of Freud's death. Said goes on:

> Above all, late style's effect on the reader or listener is alienating – that is to say, Freud and Beethoven present material that is of pressing concern to them with scant regard for satisfying, much less placating, the reader's need for closure. Other books by Freud were written with a didactic or pedagogic aim in mind: *Moses and Monotheism* is not. Reading the treatise, we feel that Freud wishes us to understand that there are other issues at stake here – other, more pressing problems to expose than ones whose solution might be comforting, or provide a sort of resting-place.[9]

Do not go gentle, then; cultivate irascibility, overturn the assumptions that have governed our own previous work, offer no closure. Said celebrates this as an indication of the liveliness of an old mind, its refusal to face death with false consolation or even perhaps to take note of death at all, but rather to press on with life's urgent tasks, the 'more pressing problems', creating new 'provocations' and, simply, becoming the most difficult version of itself. The 'grumpy old man' (Said's exemplars of late style are men, but one can imagine women too) is a stereotype that relates old age to narrowness and complaint, but here the grumpiness is a creative resistance to going quietly, a great refusal to tie things together – as if a life is ever complete, as if the dying person can be conveniently tidied away. I recall that when my own father died, my sister and I went to the residential home in which he had lived for the last few months of his life, to clear out his room. It took us about an hour and a half. This was too quick, much too quick. Too quick because a life should not be tidied up so speedily and with such ease. I took home a chair, a few books and my father's music collection;

my sister took some other things, and we gave the rest away. It was orderly and simple; my father owned little, and because he had moved out of his flat and we had cleared it already, there was not much else to do. I still feel uncomfortable with this. A full life ought to leave a lot of unfinished business behind; it ought to be complicated and time-consuming to resolve; there should be a mess that needs to be untangled, no matter how much work it makes for those who must deal with it.

Freud, weak and ill in the last years of his life, combined both elements of elderly grumpiness. Faced with the Nazis after the *Anschluss*, when hundreds of Jews and others committed suicide in Vienna, Freud's daughter Anna asked her father, 'Wouldn't it be better if we all killed ourselves?' To which Freud acerbically replied, 'Why? Because they would like us to?' As Freud's biographer Peter Gay comments:

> He might grumble that the game was not worth the candle and talk with longing for the curtain to fall, but he was not about to blow out the candle, or leave the stage, at the convenience of the enemy. The defiant mood that dominated so much of Freud's life was still stirring in him. If he had to go, he would go on his own conditions.[10]

This was Freud in resistant mood, unwilling to be mastered; and this mood carried over into his last works. There would be no reconciliation with Nazism, with his fate, with his own Jewish people (who, in *Moses and Monotheism*, he 'deprived' of their greatest hero by making Moses an Egyptian), or with his own psychoanalytic ideas. We might read this in its generality: for those used to acting on their desires, including intellectual and creative ones, there is always something missing, something to be chased after, making it impossible to arrive quietly at that good night.

Yet if intransigence is to be celebrated as a hostile, resistant approach to dying, what about acceptance, going quietly? Is that really such a failure, a kind of suicide that allows the Death

Drive, the wish for passivity and peace, to triumph over the drive for life? Is it only for those of us who cannot sustain our capacity for creative thought until the end, cannot 'curse, bless' in the way that Thomas wishes and have no late style to call upon? Or can it also be a way of moving past the agitation of resistance towards an encounter that is more open and, in that sense, more geared to the truth – after all, we are talking about dying – and so more powerfully real?

Clearly, a case can be made for late style, for staring death in the face and insisting on life until the final, irresistible moment. Yet that moment will come. Freud achieved what has long been regarded as an exemplary death for himself, living on until the pain and weakness from his cancer was too much. Reputedly, he then said to his doctor Max Schur: 'You remember our "contract" not to leave me in the lurch when the time had come; now it is nothing but torture and makes no sense.'[11] This moved Schur (or possibly Freud's daughter Anna) to implement what might now be called 'assisted dying', giving Freud a strong enough dose of morphine to ease him into death. So even for Freud, arguing with everyone until the last moment, death came as a recognition of reality and was embraced actively; he went gently, but he also went knowingly and without illusion.

Not everyone can manage this, but should we be judgemental about that? As with most things, there are surely different ways of going about departing the world in a manner that enhances both the life of the dying person and of those around them, and much depends on the circumstances of end-of-life care and social support, which are all too often inadequate. The path of resistance is a powerful one, though not necessarily easy for anyone; it demonstrates a kind of demanding heroism. As Said remarks, it implies a decision to be 'difficult' and 'intransigent', which in situations where care is needed can be a recipe for disaster. We might admire the force of someone's will without enjoying being subjected to it. More to the point, this kind of irascibility can be creative, but it can also be a way of not recognising what is happening and instead projecting anger and fear outwards, so that others suffer. At times, another path might beckon, closer perhaps to the idea of endurance that I have been working with in this book. That is to say, much as I admire the *resistance* to fading away, I can also admire the alternative of going gently, if it involves facing death accurately, not necessarily welcoming it, but seeing it as part of life.

There are people who gradually relinquish life, saying their farewells, divesting themselves of possessions, coming to terms with past losses, resolving or at least acknowledging and giving up grievances, turning their face to the wall. They go quietly, as if they do not want to trouble others too much; their deaths are grieved but also respected as something complete. Such quiet deaths have a great deal of dignity about them. They are also difficult to construct. How do we face this 'dying of the light' peacefully, when so much is unknown about it and when most of what we do is aimed at preserving our lives?

Religious people might find it easier, since most believe that they are passing 'on' rather than 'away'; yet even this may not completely remove the suffering and agitation as they approach the limit of their lives. Still, I have seen this in practice: someone who, despite being in considerable physical pain, could give himself up, could say in his last days that he had 'never felt so completely in God's hands', and could approach the end (too soon in his case, dying early of cancer) without rancour or blame, connecting with loved ones with increased intimacy and without complaint. This felt like a holy death and drew deep respect, even from those who could not share his intense religious faith. Most of us, indeed, wished we could.

But for the rest of us … For some, the process of giving up is not so much a matter of calm acceptance but of despair, because there seems nothing left to live for – the pain or infirmity is too great, the sense of pointlessness too demoralising. 'I have had enough' is the sentiment behind acceptance of this kind. The act of dying is performed with a kind of impatience, as it is by some others for whom it is the last achievement of their life, something to be got over quickly and efficiently. Once again, this is not to denigrate these feelings; all approaches to death deserve respect, everyone finds their own way if they can. If it is true that, as Freud argued, 'the aim of all life is death' and that the task of life is not to avoid death but to find, each one of us, our own way towards it, then all these different ways of doing death need acknowledgement.[12] No one can be judged, not even – certainly not – suicides, despite the turmoil they usually leave behind.

That said, perhaps it is worth going back to a crucial element of the Death Drive, that it represents a *return* to something already partly known, which while wholly new can also seem familiar, at times giving it an uncanny resonance but also allowing us to fantasise about death as a kind of peaceful return to where we belong. For Freud, drawing on what is now an outdated version of nineteenth-century neurology, the biological drives were aimed at reducing tension within the individual 'organism'. Writ large, this suggested that the drives would be satisfied when the organism was set at rest. The 'conservatism' of the drives is such as to programme the organism towards return in the sense of seeking an earlier state of affairs; rest is something that comes when we get back to that state preceding any disruption, any need to do anything at all. So the 'circuitous paths' that Freud mentions in the quote given near the start of this chapter are paths *home*; death is a familiar place.

This sounds like a fantasy as wayward as the fantasy of heaven. Despite the apparent bleakness of the idea of the Death Drive, it can become a consolation that is not all that different from the consolation of faith: we return whence we came, back into the bosom of God, or the universe, or what Freud calls the 'inorganic'. Once again, I want to emphasise that I am not criticising these 'illusions'; as Freud noted in his book on religion, they serve important psychological functions in helping people manage the demands and threats of life.[13] Without them, we face these threats naked. However, again as Freud argued, they might also be seen as a defence against reality, or more fully, a denial of the truth of our experience. If we are pursuing this truth, if we want genuinely not to look away from what is in front of us, we might need a more belligerent attitude towards death: that it is not so much a return – except in the sense that nonbeing precedes conception and follows death – as it is a shift into nothingness. Once consciousness is extinguished, nothing else remains; this could be called 'rest', but it is not really that, as there is no one left to experience it. Fantasies of continuity or of return might help us imagine this state without despairing, but this is not the same as really acknowledging it. The nothingness of death is a presence, as noted earlier, but it is not experienced as such, or as anything at all.

What we endure is not death, but the process of dying. As with my other uses of the term 'endurance', I am trying to conjure here a sense of being with someone at a time and in a condition where what matters most is not what is said or done, but what is shared. In this case, the 'someone' might be those who are gathered round to accompany the dying person, as many of us hope will be the case when we die. Acknowledging their presence, accepting the gift of their thoughtfulness and love, can be part of a process of generous relinquishment. But this 'someone' is also the self, that complex array of consciousness and unconscious wishes and desires that we have inhabited for all our life. Under some circumstances, endurance might involve an active process of reflection, thinking back over the past and reconciling ourselves with it. More often, endurance is not so much an act as a *stance*, a way of becoming real that does not depend on being able to articulate something or on putting our affairs in order but is more like a position of nonjudgemental observation. 'This is happening now and here I am.' We might call this a practice of *disenchantment*, as the necessary illusions that preserve us in life are gradually given up – illusions of permanence, of invulnerability, of how we will always be protected against the threats that lurk in the world. As such, it is part of a larger process of making-real in which what comes to the fore is recognition of the fragility of life and the fundamental, unquestionable vulnerability of every living being. This is what we share and what is genuinely a kind of return, or perhaps better a reminder of what has been true all along: that vulnerability and insecurity are fundamental to human life. The big truth of dying is not that we become visibly frail and cannot survive any longer, though this may be at some point the case, but that we have always been so, however much we might have fought against that realisation. This is certainly a kind of 'return' to the precariousness of infancy; it is also what links us to each other and what might lead us to have compassion on ourselves. The dying process, when it can be experienced fully, is one in which the things that matter become narrowed but also deepened and when the bonds that link us to others and to ourselves, in being given up, can also be lovingly mourned.

Being real involves a truthful engagement with experience that does not deny anything and that as far as possible avoids illusion and self-deceit. This is of course a state of mind that is never fully achievable, as both psychoanalysis and everyday experience show. We cannot imagine what follows death, nor can we prescribe for the pain and confusion that so often surrounds the process of dying. The circumstances may not allow it. All too often, people are not given the luxury of the good death they may crave, but are ejected from life, sometimes in a moment of violence, sometimes through accidents or rapid illnesses, sometimes simply because of the lack of accessible, high-quality end of life care. We are not in control, however much we might wish to be.

But where dying is a more gradual process, we have certain options: whether to rebel or to make peace with it, both choices requiring acceptance of what is happening. In the end, endurance is a matter of accepting reality so that it is neither repudiated nor allowed to be traumatising. Staying with a person, accompanying them on their way, recognising them for what they bring and acknowledging responsibility towards them – these are the conditions of endurance when relating to other people, but also to ourselves. We might choose to be truculent and irascible or accepting, perhaps mournful, more gradually divesting ourselves of our fears and ambitions; either way, what matters is the recognition that a finality is on the near horizon and cannot be wished away. Being real means acknowledging the reality of ending, whether it is the smaller endings we have throughout life or the large, final one. Being real involves a deep awareness and acceptance of our vulnerability and a willingness to look directly at the fragility of our life.

At this point, we are faced again with one of the underpinnings of endurance: that it acknowledges the complexity of life and of the feelings that accompany it – what I described early on in this book as 'loving in different directions at once'. There is nothing straightforward about this, which is partly why so much of this chapter has been aspirational, written in the knowledge that reality is much messier than I have allowed and that the pulls and pushes on people from others and from their own impulses are confusing, contradictory and hard to adjudicate. Loving in more than one direction means being exposed to differences and, at times, risking being torn apart by contradictory desires. Yet this is the nature of truth: it is not indivisible, because there are many truths; but it is also not relativistic, so that we can be satisfied with any truth claim, whether religious, political or intellectual. Being real means in large part acknowledging the complexity of truth in a world made up of contradictory parts and understanding the limits of what we can grasp, because we inhabit bodies and consciousnesses that are themselves erratically unstable, fragile and vulnerable. It also involves doing what we can with what we have, honestly and in recognition of the ways in which we try to protect ourselves. Looking squarely at this, in death as in life, is the only conceivable route towards deepening our sense of ourselves as real. It is the only ethical approach, because it refuses to accept lies, distortions and illusory consolations; and it recognises that while attachments and loves pull us all over the place, they are also what root us in who we might be.

Notes

Preface

1 E. M. Forster, *Howards End*, Penguin, 1971 (1910).

1. Being Real

1 A. M. Turing, 'Computing Machinery and Intelligence', *Mind* 49 (1950), 433–60.
2 Joyita Raksit, 'Subjection in the Human:Non-human Encounter Tweets and Code', unpublished MA dissertation, Birkbeck, University of London, 2020.
3 J. Weizenbaum, 'ELIZA– A Computer Program for the Study of Natural Language Communication between Man and Machine', *Communications of the ACM* 9 (1966), 36–45.
4 Eoin Fullam, 'The Social Life of Mental Health Chatbots', PhD thesis, Birkbeck, University of London, 2024.
5 John Searle, 'Minds, Brains and Programs', *Behavioral and Brain Sciences* 3 (1980), 417–57.
6 D. Cole, 'The Chinese Room Argument', in E. Zalta and U. Nodelman, eds, *The Stanford Encyclopedia of Philosophy*, Winter 2024 edn, plato.stanford.edu.
7 Daniel Miller, *Tales from Facebook*, Polity, 2011.
8 Victor Tausk, 'On the Origin of the "Influencing Machine" in Schizophrenia', *Psychoanalytic Quarterly* 2 (1933), 519–56.
9 Ibid., 521.
10 Daniel Pick, *Brainwashed: A New History of Thought Control*, Wellcome Collection, 2022.
11 Irving L. Janis, *Groupthink: Psychological Studies of Policy Decisions and Fiascoes*, Cengage Learning, 1982.
12 *American Psycho*, directed by Mary Harron, Lionsgate, 2000.
13 Christopher Lasch, *The Culture of Narcissism*, Abacus, 1979.
14 Ibid., 82.
15 Ibid., 97.
16 Nikolay Mintchev and Henrietta L. Moore, 'Brexit's Identity

Politics and the Question of Subjectivity', *Psychoanalysis, Culture and Society* 24 (2019), 452–72.
17 Judith Butler, *The Psychic Life of Power*, Stanford University Press, 1997, 140.
18 Sigmund Freud, 'Mourning and Melancholia', in *The Standard Edition of the Complete Psychological Works of Sigmund Freud*, vol. 14, *(1914–1916): On the History of the Psycho-Analytic Movement, Papers on Metapsychology and Other Works*, ed. and trans. James Strachey, Hogarth Press, 1957, 237–58.
19 D. W. Winnicott, *The Maturational Processes and the Facilitating Environment: Studies in the Theory of Emotional Development*, Hogarth Press, 1965.
20 Emmanuel Levinas, *Entre Nous: On Thinking of the Other*, Athlone, 1991.
21 D. W. Winnicott, 'The Use of an Object', *International Journal of Psychoanalysis* 50, no. 4 (1969), 711–16.
22 Sigmund Freud, 'Civilization and Its Discontents', in *The Standard Edition of the Complete Psychological Works of Sigmund Freud*, vol. 21, *(1927–1931): The Future of an Illusion, Civilization and Its Discontents, and Other Works*, ed. and trans. James Strachey, Hogarth Press, 1961, 57–146.
23 Rebecca Goldstein, 'Looking Back at Lot's Wife', *Commentary*, September 1992, 37–41.
24 Ibid., 39.
25 Ibid.
26 Ibid., 41.

2. Recovering Childhood

1 John Bowlby, *Attachment and Loss*, vol. 1, *Attachment*, Hogarth Press, 1969.
2 M. D. Ainsworth and B. A. Wittig, 'Attachment and Exploratory Behavior of One-Year-Olds in a Strange Situation', in B. M. Foss (ed.), *Determinants of Infant Behavior*, Methuen, 1969.
3 Peter Fonagy, 'The Mentalization-Focused Approach to Social Development', in Fredric N. Busch (ed.), *Mentalization: Theoretical Considerations, Research Findings, and Clinical Implications*, Analytic Press, 2008, 3–56.
4 D. W. Winnicott, 'The Capacity to Be Alone', *International Journal of Psychoanalysis* 39 (1958), 416–20.
5 S. Woodhouse, A. Miah, and M. Rutter, 'A New Look at the Supposed Risks of Early Institutional Rearing', *Psychological Medicine* 48 (2017), 1–10.

6 Salvador Minuchin, *Families and Family Therapy*, Harvard University Press, 1974.
7 André Green, 'The Dead Mother', in *On Private Madness*, Hogarth Press, 1986, 142–73.
8 Alessandra Lemma, *Transgender Identities: A Contemporary Introduction*, Routledge, 2022.
9 Ibid., 63.
10 Hilary Cass, *Independent Review of Gender Identity Services for Children and Young People: Final Report*, Cass Review, 2024.
11 Lemma, *Transgender Identities*.
12 Ibid., 58.
13 A. Freud and S. Dann, 'An Experiment in Group Upbringing', *Psychoanalytic Study of the Child* 6 (1951), 127–68.
14 Ibid., 127–8.
15 Ibid., 129–30.
16 Ibid., 130.
17 Ibid., 131.
18 Ibid., 133–4.
19 E. Young-Bruehl, *Anna Freud: A Biography*, Yale University Press, 1988, 322.

3. Hate

1 Melanie Klein, 'Envy and Gratitude', in *Envy and Gratitude and Other Works, 1946–1963*, Delta, 1975.
2 Jay R. Greenberg and Stephen A. Mitchell, *Object Relations in Psychoanalytic Theory*, Harvard University Press, 1983.
3 G. Orwell, *Nineteen Eighty-Four*, Penguin, 2000 (1949), 15.
4 Peter Gay, *Freud: A Life for Our Time*, Dent, 1988, 619.
5 Ibid., 621.
6 Mary Fulbrook, *Bystander Society: Conformity and Complicity in Nazi Germany and the Holocaust*, Oxford University Press, 2023.
7 Sigmund Freud, 'Civilization and Its Discontents', in *The Standard Edition of the Complete Psychological Works of Sigmund Freud*, vol. 21, *(1927–1931): The Future of an Illusion, Civilization and Its Discontents, and Other Works*, ed. and trans. James Strachey, Hogarth Press, 1961, 57–146.
8 Derek Hook, 'Racism and Jouissance: Evaluating the "Racism as (the Theft of) Enjoyment" Hypothesis', *Psychoanalysis, Culture and Society* 23 (2018), 244–66.
9 Judith Butler, *The Force of Nonviolence: An Etho-political Bind*, Verso, 2020.

10 Emmanuel Levinas, *Ethics and Infinity: Conversations with Philippe Nemo*, Duquesne University Press, 1985, 95.
11 Judith Butler, *Precarious Life: The Powers of Mourning and Violence*, Verso, 2004, 34.
12 Fulbrook, *Bystander Society*, 117.
13 Butler, *The Force of Nonviolence*.
14 Emmanuel Levinas, *Entre Nous: On Thinking of the Other*, Athlone, 1991.
15 Pumla Gobodo-Madikizela, *What Does It Mean to Be Human in the Aftermath of Historical Trauma? Re-envisioning the Sunflower and Why Hannah Arendt Was Wrong*, Nordic Africa Institute and Uppsala University, 2016, 8.
16 Ibid.
17 Ibid., 23.
18 Judith Butler, *Parting Ways: Jewishness and the Critique of Zionism*, Columbia University Press, 2012.

4. Defending Ourselves against Reality

1 Sándor Ferenczi, 'Confusion of Tongues between the Adults and the Child – The Language of Tenderness and of Passion', *International Journal of Psychoanalysis* 30 (1949), 225–30.
2 Ibid., 228. Italics in original.
3 Ibid., 228.
4 Sigmund Freud, 'The Interpretation of Dreams', in *The Standard Edition of the Complete Psychological Works of Sigmund Freud*, vol. 4, *(1900): The Interpretation of Dreams (First Part)*, ed. and trans. James Strachey, Hogarth Press, 1953, ix–627.
5 Ibid., 121n1.
6 Ibid., 107. Italics in original.
7 Ibid., 119.
8 David Rieff, *In Praise of Forgetting: Historical Memory and Its Ironies*, Yale University Press, 2016.
9 Christina Sharpe, *In the Wake: On Blackness and Being*, Duke University Press, 2016.
10 Yoself Hayim Yerushalmi, *Zachor: Jewish History and Jewish Memory*, University of Washington Press, 1989.
11 Roger Luckhurst, *The Trauma Question*, Routledge, 2008.
12 Didier Fassin and Richard Rechtman, *The Empire of Trauma: An Inquiry into the Condition of Victimhood*, Princeton University Press, 2009, 36.
13 Ibid., 51.
14 Pat Barker, *The Regeneration Trilogy*, Penguin, 2014.

15 Dagmar Herzog, *Cold War Freud: Psychoanalysis in an Age of Catastrophes*, Cambridge University Press, 2017.
16 Thomas Trezise, *Witnessing Witnessing: On the Reception of Holocaust Survivor Testimony*, Fordham University Press, 2013, 211.
17 Nicolas Abraham and Maria Torok, *The Shell and the Kernel: Renewals of Psychoanalysis*, ed. and trans. Nicholas T. Rand, University of Chicago Press, 1994.
18 Stephen Frosh, *Those Who Come After*, Palgrave, 2019.
19 Eva Hoffman, *After Such Knowledge: A Meditation on the Aftermath of the Holocaust*, Vintage, 2005, 66.
20 Marianne Hirsch, *The Generation of Postmemory: Writing and Visual Culture after the Holocaust*, Columbia University Press, 2012.
21 Primo Levi, *If This Is a Man/The Truce*, Penguin, 1987.
22 Primo Levi, *The Drowned and the Saved*, Abacus, 1988.
23 Ferenczi, 'Confusion of Tongues'.
24 Binjamin Wilkomirski, *Fragments: Memories of a Wartime Childhood*, Picador, 1996.
25 Hoffman, *After Such Knowledge*, 70.
26 D. W. Winnicott, 'The Use of an Object', *International Journal of Psychoanalysis* 50, no. 4 (1969), 711–16.

5. Ghosts and Ancestors

1 Luis Barrucho, 'Brazilian Vote-Pledge Stirs Memories of Military Rule', BBC, 21 April 2016, bbc.co.uk.
2 'Psicanálise e Contexto Social no Brasil: Fluxos Transnacionais, Impacto Cultural e Regime Autoritário', Projeto FAPESP 2015/11244-3. My co-researcher was Professor Belinda Mandelbaum of the University of São Paulo.
3 Sigmund Freud, 'The "Uncanny"', in *The Standard Edition of the Complete Psychological Works of Sigmund Freud*, vol. 17, *(1917–1919): An Infantile Neurosis and Other Works*, ed. and trans. James Strachey, Hogarth Press, 1955, 217–56.
4 Sigmund Freud, 'The Ego and the Id', in *The Standard Edition of the Complete Psychological Works of Sigmund Freud*, vol. 19, *(1923–1925): The Ego and the Id and Other Works*, Hogarth Press, 1961, 28.
5 Sigmund Freud, 'Mourning and Melancholia', in *The Standard Edition of the Complete Psychological Works of Sigmund Freud*, vol. 14, *(1914–1916): On the History of the Psycho-Analytic Movement, Papers on Metapsychology and Other Works*, ed. and trans. James Strachey, Hogarth Press, 1957, 248.

6 Toni Morrison, *Beloved*, Picador, 1987.
7 Mary Fulbrook, *Reckonings: Legacies of Nazi Persecution and the Quest for Justice*, Oxford University Press, 2018.
8 Mary Fulbrook, *Bystander Society: Conformity and Complicity in Nazi Germany and the Holocaust*, Oxford University Press, 2023.
9 Jennifer Teege, *My Grandfather Would Have Shot Me*, Hodder & Stoughton, 2015.
10 Roger Frie, *Not in My Family: German Memory and Responsibility after the Holocaust*, Oxford University Press, 2017.
11 Philippe Sands, *My Nazi Legacy*, directed by David Evans, British Film Institute/Wildgaze Films, 2012.
12 Niklas Frank, *In the Shadow of the Reich*, trans. Arthur S. Wensinger with Carole Clew-Hoey, Knopf, 1991.
13 Eva Hoffman, *After Such Knowledge: A Meditation on the Aftermath of the Holocaust*, Vintage, 2005, 64.
14 H. W. Loewald, 'On the Therapeutic Action of Psycho-analysis', *International Journal of Psychoanalysis* 41 (1960), 28.
15 Magda Schmukalla, *Communist Ghosts: Post-Communist Thresholds, Critical Aesthetics and the Undoing of Modern Europe*, Palgrave, 2022.
16 Walter Benjamin, 'Theses on the Philosophy of History', in *Illuminations*, Pimlico, 1999.

6. Psychopolitical Reality

1 Stephen Frosh, Ann Phoenix, and Rob Pattman, '"But It's Racism I Really Hate": Young Masculinities, Racism and Psychoanalysis', *Psychoanalytic Psychology* 17 (2000), 225–42. I have slightly changed the text; in the original we tried to imitate John's speech orthographically (for instance 'fink' for 'think'). That now seems disrespectfully stereotyping of him. A full account of the study is in Stephen Frosh, Ann Phoenix, and Rob Pattman, *Young Masculinities*, Palgrave, 2002.
2 Mark Fisher, *Capitalist Realism: Is There No Alternative?*, Zero Books, 2009, 8.
3 Margaret Thatcher, 'Interview for *Woman's Own*', 23 September 1987, Margaret Thatcher Foundation, margaretthatcher.org.
4 Ibid., 'Appendix: Statement Issued to Sunday Times, Published 10 July 1988'.
5 Louis Althusser, *Essays on Ideology*, Verso, 1972.
6 Sigmund Freud, 'Lines of Advance in Psycho-analytic Therapy', in *The Standard Edition of the Complete Psychological Works of Sigmund Freud*, vol. 17, *(1917–1919): An Infantile Neurosis and*

Other Works, ed. and trans. James Strachey, Hogarth Press, 1955, 166–7.
7 Elizabeth Danto, *Freud's Free Clinics: Psychoanalysis and Social Justice, 1918–1938*, Columbia University Press, 2005.
8 See the special issue of *Psychoanalysis and History* 24, no. 3 (December 2022), on 'Psychoanalysis for the People: Free Clinics and the Social Mission of Psychoanalysis', ed. Matt ffytche, Joanna Ryan and Raluca Soreanu.
9 Joanna Ryan, *Class and Psychoanalysis: Landscapes of Inequality*, Routledge, 2017; Lynne Layton, Nancy Caro Hollander, and Susan Gutwill (eds), *Psychoanalysis, Class and Politics: Encounters in the Clinical Setting*, Routledge, 2006.
10 Nancy Hollander, *Uprooted Minds: Surviving the Politics of Terror in the Americas*, Routledge, 2010.
11 Stephen Frosh and Belinda Mandelbaum, ' "Like Kings in Their Kingdoms": Conservatism in Brazilian Psychoanalysis during the Dictatorship', *Political Psychology* 38, no. 4 (August 2017), 591–604.
12 Lynne Layton, 'That Place Gives Me the Heebie Jeebies', in Layton, Hollander and Gutwill, *Psychoanalysis, Class and Politics*, 63.
13 Stephen Frosh, Ann Phoenix, and Rob Pattman, *Young Masculinities: Understanding Boys in Contemporary Society*, Palgrave, 2002.
14 Jean Laplanche and Jean-Bertrand Pontalis, *The Language of Psychoanalysis*, Hogarth Press, 1973, 284.
15 Jessica Benjamin, *Shadow of the Other: Intersubjectivity and Gender in Psychoanalysis*, Routledge, 1998, 61–2.
16 Luise Eichenbaum and Susie Orbach, *Outside In, Inside Out: Women's Psychology: A Feminist Psychoanalytical Approach*, Penguin, 1982.
17 Jessica Benjamin, *Like Subjects, Love Objects: Essays on Recognition and Sexual Difference*, Yale University Press, 1998.
18 Wilhelm Reich, *The Mass Psychology of Fascism*, Penguin, 1946.
19 Theodor Adorno, Else Frenkel-Brunswick, Daniel J. Levinson, and R. Nevitt Sanford, *The Authoritarian Personality*, Norton, 1982 (1950).
20 Frantz Fanon, *Black Skin, White Masks*, Pluto, 1967 (1952).

7. Endurance

1 Michael Rothberg, *The Implicated Subject: Beyond Victims and Perpetrators*, Stanford University Press, 2019.
2 Judith Butler, *The Force of Nonviolence: An Etho-political Bind*, Verso, 2020.

3 Elizabeth Hughes, *Adopted Women and Biological Fathers: Reimagining Stories of Origin and Trauma*, Routledge, 2017.
4 Jessica Benjamin, *Beyond Doer and Done To: Recognition Theory, Intersubjectivity and the Third*, Routledge, 2017.
5 *Shoah*, directed by Claude Lanzmann, Eureka Entertainment, 1985.
6 Claude Lanzmann, *The Patagonian Hare: A Memoir*, Atlantic, 2009, 434–5.
7 Agnieszka Piotrowska, *Psychoanalysis and Ethics in Documentary Film*, Routledge, 2013. The quote is from Dominick LaCapra, *History and Memory after Auschwitz*, Cornell University Press, 1998, 100.
8 Shoshana Felman, 'The Return of the Voice: Claude Lanzmann's *Shoah*', in Shoshana Felman and Dori Laub, *Testimony: Crises of Witnessing in Literature, Psychoanalysis, and History*, Routledge, 1992.
9 Ibid., 219–20.
10 The universalised saying is derived from the Talmud, Sanhedrin 37a.
11 Wilfred Bion, *Learning from Experience*, Maresfield, 1991 (1962).

8. The Sense of Ending

1 Sigmund Freud, 'The "Uncanny"', in *The Standard Edition of the Complete Psychological Works of Sigmund Freud*, vol. 17, *(1917–1919): An Infantile Neurosis and Other Works*, ed. and trans. James Strachey, Hogarth Press, 1955, 241–2.
2 Sigmund Freud, 'Beyond the Pleasure Principle', in *The Standard Edition of the Complete Psychological Works of Sigmund Freud*, vol. 18, *(1920–1922): Beyond the Pleasure Principle, Group Psychology and Other Works*, Hogarth Press, 1955, 1–64.
3 Ibid., 38–9.
4 Alphonso Lingis, *The Community of Those Who Have Nothing in Common*, Indiana University Press, 1994.
5 Ibid., 122.
6 Talmud, Ketubot 104a.
7 Dylan Thomas, 'Do not go gentle into that good night', in *Collected Poems 1934–1952*, Dent, 1952.
8 Edward Said, *Freud and the Non-European*, Verso, 2003, 29.
9 Ibid., 30.
10 Peter Gay, *Freud: A Life for Our Time*, Dent, 1988, 622.
11 Ibid., 651.
12 Freud, 'Beyond the Pleasure Principle', 38.

13 Sigmund Freud, 'The Future of an Illusion', in *The Standard Edition of the Complete Psychological Works of Sigmund Freud*, vol. 21, *(1927–1931): The Future of an Illusion, Civilization and Its Discontents, and Other Works*, ed. and trans. James Strachey, Hogarth Press, 1961, 1–56.